THE HOUSE THAT RACE BUILT

Wahneema Lubiano

THE
HOUSE
THAT
RACE BUILT

Wahneema Lubiano is an associate professor in the
Program in Literature and the Program in African
and African American Studies at Duke University.
She lives in Durham, North Carolina.

WITHDRAWN

THE
HOUSE
THAT
RACE BUILT

■

*Original Essays by Toni Morrison,
Angela Y. Davis, Cornel West, and Others
on Black Americans and Politics
in America Today*

*Edited and with an Introduction
by Wahneema Lubiano*

Vintage Books
A Division of Random House, Inc.
New York

First Vintage Books Edition, March 1998

Introduction and compilation copyright ©1997 by Wahneema Lubiano • Afterword copyright © 1997 by Cornel West • "Home" copyright © 1997 by Toni Morrison • "The Liberal Retreat from Race During the Post-Civil Rights Era" copyright © 1997 by Stephen Steinberg • "White Workers, New Democrats, and Affirmative Action" copyright © 1997 by David Roediger • "Tales of Two Judges: Joyce Karlin in *People v. Soon Ja Du*; Lance Ito in *People v. O.J. Simpson*" copyright © 1997 by Neil Gotanda • "Racial Dualism at Century's End" copyright © 1997 by Howard Winant • "'Ain't Nothin' Like the Real Thing'; Black Masculinity, Gay Sexuality, and the Jargon of Authenticity" copyright © 1997 by Kendall Thomas • "Living at the Crossroads: Explorations in Race, Nationality, Sexuality, and Gender" copyright © 1997 by Rhonda M. Williams • "Rethinking Vernacular Culture: Black Religion and Race Records in the 1920s and 1930s" copyright © 1997 by Evelyn Brooks Higginbotham • "What Is Black Culture?" copyright © 1997 by David Lionel Smith • "Playing for Keeps: Pleasure and Profit on the Postindustrial Playground" copyright © 1997 by Robin D. G. Kelley • "Black Nationalism and Black Common Sense: Policing Ourselves and Others" copyright © 1997 by Wahneema Lubiano • "The Ethnic Scarring of American Whiteness" copyright © 1997 by Patricia J. Williams • "Race and Criminalization: Black Americans and the Punishment Industry" copyright © 1997 by Angela Y. Davis • "Color Blindness, History, and the Law" copyright © 1997 by Kimberlé Williams Crenshaw • "Subjects in History: Making Diasporic Identities" copyright © 1997 by Stuart Hall. (This copyright page is continued on page 324.)

The Library of Congress has cataloged the Pantheon edition as follows:

The house that race built / edited and with an introduction by Wahneema Lubiano.
p.   cm.
Includes bibliographical references and index.
ISBN 0-679-44090-9
1. Racism—United States. 2. United States— Race relations. 3. Afro-Americans—
Social conditions—1975– I. Lubiano, Wahneema H.
E185.615.H68   1997
305.8'00973—dc20
96-25159
CIP

Vintage ISBN: 0-679-76068-7

Random House Web address: http://www.randomhouse.com

Printed in the United States of America
10 9 8 7 6 5 4

CONTENTS

■

INTRODUCTION

Wahneema Lubiano

∎

THE IDEA OF RACE and the operation of racism are the best friends that the economic and political elite have in the United States. They are the means by which a state and a political economy largely inimical to most of the U.S. citizenry achieve the consent of the governed. They act as a distorting prism that allows that citizenry to imagine itself functioning as a moral and just people while ignoring the widespread devastation directed at black Americans particularly, but at a much larger number of people generally.* Poverty has a black face—not in reality, but in the public imagination. Crime has a black face—again, not in reality, but in the public imagination. And I use the word "public" without a race adjective because the operation of racism is so thoroughgoing that even those individuals who are its objects are not exempt from thinking about the world through its prism.

The United States is not just the domicile of a historically specific form of racial oppression, but it sustains itself as a structure through that oppression. If race—and its strategic social and ideological deployment as racism—didn't exist, the United States' severe inequalities and betrayal of its formal commitments to social equality and social justice would be readily apparent to anyone existing on this ground.

The essays gathered here were produced by a group of scholars who answered a call sent by myself and several of my colleagues at Princeton University, including Toni Morrison, Cornel West, and Arnold Rampersad, to address the issue of race and black Americans on the ground of the United States. It was necessary, many of us thought, to mark again, in the present moment, a recognition that the basic character of the United States not only harbored, but depended upon, a profound violation of the spirit of democracy, and that that fundamental violation is racism.

Central to the existence of racism is the politics of its denial. It is in the best interests of the right to assert the nonexistence of racism except as a manifestation of individual pathology—a matter simply of individuals with bad attitudes. But it is the shame of liberals who think of themselves as guardians and witnesses of corrective concern and conscience that they too have elected to treat racism as a problem of individual social relations and not the systematic operation of power at work throughout our political economy. These essays call into question and to account a liberal majority that trivializes racism by turning its attention to individual remedies, to attitude adjustment, to "color-blind" legal adjudication.

This book also presents work that addresses within-the-group dynamics of black Americans. It addresses the way these dynamics operate through and help define gender, sexuality, and cultural production. Aesthetics, everyday common sense, and the urban landscape are grappled with and complicated by analyses that do justice to the intricate ways by which black Americans make their presence known—to each other and to the dominant culture. For those of us who know the interesting work in cultural analysis being produced in the academy, the conference and book offered a chance to make available that analysis even as public discourse was being increasingly narrowed and degraded by the recycling of a small group of pundits' pronouncements meant to serve the purposes of exhortation and sloganeering rather than reasoned debate and democratic self-determination.

The scholars who gathered at Princeton University for the Race Matters Conference were not there because they necessarily agreed with the analyses offered by Cornel West in his book of that title. They did, however, all agree that race not only mattered but is central to a profound betrayal of democracy taking place throughout contemporary American culture.

These essays do not attempt a scholarly synthesis. This is an openly political collection that offers a range of analyses of how racial politics matter, and attempts to hold the culture intellectually attentive to—even accountable for—the racism by which it functions against a tide of increasingly popular denial. Not least, it seeks to demonstrate the lethal inadequacy of the terms of debate now at the center of American political discourse.

This book tries to offer decisive change in the work of antiracism by providing a sample of some of the best new thinking on the subject of race. Finally, this book attempts to foster, in clear and forceful terms, the recognition that we are at a moment in which a consolidation of forces is working to roll back real gains made in racial democracy in recent years. It argues that we are currently in the midst of a dangerous reconsolidation of white racial nationalism and racial domination taking place under new and quasi-respectable ideologies. These developments can only harden the state of racial apartheid already in effect in this country.

* I use "black Americans" rather than the more conventional "African Americans" to refer to the history of racial demonizing and binarism that has supported, and continues to support, the white supremacy that structures U.S. democracy. Using "black Americans" is simultaneously a way to remember the defiance of that demonization and binarism articulated in the militant antiracists' reclamation of the term.

THE
HOUSE
THAT
RACE BUILT

HOME

Toni Morrison

■

FROM THE BEGINNING I was looking for a sovereignty—an authority—that I believed was available to me only in fiction writing. In that activity alone did I feel coherent, unfettered. There, in the process of writing, was the willed illusion, the control, the pleasure of nestling up ever closer to meaning. There alone the delight of redemption, the seduction of origination. But I have known for a good portion of the past twenty-nine years that those delights, those seductions, are deliberate inventions necessary to both do the work and legislate its mystery. It became increasingly clear how language both liberated and imprisoned me. Whatever the forays of my imagination, the keeper, whose keys tinkled always within earshot, was race.

I have never lived, nor has any of us, in a world in which race did not matter. Such a world, one free of racial hierarchy, is usually imagined or described as dreamscape—Edenesque, utopian, so remote are the possibilities of its achievement. From Martin Luther King's hopeful language, to Doris Lessing's four-gated city, to Jean Toomer's "American," the race-free world has been posited as ideal, millennial, a condition possible only if accompanied by the Messiah or situated in a protected preserve—a wilderness park.

But, for the purposes of this talk and because of certain projects I am engaged in, I prefer to think of a-world-in-which-race-does-*not*-matter as something other than a theme park, or a failed and always-failing dream, or as the father's house of many rooms. I am thinking of it as home. "Home" seems a suitable term because, first, it lets me make a radical distinction between the metaphor of house and the metaphor of home and helps me clarify my thoughts on racial construction. Second, the term domesticates the racial project, moves the job of unmattering race away from pathetic yearning and futile desire; away from an impossible future or an irretrievable and probably nonexistent Eden to a manageable, doable, modern human activity. Third, because eliminating the potency of racist constructs in language is the work I can do. I can't wait for the ultimate liberation theory to imagine its practice and do its work. Also, matters of race and matters of home are priorities in my work and both have in one way or another initiated my search for that elusive sovereignty as well as my abandonment of the search once I recognized its disguise.

As an already- and always-raced writer, I knew from the very beginning that I could not, would not, reproduce the master's voice and its assumptions of the all-knowing law of the white father. Nor would I substitute his voice with that of his fawning mistress or his worthy opponent, for both of these positions (mistress or opponent) seemed to confine me to his terrain, in his arena, accepting the house rules in the dominance game. If I had to live in a racial house, it was important, at the least, to rebuild it so that it was not a windowless prison into which I was forced, a thick-walled, impenetrable container from which no cry could be heard, but rather an open house, grounded, yet generous in its supply of windows and doors. Or, at the most, it became imperative for me to transform this house completely. Counterracism was never an option.

I was tempted to convert it into a palace where racism didn't hurt so much; to crouch in one of its many rooms where coexistence offered the delusion of agency. At some point I tried to use the race house as a scaffolding from which to launch a movable feast that could operate, be celebrated, on any number of chosen sites. That was the authority, the glossy comfort, the redemptive quality, the freedom writing seemed at first to promise.

Yet in that freedom, as in all freedoms (especially stolen ones), lies danger. Could I redecorate, redesign, even reconceive the racial house without forfeiting a home of my own? Would life in this renovated house mean eternal homelessness? Would it condemn me to intense bouts of nostalgia for the race-free home I have never had and would never know? Or would it require intolerable circumspection, a self-censoring bond to the locus of racial architecture? In short, wasn't I (wouldn't I always be) tethered to a death-dealing ideology even (and especially) when I honed all my intelligence toward subverting it?

These questions, which have engaged so many, have troubled all of my work. How to be both free and situated; how to convert a racist house into a race-specific yet nonracist home. How to enunciate race while depriving it of its lethal cling? They are questions of concept, of language, of trajectory, of habitation, of occupation, and, although my engagement with them has been fierce, fitful, and constantly (I think) evolving, they remain in my thoughts as aesthetically and politically unresolved.

Frankly, I look to the contributors of this conference for literary and extraliterary analyses and for much of what can be better understood about matters of race. I believe, however, that my own writerly excursions and my use of a house/home antagonism are related to the topics addressed at this conference because so much of what seems to lie about in discourses on race concerns legitimacy, authenticity, community, belonging. In no small way, these discourses are about home: an intellectual home; a spiritual home; family and community as home; forced and displaced labor in the destruction of home; dislocation of and alienation within the ancestral home; creative responses to exile, the devastations, pleasures, and imperatives of homelessness as it is manifested in discussions on feminism, globalism, the diaspora, migrations, hybridity, contingency, interventions, assimilations, exclusions. The estranged body, the legislated body, the violated, rejected, deprived body—the body as consummate home. In virtually all of these formations, whatever the terrain, race magnifies the matter that matters.

Let me try to be explicit in the ways the racial house has troubled my work.

There was a moment of some significance to me that followed the publication of *Beloved*. It concerns the complex struggle and frustration inherent in creating figuratively logical narrative language that insists on race-specificity without race prerogative.

Someone saw the last sentence of *Beloved* as it was originally written. In fact, it was the penultimate sentence if one thinks of the last word in the book (the resurrection of the title, the character, and the epigraph) as the very last sentence. In any case the phrase "Certainly no clamor for a kiss," which appears in the printed book, is not the one with which I had originally closed the book. My friend was startled by the change. I told him that my editor had suggested an alteration in the language of the sentence without, of course, offering a sample of what the change might be.

The friend railed at my editor for his audacity and at me, too, for considering, let alone agreeing to, the change. I then went to some pains to explain to him why I did it, but became entangled in what the original phrase had meant, or rather what the original last word of the phrase had meant to me. How long it took to arrive at it, how I thought it was the perfect final word; that it connected everything together from the epigraph and the difficult plot to the struggles of the characters through the process of re-membering the body and its parts, re-membering the family, the neighborhood, and our national history. How it reflected this remembering, revealed its necessity, clarified its complexity, and provided the bridge I wanted from the beginning of the book to its end, as well as the beginning of the book that was to follow.

As I went on belaboring the importance of the word, my friend became angrier and angrier. It seemed clear to him from my sustained defense of the word I had abandoned that I was still convinced of its rightness. Nevertheless, I said, I thought there was something to be considered in the editor's objection (which was simply that—not a command). The editor wondered if a better word could be found to end the book because the one I had chosen was too dramatic, too theatrical. At first I disagreed with him: it was a simple, common word. But I was open to his opinion that, in the context of the previous passages, it stood out like a sore thumb. That may even have been his phrase.

Still I resisted the revision for some time (a long time, considering that we were in the galley or late manuscript stage—I am not sure which). I went away and thought about how completely reliable the editor's instincts and recommendations had always been. I decided, finally, to let the decision rest on whether I could indeed find a better word. One that produced the same meaning and had the same effect.

I was eager to find a satisfactory replacement, because the point that gripped me was that even if the word I had chosen was the absolute right one, something was wrong with it if it called attention to itself—

awkwardly, inappropriately—and did not complete the meaning of the text, but dislodged it. It wasn't a question of simply substituting one word for another that meant the same thing: I might have to rewrite a good deal in order to assure myself that a certain synonym was preferable. Eventually, I did discover a word that seemed to accomplish what the original one did with less mystification: "kiss."

The discussion with my friend made me realize that I am still unhappy about it because "kiss" works at a level a bit too shallow. It searches for and locates a quality or element of the novel that was not, and is not, its primary feature. The driving force of the narrative is not love, or the fulfillment of physical desire. The action is driven by necessity, something that precedes love, follows love, informs love, shapes it, and to which love is subservient. In this case the necessity was for connection, acknowledgment, a paying-out of homage still due. "Kiss" clouds that point.

I was inclined to believe that there were poorly lit passages leading up to that original word if indeed it was so very misunderstood and so strongly and wrongly unsettling. I have been reading recently some analyses of revisions of texts out of copyright and thinking about the ways in which books get not only reread but also rewritten—both in one's own language (with the ambivalence of the writer and the back-and-forth between editor and writer), and in translation. The liberties translators take that enhance; the ones taken that diminish. And for me, the alarm. There is always the threat of not being taken seriously, of having the work reduced to social anthropology, of having the politics of one's own language, the politics of another language bury, rather than expose, the reader's own politics.

My effort to manipulate American English was not to take standard English and use vernacular to decorate it, or to add "color" to dialogue. My efforts were to carve away the accretions of deceit, blindness, ignorance, paralysis, and sheer malevolence embedded in raced language so that other kinds of perception were not only available but were inevitable. That is the work I thought my original last word accomplished; then I became convinced that it did not, and now am sorry I made the change. The trouble it takes to find just one word and know that it is that note and no other that would do is an extraordinary battle. To have found it and lost it is, in retrospect, infuriating. Well, what does it matter? Can a book really fall apart because of one word, even if it's in a critical position? Probably not.

But maybe it can, if the writing is emphasizing racial specificity minus racist hierarchy in its figurative choices. In this instance I settled for the latter. I gave up a word that was racially charged and figuratively coherent for one that was only the latter, because my original last word was so clearly disjunctive, a sore thumb, a jarring note combining as it did two linguistically incompatible functions—except when signaling racial exoticism. It is difficult to sign race while designing racelessness.

Actually, I think my editor was right. The original word was the "wrong" word. But I also know that my friend was right: the "wrong" word, in this case, was also the only word. Since language *is* community, if the cognitive ecology of a language is altered, so is the community. As you can see, my assertion of agency outside the raced house turned into genuflection in its familiar yard.

That experience of regret highlights for me the need to rethink the subtle yet persuasive attachments we may have to the architecture of race. We need to think about what it means and what it takes to live in a redesigned racial house and—evasively and erroneously—call it diversity or multiculturalism as a way of calling it home. We need to think about how invested some of the best theoretical work may be in clinging to the house's redesign as simulacrum. We need to think about what new dangers present themselves when escape or self-exile from the house of racial construction is announced or achieved.

I risk here, perhaps, charges of encouraging futile attempts to transcend race or pernicious efforts to trivialize it. It would worry me a great deal if my remarks—or my narratives—were to be so completely misunderstood. What I am determined to do is to take what is articulated as an elusive race-free paradise and domesticate it. I am determined to concretize a literary discourse that (outside of science fiction) resonates exclusively in the register of permanently unrealizable dream. It is a discourse that (unwittingly) allows racism an intellectual weight to which it has absolutely no claim. My confrontation is piecemeal and very slow. Unlike the successful advancement of an argument, narration requires the active complicity of a reader willing to step outside established boundaries of the racial imaginary. And, unlike visual media, narrative has no pictures to ease the difficulty of that step.

In writing novels the adventure for me has been explorations of seemingly impenetable, race-inflected, race-clotted topics. In the first book I was interested in racism as a cause, consequence, and manifestation of individual and social psychosis. In the second I was preoccupied with the culture of gender and the invention of identity, both of which acquired astonishing meaning when placed in a racial context. In *Song of Solomon* and *Tar Baby* I was interested in the impact of race on the romance of community and individuality. In *Beloved* I wanted to explore the revelatory possibilities of historical narration when the body-mind, subject-object, past-present oppositions, viewed through the lens of race, collapse. In *Jazz* I tried to locate American modernity as a response to the race house. It was an attempt to blow up its all-encompassing shelter, its all-knowingness, and its assumptions of control. In the novel I am now writing, I am trying first to enunciate and then eclipse the racial gaze altogether.

In *Jazz* the dynamite fuse to be lit was under the narrative voice—the voice that could begin with claims of knowledge, inside knowledge, and indisputable authority ("I know that woman. . . .") and end with the blissful epiphany of its vulnerable humanity and its own needs. In my current project I want to see whether or not race-specific, race-free language is both possible and meaningful in narration. And I want to inhabit, walk around, a site clear of racist detritus; a place where race both matters and is rendered impotent; a place "already made for me, both snug and wide open. With a doorway never needing to be closed, a view slanted for light and bright autumn leaves but not rain. Where moonlight can be counted on if the sky is clear and stars no matter what. And below, just yonder, a river called Treason to rely on." I want to imagine not the threat of freedom, or its tentative panting fragility, but the concrete thrill of border-lessness—a kind of out of doors safety where "a sleepless woman could always rise from her bed, wrap a shawl around her shoulders and sit on the steps in the moonlight. And if she felt like it she could walk out the yard and on down the road. No lamp and no fear. A hiss-crackle from the side of the road would never scare her because what ever it was that made that sound, it wasn't something creeping up on her. Nothing for miles around thought she was prey. She could stroll as slowly as she liked, thinking of food preparations, of family things, or lift her eyes to stars and think of war or nothing at all. Lampless and without fear she could make her way. And if a light shone from a window up a ways and the cry of a colicky baby caught her attention, she might step over to the house and call out softly to the woman inside trying to soothe the baby. The two of them might take turns massaging the infant stomach, rocking, or trying to get a little soda water down. When the baby quieted they could sit together for a spell, gossiping, chuckling low so as not to wake anybody else. The woman could decide to go back to her bed then, refreshed and ready to sleep, or she might stay her direction and walk further down the road—on out, beyond, because nothing around or beyond considered her prey."

■

That description is meant to evoke not only the safety and freedom outside the race house, but to suggest contemporary searches and yearnings for social space that is psychically and physically safe.

■

The overweening, defining event of the modern world is the mass movement of raced populations, beginning with the largest forced transfer of people in the history of the world: slavery. The consequences of which transfer have determined all the wars following it as well as the current ones being waged on every continent. The contemporary world's work has become policing, halting, forming policy regarding, and trying to administer the movement of people. Nationhood—the very definition of citizenship—is constantly being demarcated and redemarcated in response to exiles, refugees, *Gastarbeiter*, immigrants, migrations, the displaced, the fleeing, and the besieged. The anxiety of belonging is entombed within the central metaphors in the discourse on globalism, transnationalism, nationalism, the break-up of federations, the rescheduling of alliances, and the fictions of sovereignty. Yet these figurations of nationhood and identity are frequently as raced themselves as the originating racial house that defined them. When they are not raced, they are, as I mentioned earlier, imaginary landscape, never inscape; Utopia, never home.

I applaud and am indebted to scholars here and elsewhere who are clearing intellectual and moral space where racial constructs are being forced to reveal their struts and bolts, their technology and their carapace, so that political action, legal and social thought, and cultural production can be generated sans racist cant, explicit or in disguise.

The defenders of Western hegemony sense the encroachment and have already defined the possibility of imagining race without dominance—without hierarchy—as "barbarism." We are already being asked to understand such a world as the destruction of the four-gated city, as the end of history. We are already being asked to know such a world as aftermath—as rubbish, as an already damaged experience, as a valueless future. Once again, the political consequences of new and threatening theoretical work is the ascription of an already-named catastrophe. It is therefore more urgent than ever to develop nonmessianic language to refigure the raced community, to decipher the deracing of the world. It is more urgent than ever to develop an epistemology that is neither intellectual slumming nor self-serving reification. Participants in this conference are marking out space for critical work that neither bleeds the raced house for the gains it provides in authenticity and insiderdom, nor abandons it to its own signifying gestures. To the extent the world-as-home that we are working for is already described in the raced house as waste, the work this conference draws our attention to is not just interesting—it may save our lives.

The campuses where we mostly work and frequently assemble will not, under the close scrutiny of conferences such as this one, remain alien terrain. Our campuses will not retain their fixed borders while tolerating travel from one kind of race-inflected community to another as interpreters, native guides. They will not remain a collection of segregated castles from whose balustrades we view—even invite—the homeless. They will not remain markets where we permit ourselves to be auctioned, bought, silenced, downsized, and vastly compromised depending on the whim of the master and the going rate. Nor will they remain oblivious to the work of conferences such as this one because they cannot enforce or afford the pariah status of race theory without forfeiting the mission of the university itself.

Hostility to race studies, however, is not limited to political and academic critics. There is much wariness in off-campus communities, especially minority communities where resentment against being described and spoken for can be intense, regardless of the researcher's agenda. The distrust that race studies often receive from the authenticating off-campus community is legitimate only when the scholars themselves have not recognized their own participation in the maintenance of the race house. The wariness is justified only when scholars have not unapologetically recognized that the valuable work they do can be done best in this environment; when they have not envisioned academic life as straddling opposing worlds or as escapist flight. W. E. B. Dubois's observation about double consciousness is a strategy, not a prophecy or a cure. Beyond the dichotomous double consciousness, the new space this conference explores is formed by the inwardness of the outside, the interiority of the "othered," the personal that is always embedded in the public. In this new space one can imagine safety without walls, can iterate difference that is prized but unprivileged, and can conceive of a third, if you will pardon the expression, world "already made for me, both snug and wide open, with a doorway never needing to be closed."

Home.

THE LIBERAL RETREAT FROM RACE DURING THE POST–CIVIL RIGHTS ERA

Stephen Steinberg

■

The liberal is an aesthete, much preoccupied with form and means and techniques. He looks out on a raging battlefield and sees error everywhere, and he thinks he can find the truth by avoiding error.

—Lerone Bennett, "Tea and Sympathy:
Liberals and Other White Hopes," 1964

A moderate is a cat who will hang you from a low tree.

—Dick Gregory, c. 1964

MARTIN LUTHER KING, JR.'S 1963 "Letter from Birmingham Jail" has become a part of this nation's political folklore. However, its specific contents have been all but expunged from our collective memory. The letter was not a condemnation of racism. Nor was it, like his celebrated "I Have a Dream" oration—whose contents *are* remembered—an evocation of American ideals or a prophetic vision of better times ahead. King was responding to a letter signed by eight priests, rabbis, and ministers that appeared in the *Birmingham News* while he was imprisoned. The letter spoke sympathetically of "rights consistently denied," but criticized King's tactics as "unwise and untimely" and called for a "constructive and

13

realistic approach," one that would substitute negotiation for confrontation. In his response King acknowledged their sincerity in seeking "a better path," but explained why confrontation and crisis were necessary in order to shake white society out of its apathy and intransigence. Mincing no words, King issued the following indictment of the so-called moderate:

> I have almost reached the regrettable conclusion that the Negro's great stumbling block in the stride toward freedom is not the White Citizens Counciler or the Ku Klux Klanner, but the white moderate who is more devoted to "order" than to justice; who prefers a negative peace which is the absence of tension to a positive peace which is the presence of justice; who constantly says, "I agree with you in the goal you seek, but I can't agree with your methods of direct action"; who paternalistically feels that he can set the timetable for another man's freedom; who lives by the myth of time and who constantly advises the Negro to wait until "a more convenient season."[1]

In his remonstration of "the white moderate," King anticipated the liberal retreat from race that would become a hallmark of the post–civil rights era. By 1963 there were already signs of increasing disaffection on the part of liberals in the North as well as the South. Indeed, this was the subject of a prescient article in the *Atlantic Monthly* entitled "The White Liberal's Retreat." Its author, Murray Friedman, observed that "the liberal white is increasingly uneasy about the nature and consequences of the Negro revolt."[2] According to Friedman, a number of factors contributed to the white liberal retreat. For one thing, after school desegregation came to northern cities, white liberals realized that the Negro was not just an abstraction, and not just a southern problem. Second, the rise of black nationalism exacerbated tensions with liberals, especially when white liberals were ejected from some civil rights organizations. Third, the escalating tensions and violence tested the limit of liberal support. "In the final analysis," Friedman wrote, "a liberal, white, middle-class society wants to have change, but without trouble."[3]

As Friedman observed, there was nothing new in the tendency for white liberals to withdraw support from the liberation movement—essentially the same thing had happened during Reconstruction. In both cases advances made by blacks were followed by periods of racism and reaction, each feeding on the other, and liberals capitulated to this white backlash by urging blacks to curb their demands. Friedman described the situation in 1963 in these epigrammatic terms: "to the Negro demand for 'now,' to which the Deep South has replied 'never,' many liberal whites are increasingly responding 'later.'"[4]

It did not take long for the intensifying backlash and the liberal retreat to manifest themselves politically. The critical turning point was 1965, the year the civil rights movement reached its triumphant finale. The 1964 Civil Rights Act—passed after a decade of black insurgency—ended segregation in public accommodations and, at least in theory, proscribed discrimination in employment. The last remaining piece of civil rights legislation—the 1965 Voting Rights Act—was wending its way through Congress and, in the wake of Johnson's landslide victory, was assured of eventual passage. In a joint session of Congress on voting rights in March 1965—the first such session on a domestic issue since 1946—President Johnson electrified the nation by proclaiming, in his southern drawl, "And we *shall* overcome." As a senator from Texas, Johnson had voted against anti-lynching legislation. Now, in the midst of a crisis engineered by a grassroots protest movement, Johnson embraced the battle cry of that movement as he proposed legislation that would eliminate the last and most important vestige of official segregation.

In retrospect, Johnson's speech represented not the triumph of the civil rights movement but its last hurrah. Now that its major legislative objectives had been achieved, not only the future of the movement, but also the constancy of liberal support, were thrown into question. By 1965, leaders and commentators, both inside and outside the movement, were asking, "What's next?" However, this question had an ominous innuendo when it came from white liberals, as King noted in *Why We Can't Wait*, published in 1963. King provides this account of his appearance with Roy Wilkins on *Meet the Press*:

> There were the usual questions about how much more the Negro wants, but there seemed to be a new undercurrent of implications related to the sturdy new strength of our movement. Without the

courtly complexities, we were, in effect, being asked if we could be trusted to hold back the surging tides of discontent so that those on the shore would not be made too uncomfortable by the buffeting and onrushing waves. Some of the questions implied that our leadership would be judged in accordance with our capacity to "keep the Negro from going too far." The quotes are mine, but I think the phrase mirrors the thinking of the panelists as well as of many other white Americans.[5]

By 1965—even before Watts exploded—there was a growing awareness among black leaders that political rights did not go far enough to compensate for past wrongs. Whitney Young epitomized this when he wrote that "there is little value in a Negro's obtaining the right to be admitted to hotels and restaurants if he has no cash in his pocket and no job."[6] As Lee Rainwater and William Yancey have suggested, "The year 1965 may be known in history as the time when the civil rights movement discovered, in the sense of becoming explicitly aware, that abolishing legal racism would not produce Negro equality."[7]

If laws alone would not produce equality, then the unavoidable conclusion was that some form of "special effort"—to use Whitney Young's term—was necessary to compensate for the accumulated disadvantages of the past. By 1965 the words "compensation," "reparations," and "preference" had already crept into the political discourse, and white liberals were beginning to display their disquiet with this troublesome turn of events.[8] In *Why We Can't Wait*, King observed: "Whenever this issue of compensatory or preferential treatment for the Negro is raised, some of our friends recoil in horror. The Negro should be granted equality, they agree; but he should ask nothing more."[9]

The demand for "something more" than legal equality precipitated a crisis among white liberals. This crisis was already evident in February 1964 when *Commentary* magazine sponsored a roundtable discussion, "Liberalism and the Negro."[10] The event took place at Town Hall in New York City before an invited audience, which included many of the leading liberal intellectuals of the period. Norman Podhoretz introduced the discussion:

I think it may be fair to say that American liberals are by now divided into two schools of thought on what is often called the Negro problem. . . . On the one side, we have those liberals whose ultimate perspective on race relations . . . envisages the gradual absorption of deserving Negroes one by one into white society. . . . Over the past two or three years, however, a new school of liberal (or perhaps it should be called radical) thought has been developing which is based on the premise . . . that "the rights and privileges of an individual rest upon the status attained by the group to which he belongs." From this premise certain points follow that are apparently proving repugnant to the traditional liberal mentality.[11]

Behind this elliptical language was the specter of "preference." Traditional liberalism, Podhoretz explained, sought to integrate "deserving Negroes one by one into white society." But a newer school of liberals had emerged that "maintains that the Negro community *as a whole* has been crippled by three hundred years of slavery and persecution and that the simple removal of legal and other barriers to the advancement of individual Negroes can therefore only result in what is derisively called 'tokenism.'" Finally, Podhoretz laid his cards on the table:

This school of thought insists that radical measures are now needed to overcome the Negro's inherited disabilities. Whitney Young of the National Urban League, for example, has recently spoken of a domestic Marshall Plan, a crash program which he says need last only ten years, in order to bring the Negro community to a point where it can *begin* to compete on equal terms with the white world. Other Negro leaders have similarly talked about 10 percent quotas in hiring, housing, and so on. Negroes, they say, ought to be represented in all areas of American life according to their proportion in the population, and where they are not so represented, one is entitled to draw an inference of discrimination. The slogan "preferential treatment for Negroes" is the most controversial one that has come up in this discussion.[12]

The other white participants in the roundtable—Nathan Glazer, Sidney Hook, and Gunnar Myrdal—declared their blanket opposition to any system of racial preference. Glazer touted the success of New York's Fair Employment Practices Law, implying that racial justice could be achieved within the same liberal framework that worked for other groups. Hook argued that, by lowering standards for Negroes, preference was patronizing and, in effect, treated blacks as second-class citizens. Myrdal cautioned that preference amounted to tokenism and that what was needed was a program to lift *all* poor people out of poverty.

James Baldwin stood alone, parrying the arguments thrust at him with his usual eloquence and resolve. To the optimistic view that the nation was making progress ("not enough progress, to be sure, but progress nevertheless"), Baldwin had this to say:

> I'm delighted to know there've been many fewer lynchings in the year 1963 than there were in the year 1933, but I also have to bear in mind—I have to bear it in mind because my life depends on it—that there are a great many ways to lynch a man. The impulse in American society, as far as I can tell from my experience in it, has essentially been to ignore me when it could, and then when it couldn't, to intimidate me; and when that failed, to make concessions.[13]

As the discussion wore on, it became increasingly obvious that a vast difference in worldview separated Baldwin and the others. When Hook gloated over the expansion of ethical principles in American society, Baldwin retorted:

> What strikes me here is that you are an American talking about American society, and I am an American talking about American society—both of us very concerned with it—and yet your version of American society is really very difficult for me to recognize. My experience in it has simply not been yours.[14]

Speaking from the audience, Kenneth Clark was even more blunt in declaring his disaffection with liberalism:

> How do I—a Negro in America who throughout his undergradu-
> ate years and the early part of his professional life identified him-
> self with liberalism—how do I now see American liberalism? I
> must confess bluntly that I now see white American liberalism
> primarily in terms of the adjective, "white."[15]

Indeed, the day's proceedings seemed only to corroborate Podhoretz's initial observation of "a widening split between the Negro movement and
the white liberal community."

Here in the spring of 1964 was an early sign of the imminent breakup
of the liberal coalition that had functioned as a bulwark of the civil rights
movement. One faction would gravitate to the nascent neoconservative
movement. Another faction would remain in the liberal camp, committed in principle to both liberal reform and racial justice. This, however,
was to prove a difficult balancing act, especially when confronted with an
intensifying racial backlash. Even in the best of times, racial issues tended
to exacerbate divisions in the liberal coalition on which Democratic electoral victories depended. As the polity swung to the right, liberals in the
Democratic Party came under mounting pressure to downplay or sidestep
racial issues.

Thus, the liberal retreat from race was rationalized in terms of
realpolitik. The argument ran like this: America is too racist to support
programs targeted for blacks, especially if these involve any form of
preference, which is anathema to most whites. Highlighting racial issues,
therefore, only serves to drive a wedge in the liberal coalition, driving
whites from the Democratic Party, and is ultimately self-defeating. That
this reasoning amounted to a capitulation to the white backlash did not
faze the political "realists" since their motives were pure. Indeed, unlike
the racial backlash on the right, the liberal backlash was *not* based on
racial animus or retrograde politics. On the contrary, these dyed-in-the-
wool liberals were convinced that the best or only way to help blacks was
to help "everybody." Eliminate poverty, they said, and blacks, who count
disproportionately among the poor, will be the winners. Achieve full employment, and black employment troubles will be resolved. The upshot,
however, was that blacks were asked to subordinate their agenda to a
larger movement for liberal reform. In practical terms, this meant forgo-

ing the black protest movement and casting their lot with the Democratic Party.

Thus, after 1965 many white liberals who were erstwhile supporters of the civil rights movement placed a kiss of death on race-based politics and race-based public policy. They not only joined the general retreat from race in the society at large, but in fact cited the white backlash as reason for their own abandonment of race-based politics. In this sense the liberal retreat from race can be said to represent the left wing of the backlash.

THE HOWARD ADDRESS:
A CASE OF "SEMANTIC INFILTRATION"

The ideological cleavage that would split the liberal camp was foreshadowed in a commencement address that President Johnson delivered at Howard University on June 4, 1965. The speech, written by Richard Goodwin and Daniel Patrick Moynihan, was riddled with contradictions, and for this very reason epitomizes the political limbo that existed in 1965, as well as the emerging lines of ideological and political division within the liberal camp.[16]

The speech, aptly entitled "To Fulfill These Rights," began with the most radical vision on race that has ever been enunciated by a president of the United States. After reviewing the series of civil rights acts that secured full civil rights for African Americans, Johnson declared: "But freedom is not enough." He continued:

> You do not take a person who, for years, has been hobbled by chains and liberate him, bring him up to the starting line of a race and then say, "you are free to compete with all the others," and still justly believe that you have been completely fair. Thus it is not enough just to open the gates of opportunity. All our citizens must have the ability to walk through those gates.

Johnson's oratory went a critical step further:

This is the next and more profound stage of the battle for civil rights. We seek not just freedom but opportunity—not just legal equity but human ability—*not just equality as a right and a theory but equality as a fact and as a result.*

With these last words, Johnson adopted the logic and the language of those arguing for compensatory programs that would redress past wrongs. Equality, not liberty, would be the defining principle of "the next and more profound stage" in the liberation struggle.[17]

So far so good. Johnson's speech then took an abrupt detour away from politics to sociology, reflecting the unmistakable imprint of Daniel Patrick Moynihan, who only a month earlier had completed an internal report focusing on problems of the black family. Johnson said:

. . . equal opportunity is essential, but not enough. Men and women of all races are born with the same range of abilities. But ability is not just the product of birth. Ability is stretched or stunted by the family you live with, and the neighborhoods you live in, by the school you go to and the poverty or the richness of your surroundings. It is the product of a hundred unseen forces playing upon the infant, the child, and the man.

Compare the language and logic of this passage with the one that follows:

Overt job discrimination is only one of the important hurdles which must be overcome before color can disappear as a determining factor in the lives and fortunes of men. . . . The prevailing view among social scientists holds that there are no significant differences among groups as to the distribution of innate aptitudes or at most very slight differences. On the other hand, differences among individuals are very substantial. The extent to which an individual is able to develop his aptitudes will largely depend upon the circumstances present in the family within which he grows up and the opportunities which he encounters at school and in the larger community.

This latter passage comes from a 1956 book, *The Negro Potential*, by Eli Ginzberg, who was a leading liberal economist of that period.[18] My point is not that Johnson's speechwriters were guilty of plagiarism. Rather it is to take note of their Machiavellian genius. With a rhetorical sleight of hand, Goodwin and Moynihan shifted the discourse away from the radical vision of "equal results" that emanated from the black protest movement of the 1960s back to the standard liberal cant of the 1950s, which held that the black child is stunted by "circumstances present in the family within which he grows up." The conceptual groundwork was being laid for a drastic policy reversal: the focus would no longer be on white racism, but rather on the deficiencies of blacks themselves.

Having planted the seeds of equivocation, the speech then shifted back to a fretful discussion of the "widening gulf" between poor blacks and the rest of the nation, including the black middle class. Johnson cited a litany of statistics on black employment and income. Logically, this might have led to a discussion of policies that would move the nation in the direction of "equal results" in employment and income. However, as Tom Wicker astutely observed in the *New York Times:* "Mr. Johnson did not mention such specific remedies as job quotas or preferential hiring, which some civil rights leaders have advocated."[19] Instead, the speech shifted to more generalities on "the special nature of Negro poverty" and "the breakdown of the Negro family structure." Centuries of oppression, Johnson asserted, had eroded the ability of Negro men to function as providers for their family, and, as a result, fewer than half of Negro children currently live out their lives with both parents. Inasmuch as the family "is the cornerstone of our society," the collapse of the family has dire consequences for individuals and communities alike. "So," Johnson concluded, "unless we work to strengthen the family . . . all the rest: schools and playgrounds, public assistance and private concern, will never be enough to cut completely the circle of despair and deprivation."

This last comment probably passed over Johnson's audience at Howard as mere political oratory. Only in retrospect can we fully appreciate the dire political implications of suggesting that government programs were futile "unless we work to strengthen the family." With another rhetorical sleight of hand, Johnson (via Goodwin and Moynihan) shifted the focus from "equal results" to the black family which, it was said, was perpetuating "the circle of despair and deprivation." The speech conspicuously avoided any policy prescriptions, deferring these to a planned White House conference under the title "To Fulfill These Rights." However, the conceptual groundwork was being laid for policies that would change "them," not "us."

Thus, a presidential speech that began on a progressive note ended up in abysmal political regression. Was this self-contradiction merely the result of careless or muddled thought? Or did it reflect political calculation? There is reason to think that Johnson's advisors acted with deliberation and foresight. In a *New York Times* story on June 5, the day after the Howard speech, unnamed "White House sources" are quoted to the effect that the Howard address was the first major presidential civil rights speech conceived independently of the direct pressure of racial crisis. Reading between these lines, it would appear that Johnson's political strategists were seeking to wrest control over the troublesome direction that racial politics were headed. Indeed, the Howard speech is a prime example of what Moynihan calls "semantic infiltration."[20] This term refers to the appropriation of the language of one's political opponents for the purpose of blurring distinctions and molding it to one's own political position. In this instance Moynihan invoked the language of "equal results" only to redefine and redirect it in a politically safe direction. When semantic infiltration is done right, it elicits the approbation even of one's political opponents who, as in the case of the audience at Howard, may not fully realize that a rhetorical shill game has been played on them.[21]

Moynihan was already on record as opposing public policies targeted specifically for blacks. In a conference sponsored by *Daedalus* and the American Academy of Arts and Sciences only a month earlier, "preference" emerged as a key issue of debate. Below is an excerpt in which Moynihan presents his case against race-specific policies, insisting that they must be embedded in a race-neutral framework.[22] The other speakers are Everett C. Hughes, the eminent sociologist from Brandeis, and Jay Saunders Redding, professor of English at the Hampton Institute in Virginia:

HUGHES: May I ask all these gentlemen a question? Are they or
are they not saying that any reduction in the number and proportion of the very poor among the Negro will be accomplished not by addressing ourselves so much to the Negro but
by addressing ourselves to the whole state of the economy in
our society, to the nature of poverty in general?

MOYNIHAN: I will answer the question by saying that in order to
do anything about Negro Americans on the scale that our
data would indicate, we have to declare that we are doing it
for *everybody*. I think, however, that the problem of the Negro American *is* now a special one, and is not just an intense
case of the problem of all poor people.

REDDING: Why do we have to announce that we are doing this for
everyone?

MOYNIHAN: Congressmen vote for everyone more readily than
they vote for any one. Because the poverty program is a color-
blind program, we can do what we could not have done otherwise. We could not have done it for West Virginia or for
Harlem—either one of those opposite extremes—but we can
do it in generalized terms—for people.

REDDING: Do you think, then, that the idea of compensatory or
preferential treatment for the Negro specifically is a bad idea?

MOYNIHAN: I do not know about "good" or "bad." I would say that
in terms of the working of the system we are trying to influence by our thinking here, it will be done for "everybody,"
whatever may be in the back of the minds of the people who
do it.

Here Moynihan speaks with the dispassionate voice of the political pragmatist, brushing aside questions of "good" or "bad," "right" or "wrong,"
and guided solely by realpolitik—one that accepts white racism as a given,
or, at best, a political impediment to be circumvented. This leads him to
a blanket rejection of policies targeted for blacks. Within this political
framework, the politics of "equal results" has no place.

Aside from its intent, the significance of the Howard address was that it drew a line in the political sand marking how far the Johnson administration would go in supporting the escalating demands of the protest movement. In throwing his support behind the Voting Rights Act, Johnson had gone further than any of his predecessors in jeopardizing the Solid South. The rhetoric of "equal results" also threatened to antagonize blue-collar workers, Jews, and other elements of the Democratic coalition. The covert message in the Howard speech was that, as far as the Democratic Party was concerned, the impending Voting Rights Act marked the end of the civil rights revolution ("the end of the beginning," Johnson said disingenuously, quoting Churchill). If blacks were "to fulfill these rights," they would have to get their own house in order. Literally!

Thus, behind the equivocal language in Johnson's address was a key policy issue concerning the role of the state in the post–civil rights era. Would future progress depend on an expansion of antiracist policies— aimed not only at forms of intentional discrimination but also at the insidious forces of institutionalized racism that have excluded blacks categorically from whole job sectors and other opportunity structures? Or would future progress depend on programs of social uplift that contemplate "the gradual absorption of deserving Negroes one by one into white society"?

These alternative policy options were predicated on vastly different assumptions about the nature and sources of racism. The one located the problem within "white" society and its major institutions, and called for policies to rapidly integrate blacks into jobs, schools, and other institutional sectors from which they had historically been excluded. The other assumed that racism was waning, but that blacks generally lacked the requisite education and skills to avail themselves of expanding opportunities. This latter school included both traditional liberals who supported government programs that "help blacks to help themselves," and conservatives, including a new genre of black conservatives, who adamantly opposed government intervention, insisting that blacks had to summon the personal and group resources to overcome disabilities of race and class.

What was most flagrantly Machiavellian about Johnson's speech is that it camouflaged "self-help" behind a rhetorical facade of "equal results." For the most part, the liberal press responded with predictable gullibility. For example, the *New York Times* editorialized: "President Johnson has addressed himself boldly to what is unquestionably the most basic and also the most complicated phase of the civil rights struggle—the need for translating newly reinforced legal rights into genuine equality."[23] On the other hand, based on unnamed White House aides, Mary Mc-Grory of the *Washington Star* gave the speech a very different spin: "President Johnson suggested that the time had come for them [Negroes] to come to grips with their own worst problem, 'the breakdown of Negro family life.'"[24]

FROM INFILTRATION TO SUBVERSION:
THE MOYNIHAN REPORT

The polarity between antiracism and social uplift became even more sharply defined by the controversy surrounding the publication of the Moynihan Report three months after Johnson's address at Howard University. Officially titled *The Negro Family: The Case for National Action*, the report presented a mound of statistics showing high rates of divorce, illegitimacy, and female-headed households. Although Moynihan paid lip service to the argument that unemployment and low wages contributed to family breakdown, he was practically obsessed with a single statistic showing that Aid to Families with Dependent Children (AFDC) continued to increase between 1962 and 1964, despite the fact that unemployment was decreasing.[25] On this meager empirical basis, Moynihan concluded that poverty was "feeding upon itself," and that the "disintegration of the Negro family" had assumed a dynamic all its own, independent of joblessness and poverty. In yet another leap of faith, he asserted that family breakdown was the *source* of most of the problems that afflict black America. In Moynihan's own words: ". . . at the center of the tangle of pathology is the weakness of the family structure. Once or twice removed, it will be found to be the principal source of most of the aberrant, inadequate, or antisocial behavior that did not establish, but now serves to perpetuate, the cycle of poverty and deprivation."[26]

Moynihan's critics accused him of inverting cause and effect, and, in doing so, shifting the focus of blame away from societal institutions onto blacks themselves. For example, Christopher Jencks wrote in 1965:

> Moynihan's analysis is in the conservative tradition that guided the drafting of the poverty program (in whose formulation he participated during the winter of 1963–4). The guiding assumption is that social pathology is caused less by basic defects in the social system than by defects in particular individuals and groups which prevent their adjusting to the system. *The prescription is therefore to change the deviants, not the system.*[27]

The regressive implications of Moynihan's report for public policy were also noted by Herbert Gans:

> The findings on family instability and illegitimacy can be used by right-wing and racist groups to support their claim that Negroes are inherently immoral and therefore unworthy of equality. Politicians responding to more respectable white backlash can argue that Negroes must improve themselves before they are entitled to further government aid. . . . Worse still, the report could be used to justify a reduction of efforts in the elimination of racial discrimination and the War on Poverty. . . .[28]

Thus, at this critical juncture in race history—when there was political momentum for change and when even the president of the United States gave at least verbal support for "a new phase" that would go beyond political rights to assuring equal results—Moynihan succeeded in deflecting policy debate to a useless dissection of the black family. With his considerable forensic skill as speechwriter for Johnson, Moynihan had brought the nation to the threshold of truth—racial equality as a moral and political imperative—and then, with rhetorical guile, deflected the focus onto the tribulations within black families. By the time that the promised White House conference "To Secure These Rights" actually took place, it degenerated into a debate over the Moynihan Report, which by then had become public. Whether by design or not, Moynihan had acted as a political decoy, drawing all the fire to himself while the issue of "equal results" receded into oblivion.[29]

Notwithstanding the efforts of a number of writers, including Moynihan himself, to portray the controversy over the Moynihan Report as fruitless and even counterproductive, it proved to be one of the most formative debates in modern social science. The debate crystallized issues, exposed the conservative assumptions and racial biases that lurked behind mainstream social science, and prompted critics of the report to formulate alternative positions that challenged the prevailing wisdom about race in America. The principal counterposition—encapsulated by psychologist William Ryan's ingenious phrase "blaming the victim"—blew the whistle on the tendency of social science to reduce social phenomena to an individual level of analysis, thereby shifting attention away from the structures of inequality and focusing on the behavioral responses of the individuals suffering the effects of these adverse structures. The controversy also stimulated a large body of research—the most notable example is Herbert Gutman's now classic study *The Black Family in Slavery and Freedom*. This study demolished the myth that "slavery destroyed the black family"—a liberal myth that allowed social scientists and policymakers to blame "history" for the problems in the black family, thus deflecting attention away from the factors in the here and now that tear families apart.[30]

Yet leading liberals today contend that Moynihan was the victim of unfair ideological attack. Moynihan set the tone for this construction of history in an article that was published in *Commentary* (February 1967) under the title "The President and the Negro: The Moment Lost." Again, Moynihan begins on the threshold of truth: "For the second time in their history, the great task of liberation has been left only half-accomplished. It appears that the nation may be in the process of reproducing the tragic events of the Reconstruction: giving to Negroes the forms of legal equality, but withholding the economic and political resources which are the bases of social equality."[31] Moynihan goes on to argue, as I have here, that 1965 represented a moment of opportunity: "The moment came when, as it were, the nation had the resources, and the leadership, and the will to make a *total* as against a partial commitment to the cause of Negro equality. It did not do so."[32]

Why was the opportunity missed? According to Moynihan, the blame lies not with the forces of racism and reaction, and certainly not with himself, but with "the liberal Left" who opposed his initiative to address problems in the black family. Specifically, opposition emanated

> from Negro leaders unable to comprehend their opportunity; from civil-rights militants, Negro and white, caught up in a frenzy of arrogance and nihilism; and from white liberals unwilling to expend a jot of prestige to do a difficult but dangerous job that had to be done, and could have been done. But was not.[33]

Thus, in Moynihan's recapitulation of events, it was his political enemies who, in "a frenzy of arrogance and nihilism," had aborted the next stage in the Negro revolution that Moynihan had engineered as an influential adviser to the president.

Moynihan's account is predicated on the assumption that "the civil-rights movement had no program for going beyond the traditional and relatively easy issues of segregation and discrimination."[34] But this is an inaccurate and patently self-serving construction of events. The civil rights movement was evolving precisely such a program, and it involved a surefire method for achieving equal results: instituting a system of preference that would rapidly integrate blacks into job markets and other institutions from which they had been excluded historically. Moynihan, as we have seen, was adamantly opposed to such an approach, and he did what he could, as speechwriter for Johnson's duplicitous Howard address and as author of the report on the Negro family, to derail any movement in this direction. Yet he portrays himself sanctimoniously as the innocent victim of "the liberal Left," and shifts the blame for "the moment lost" to his critics. He seems to forget that these critics were only reacting to a political position that he had advanced—one that, despite Moynihan's many disclaimers, did shift the focus of policy away from a concerted attack on racist structures to an inconsequential preoccupation with the black family.

In recent years there have been attempts to rehabilitate Moynihan, and to portray him as the hapless victim of the ideological excesses of the sixties. For example, in *The Undeserving Poor*—a book that traces the poverty debates since the 1960s—historian Michael Katz asserts that "because most critics distorted the report, the debate generated more passion than insight." One result of the attack on Moynihan, he adds mournfully, "was to accelerate the burial of the culture of poverty as an acceptable concept in liberal reform."[35] William Julius Wilson goes even further in suggesting that "the controversy surrounding the Moynihan report had the effect of curtailing serious research on minority problems in the inner city for over a decade." Wilson would have us believe that, like the character in Woody Allen's film *Sleeper*, social scientists fell into a fifteen-year coma, and when they emerged from ideological torpor, "they were dumbfounded by the magnitude of the changes that had taken place."[36]

THE INTELLECTUAL REINCARNATION
OF DANIEL PATRICK MOYNIHAN

Joyce Ladner's 1973 declaration of "the death of white sociology" turns out to have been premature.[37] A remarkable thing happened: "white sociology" underwent a black reincarnation. In the case of Daniel Patrick Moynihan, his theoretical and political positions were essentially resurrected twenty years later by William Julius Wilson. Indeed, Moynihan would be able to gloat over the fact that Wilson and other black scholars had taken up the very positions for which he had been vilified years earlier. As he commented in his Godkin lectures at Harvard in 1984: "The family report had been viewed as mistaken; the benign neglect memorandum was depicted as out-and-out racist. By mid-decade, however, various black scholars were reaching similar conclusions, notably William Julius Wilson in his 1978 study, *The Declining Significance of Race*."[38]

In point of fact, Wilson struck a number of themes that were at the heart of Moynihan's political analysis in 1965: that blacks had their political rights, thanks to landmark civil rights legislation; that there was "a widening gulf" between the black middle class, which was reaping the benefits of an improved climate of tolerance, and the black lower class, which was as destitute and isolated as ever; that blacks were arriving in the nation's cities at a time when employment opportunities, especially in the manufacturing sector, were declining; and that future progress would depend less on tearing down racist barriers than on raising the level of education and skills among poor blacks.[39] The underlying assumption in both cases was that the civil rights revolution was a watershed that more or less resolved the issue of "race," but that left unaddressed the vexing problems of "class." By "class," however, neither Moynihan nor Wilson were advancing a radical theory that challenged structures of inequality, or that envisioned a radical restructuring of major political and economic institutions. All they meant was that lower class blacks needed to acquire the education and skills that are a prerequisite for mobility and that explain the success of the black middle class.

In *The Truly Disadvantaged*, published in 1987, Wilson spelled out the implications of his "declining significance" thesis for politics and public policy. Again, he arrived at a position that Moynihan had articulated in 1965: that there was no political constituency for policies targeted specifically for blacks, and therefore "we have to declare that we are doing it for *everybody*." In the very next sentence, Moynihan added an important caveat: "I think, however, that the problem of the Negro American *is* now a special one, and is not just an intense case of the problem of all poor people."[40] But, he insisted, blacks could be helped only through color-blind programs that defined poverty—not race—as the basis for social action. Here, alas, was the "hidden agenda" that Wilson proposed twenty-two years later.

Wilson originally intended to use "The Hidden Agenda" as the title of *The Truly Disadvantaged*.[41] Instead, he used this as the title of chapter 7, in which he contended that, because there is no political constituency for policies targeted for blacks, it becomes necessary to "hide" such programs behind universal programs "to which the more advantaged groups of all races and class backgrounds can positively relate."[42] Ironically, Wilson's language reveals that he is a poor social democrat. It suggests that his first priority is to help the ghetto underclass, and that he opts for "universal programs" only out of political expediency.

The notion of a "hidden agenda" also contradicts Wilson's claim that racism is of "declining significance." Indeed, it is *because* of racism that

Wilson feels compelled to "hide" his agenda in the first place. The under-lying premise is that America is *so* racist—so utterly indifferent to the plight of black America, so implacably opposed to any kind of indemnifi-cation for three centuries of racial oppression—that it becomes necessary to camouflage policies intended for blacks behind policies that offer ben-efits to the white majority.

At first blush, it might appear odd to portray Wilson as a political clone of Moynihan. Wilson, after all, is an ivory-tower scholar and a po-litical outsider who has described himself as a social democrat. Moynihan gave up any pretense of political chastity to become a major entity within the Democratic Party. On closer scrutiny, however, Wilson is far from a detached intellectual. In two national elections he has gone on record, via op-ed pieces in the *New York Times*, to advocate race-neutral politics in order to enhance Democratic electoral prospects.[43] And he has quietly served as President Clinton's exculpation for the administration's failure to develop policies to deal with the plight of the nation's ghettos. When-ever Clinton is confronted with this issue, his stock answer is to defend his do-nothing policy by invoking the name of "the famous African-American sociologist William Julius Wilson," explaining how profoundly influenced he was by his book *The Truly Disadvantaged*, and ending with glowing projections about how blacks stand to benefit from his economic policies.[44] It should come as no surprise that Wilson has been mentioned as a possible cabinet appointee.[45]

Thus, whatever differences exist between Moynihan and Wilson, the factor of overriding importance is that both repudiated race-based politics and race-based public policy. Here we come to the delicate but unavoid-able issue concerning the role that the race of a social theorist plays in de-termining what Alvin Gouldner refers to as "the *social* career of a theory."[46] Not only was Moynihan white, but he wrote at a time of height-ened racial consciousness and mobilization, both inside and outside the university. As a white, he was susceptible to charges of racism and of re-sorting to stereotypes in his depiction of black families. Even the voluble Moynihan was reduced to silence when it came to parrying the charges leveled against him by black scholars and activists.

Wilson, too, has had his critics, but at least he has been immune to charges of "racism." Furthermore, Wilson appeared on the stage of history at a time when racial militancy was ebbing. The nation, including the academic establishment, had grown weary of racial conflict, and was eager, like the Democratic Party, to "get beyond race." Wilson, clearly, was the right person in the right place and the right time, and, as if this were not enough, his book *The Declining Significance of Race* had the right title—one that satisfied the nation's yearning to put race behind, to pretend that racism was no longer the problem it had been in times past.

To be sure, Wilson did not cause the retreat from race that has occurred over the past two decades. He did, however, confer on it an indispensable mark of legitimacy. This is the significance of Wilson's elevation to national prominence and even to celebrity status. It has meant that the retreat from race could no longer be equated with racism and reaction.[47]

CORNEL WEST:
THE LEFT WING OF THE BACKLASH

If books could be judged by their titles, one would think that a book entitled *Race Matters* would be the antithesis of a book entitled *The Declining Significance of Race*. But then again, one must beware of semantic infiltration, and the possibility that titles are subversive of meaning.

Of course, the title has an intentional double meaning. The first—*race* matters—serves as a catchall for the disparate essays that West has compiled in this volume. The second meaning—race *matters*—is more substantive, but still leaves the reader to wallow in ambiguity. In what sense does race "matter" in the *Weltanschauung* of Cornel West? Is this an ironic comment on whites' obsessive preoccupation with the happenstance of skin color? Or does it allude to the fateful influence that race has on the lives of African Americans? Nor is the meaning of "race" clear. Is this an affirmation of race—that is, of black culture and identity? Or does "race" refer to "racism" and the extent that *it* "matters" in the lives of African Americans? Or is the ambiguity purposeful, to point up the paradoxical and sometimes contradictory nature of the phenomenon itself?

Suffice it to say that many or all of these elements appear in West's book: topics range from the crisis in black leadership, to black conservatism, to black-Jewish relations, to black sexuality. These are all race matters, to be sure, but they are only marginally related to the question that preoccupies us here: the extent that race (read racism) matters, and the consequences that ensue for politics and public policy. These issues are explored in two of West's essays that serve as the basis of the following discussion: "Nihilism in Black America" and "Beyond Affirmative Action: Equality and Identity."[48]

The term "nihilism" invites semantic confusion. Invoked by a professor of philosophy, the term conjures up hoary philosophical debates concerning the nature of existence and the possibility of objective knowledge. But West surely is not claiming that the ghetto is an enactment of some dubious philosophical doctrine. Invoked by a political activist, "nihilism" calls up associations with Russian revolutionaries who believed that the old order must be utterly eradicated to make way for the new. Again, it is doubtful that West, the political activist, is imputing these motives to ghetto youth. Nor does his use of "nihilism" suggest the angst and denial of meaning that are often viewed as endemic to modernity. No doubt West could expound on all of these themes, but in describing the urban ghetto, he uses the word specifically to refer to destructive and self-destructive behavior that is unconstrained by legal or moral norms. But this meaning comes dangerously close to the prevailing view of ghetto youth as driven by aberrant and antisocial tendencies. Alas, does "nihilism" merely provide an intellectual gloss for ordinary assumptions and claims?

Any such doubts are seemingly dissipated by the book's opening sentence: "What happened in Los Angeles in April of 1992 was neither a race riot nor a class rebellion. Rather, this monumental upheaval was a multiracial, trans-class, and largely male display of justified social rage." With this manifesto, West establishes his credentials as a person on the left. By the end of the same paragraph, however, West says that "race was the visible catalyst, not the underlying cause."[49] Already the reader is left to wonder: does race matter or doesn't it?

In the next paragraph West assumes the rhetorical stance that pervades his book: his is the voice of reason and moderation between liberals and conservatives, each of which is allegedly trapped in rigid orthodoxies that leave us "intellectually debilitated, morally disempowered, and personally depressed."[50] Liberals, West avers, are burdened with a simplistic faith in the ability of government to solve our racial problems. Conservatives, on the other hand, blame the problems on blacks and ignore "public responsibility for the immoral circumstances that haunt our fellow citizens." Both treat blacks as "a problem people." West presents himself as mediator between these ideological poles. He is a leftist who does not resort to a crude economic determinism that denies human freedom and that relieves the poor of moral responsibility for their actions. And he is a theologian who does not use morality to evade public responsibility for social wrongs.

Thus for West racism and poverty are only part of the problem. Of equal concern is the "pervasive spiritual impoverishment" that afflicts ghetto dwellers. With these false dichotomies, West has set the stage for a morality play involving a contest between material and spiritual forces and between left and right. Enter the protagonist: a Man of Vision who sees through the mystifications of both sides, a Great Conciliator who transcends political schism and will point the way to an Eden of racial harmony and social justice.

A captivating tale, to be sure. But the critical issue is this: where does West's laudatory attempt to bridge the ideological chasm lead him? According to West, "the liberal/conservative discussion conceals the most basic issue now facing black America." The reader waits with bated breath: what is this "most basic issue"? West has already conveyed his skepticism of the left's monistic emphasis on issues of racism and political economy. And he claims to reject the conservative emphasis on "behavioral impediments" with its bootstrap morale. The most basic issue now facing black America, according to Cornel West, is *"the nihilistic threat to its very existence."*[51] West continues:

This threat is not simply a matter of relative economic deprivation and political powerlessness—though economic well-being and political clout are requisites for meaningful black progress. It is primarily a question of speaking to the profound sense of psychological depression, personal worthlessness, and social despair so widespread in black America.[52]

Now, there can be no doubt that "psychological depression, personal worthlessness, and social despair" abound in ghettos across America. So do "battered identities," "spiritual impoverishment," "social deracination," "cultural denudement," and a host of related afflictions that leave West groping for words to convey the gravity and horror of this situation. Certainly, West should not be faulted for bringing such conditions to light. This point is worth underscoring because Wilson and others have claimed that discussion of ghetto "pathologies" has been taboo ever since Moynihan was clobbered, as they would have it, for reporting some unpleasant statistics on black families. This is a totally unfounded allegation. The only issue, both then and now, concerns the theoretical claims that are advanced concerning the *causes* of these well-known afflictions, together with the related issue of what is to be *done* about them. This was the basis of the attack on Moynihan, and it is on these same issues that West must be judged.

According to West, despite the tribulations going back to slavery, blacks have always been endowed with "cultural armor to beat back the demons of hopelessness, meaninglessness, lovelessness."[53] He points out that until the 1970s the rate of suicide was comparatively low among blacks, but today young blacks have one of the highest rates of suicide. Thus, for West the question becomes: what has happened to "the cultural structures that once sustained black life in America" and "are no longer able to fend off the nihilistic threat?" His answer focuses on two factors:

1. *The saturation of market forces and market moralities in black life.*
   By this West means that blacks have succumbed to the materialism and hedonism that pervade American culture, and that "edge out nonmarket values—love, care, service to others—handed down by preceding generations." If blacks are more susceptible to these corrupting influences than others, it is because the poor have "a limited capacity to ward off self-contempt and self-hatred."[54]

2. *The crisis in black leadership.* Here West bemoans the failure of black leaders to carry on a tradition of leadership that was at once aggressive and inspirational. One reason for this failure is that the new middle class has been corrupted by their immersion into mass culture. But another reason that "quality leadership is on the wane" has to do with "the gross deterioration of personal, familial, and communal relations among African-Americans."[55] With families in decline and communities in shambles, the basis for effective leadership is lost.

West harkens back to the halcyon days when there was "a vital community bound by its ethical ideals."[56] Unfortunately, oppression does not always produce such felicitous outcomes, and the victims of oppression are not always ennobled by their experience and an inspiration to the rest of us.

West's problem, to repeat, is not that he discusses crime, violence, drugs, and the other notorious ills of ghetto life. Rather, the problem is that he presents social breakdown and cultural disintegration as a problem *sui generis*, with an existence and momentum independent of the forces that gave rise to it in the first place. Moynihan, too, had held that centuries of injustice had "brought about deep-seated structural distortions in the life of the Negro American." But he added a remarkable addendum: "At this point, the present pathology is capable of perpetuating itself without assistance from the white world."[57] Similarly, West traces nihilism to centuries of injustice, but goes on to claim that nihilism is so embedded in the life of the ghetto that it assumes a life all its own. At least this is what West implies when he writes that "culture is as much a structure as the economy or politics."[58] Indeed, the whole point of West's critique of "liberal structuralism" is that nihilism is not reducible to political economy. It is precisely because nihilism is so deeply embedded that this "cultural structure" must be addressed as a force in its own right.

It takes hairsplitting distinctions that do not bear close scrutiny to maintain that West's view of nihilism is different from the conservative view of ghetto culture as deeply pathological, and as the chief source of the problems that beset African Americans. Despite his frequent caveats,

West has succeeded in shifting the focus of blame onto the black community. The affliction is *theirs*—something we shall call "nihilism."

It is also theirs to resolve. As with the Moynihan Report, the regressive implications of West's theory become clear when one examines his
praxis. West calls for "a politics of conversion"—a frail attempt to use radical vernacular as a cover for ideas that are anything but radical. "Like al-
coholism and drug addiction," West explains, "nihilism is a disease of the
soul."[59] How does one cure a disease of the soul? West's prescription (to
paraphrase Jencks) is to change the nihilist, not the system. In West's own
words:

> Nihilism is not overcome by arguments or analysis; it is tamed by
> love and care. Any disease of the soul must be conquered by a
> turning of one's soul. This turning is done through one's own af-
> firmation of one's worth—an affirmation fueled by the concern of
> others. A love ethic must be at the center of a politics of conver-
> sion.[60]

One can almost hear the national sigh of relief from those who feared
that expensive new programs of social reconstruction and a renewed commitment to affirmative action might become necessary to control the
disorder emanating from the ghettos of America. Instead, we have an
inexpensive palliative: a crusade against nihilism to be waged from within
the black community. So much the better that this proposal is advanced
not by another black conservative whose politics might be suspect, but by
a self-proclaimed socialist. Unfortunately, West, the philosopher and activist, adopts the idiom of the preacher who mounts the pulpit, pounds
the lectern, and enjoins his flock to "have the audacity to take the nihilistic threat by the neck and turn back its deadly assaults."[61]

One cannot fault West for trying to bridge the chasm between religion and politics. However, he has not placed himself in the tradition of
Martin Luther King, Jr., who invoked religious symbols and appealed to
spiritual values in order to mobilize popular support behind a political
movement. King did not believe that a love ethic could ever serve as an
antidote to spiritual breakdown. The only remedy was a political transfor-

mation that eliminated the conditions that eat away at the human spirit. West, on the other hand, offers no political framework for his so-called politics of conversion. Indeed, he explicitly divorces nihilism from political economy, thus implying that moral redemption is to be achieved through some mysterious "turning of one's soul."[62]

West cannot escape the retrograde implications of his position with the disclaimer that "unlike conservative behaviorists, the politics of conversion situates these actions within inhumane circumstances."[63] He ignores his own admonition that "to call on black people to be agents makes sense only if we also examine the dynamics of this victimization against which their agency will, in part, be exercised."[64] And while he is guided by "a vision of moral regeneration and political insurgency for the purpose of fundamental social change for all who suffer from socially induced misery,"[65] he fails to translate this prophetic ideal into a political praxis. On the contrary, the practical implication of West's position is to substitute a vapid and utterly inconsequential "politics of conversion" for a genuine political solution—one that would call upon the power and resources of the national government for what is at bottom a national problem and a national disgrace.

It should come as no surprise that the most prominent convert to West's politics of conversion is President Clinton. In a speech delivered to a Memphis church in 1993, Clinton practically echoed West in asserting that there is a crisis of the spirit. The ramifications for public policy should have been predictable: "Sometimes, there are no answers from the outside in. Sometimes, all of the answers have to come from the values and the stirrings and the voices that speak to us from within."[66] Thus are legitimate spiritual concerns used as a subterfuge for political and moral abdication. The irony is made still more bitter by the fact that Clinton gave his speech in the same Memphis church where Martin Luther King, Jr., delivered his last sermon the night before his 1968 assassination.

Not only does West shift the focus of analysis and of blame away from the structures of racial oppression, but in his chapter entitled "Beyond Affirmative Action" he undercuts the single policy that has gone a decisive step beyond equal rights in the direction of equal results. West is *not* opposed to affirmative action, but he engages in a tortuous reasoning that subverts the whole logic behind it. He begins on the one hand by declaring that in principle he favors a class-based affirmative action (as does William Julius Wilson).[67] On the other hand, he knows that such a policy is politically unrealistic. He also knows that if affirmative action in its present form were abolished, then "racial and sexual discrimination would return with a vengeance."[68] Why, then, all this hairsplitting? Even if a class-based affirmative action could be enacted, few of the benefits would filter down to African Americans, who are not only most in need but also have unique claims for compensatory treatment. Nor would working-class whites who become lawyers and doctors on the basis of affirmative action provide the black community with the professional talent that it sorely needs. Finally, advocates of class-based affirmative action overlook the fact that, unlike blacks, working-class whites do not need governmental protection to assure them of access to working-class jobs.

In short, affirmative action is meant to counteract the evils of *caste*, not of class. It is predicated on a realization that blacks have been victims of a system of oppression that goes far beyond the disabilities associated with class disadvantage, and therefore warrants a special remedy. West's equivocation with respect to race-based affirmative action is the clearest indication of how little race matters in his theoretical framework and in his agenda for change.

Reminiscent of Moynihan and Wilson, West's approach for helping blacks is to help "everybody." Like them, he provides a respectable liberal cover for evading the issue of race, and still worse, backing off from race-targeted policies like affirmative action, all in the name of getting "beyond race." West prides himself on steering "a course between the Scylla of environmental determinism and the Charybdis of a blaming-the-victims perspective."[69] Unfortunately, he ends up in a political never-never land where, as Du Bois once said in his critique of historiography, "nobody seems to have done wrong and everybody was right."[70] And nothing changes.

This nation's ruling elites need to be told that there is no exit from the current morass until they confront the legacy of slavery and resume the unfinished racial agenda. It is *their* nihilism that deserves our condemnation—the crime, the immorality, the self-destructive folly of tolerating racial ghettos and excluding yet another generation of black youth from the American dream.

CONCLUSION

Was there hyperbole in King's assertion that the great stumbling block in the stride for freedom was not the Council or the Klan but those who seek a middle ground and would settle for a negative peace? Perhaps. As is often argued, liberals are not *the* enemy. However, the "enemy" depends on the so-called liberal to put a kinder and gentler face on racism; to subdue the rage of the oppressed; to raise false hopes that change is imminent; to modulate the demands for complete liberation; to divert protest; and to shift the onus of responsibility for America's greatest crime away from powerful institutions that *could* make a difference onto individuals who have been rendered powerless by these very institutions.

The liberal retreat from race during the post–civil rights era is full of political paradox. When forced to confront the issue, the liberal will argue that in a racist society, race-based politics are not viable precisely because blacks are an isolated and despised minority. As with much race-think, this is upside down and inside out. It is precisely because blacks were an isolated and despised minority that they were forced to seek redress outside of the framework of electoral politics. The civil rights movement was triumphant in part because it tapped the lode of revolutionary potential within the black community, and in part because it galvanized the support of political allies outside the black community, including white liberals. Furthermore, this movement not only achieved its immediate objectives, but also was the major catalyst for progressive change in the twentieth century. As Aldon Morris writes at the conclusion of *The Origins of the Civil Rights Movement:* "The civil rights movement served as a training ground for many of the activists who later organized movements within their own communities. Indeed, the modern women's movement, student movement, farm workers' movement, and others of the period were triggered by the unprecedented scale of non-traditional politics in the civil rights movement."[71]

A common refrain from the right is that advocates of affirmative action are guilty of the very thing that they say they are against—namely, treating blacks as a separate class. Again, this reasoning is upside down and inside out. The truth is that it is the *refusal* to see race—the willful color blindness of the liberal camp—that acquiesces to the racial status quo, and does so by consigning blacks to a twilight zone where they are politically invisible. In this way elements of the left unwittingly join the right in evading any reckoning with America's greatest crime—slavery—and its legacy in the present.

NOTES

1. Martin Luther King, Jr., "Letter from Birmingham Jail," in *I Have a Dream: Writings and Speeches That Changed the World,* ed. James Melvin Washington (New York: HarperCollins, 1986), 91.
2. Murray Friedman, "The White Liberal's Retreat," *Atlantic Monthly* 211 (January 1963): 43.
3. Ibid., 44.
4. Ibid., 46.
5. Martin Luther King, Jr., *Why We Can't Wait* (New York: Harper & Row, 1963), 147.
6. Whitney M. Young, Jr., *To Be Equal* (New York: McGraw-Hill, 1963), 54. This was to become a common refrain among civil rights leaders. In 1964, Bayard Rustin wrote, "What is the value of winning access to public accommodations for those who lack money to use them?" That same year Hubert Humphrey commented in congressional debate, "What good does it do a Negro to be able to eat in a fine restaurant if he cannot afford to pay the bill?" In 1968, Martin Luther King, Jr., wrote, "What good is it to be allowed to eat in a restaurant if you can't afford a hamburger?" Bayard Rustin, "From Protest to Politics: The Future of the Civil Rights Movement," *Commentary* 39 (February 1964): 25; Hubert Humphrey, quoted in Richard A. Epstein, *Forbidden Grounds* (Cambridge, Mass.: Harvard University Press, 1992), 400; Martin Luther King, Jr., quoted in "Showdown for Non-Violence," *Look,* April 16, 1968, 24.
7. Lee Rainwater and William L. Yancey, eds., *The Moynihan Report and the Politics of Controversy* (Cambridge, Mass.: MIT Press, 1967), 11.
8. In October 1963, the issue of "compensation" was debated in no less public a forum than the *New York Times Magazine:* Whitney M. Young, Jr., and Kyle Haselden, "Should There Be 'Compensation' for Negroes?" *New York*

Times Magazine (October 6, 1963), 43ff. Already on the defensive, Young wrote: ". . . the Urban League is asking for a special effort, not for special privileges. This effort has been described as 'preferential treatment,' 'indemnification,' 'special consideration,' 'compensatory activity.' These are 'scare' phrases that obscure the meaning of the proposal and go against the grain of our native sense of fair play. What we ask now is for a brief period there be a deliberate and massive effort to include the Negro citizen in the mainstream of American life." Kyle Haselden, who was an editor at *Christian Century* and author of a book entitled *The Racial Problems in Christian Perspective*, argued that "our goal should be parity, not preferment," and struck the chord that would pervade the antiaffirmative discourse: that "compensation for Negroes is a subtle but pernicious form of racism."

9. King, *Why We Can't Wait*, 147.

10. James Baldwin, Nathan Glazer, Sidney Hook, and Gunnar Myrdal took part in this discussion. The proceedings were published as "Liberalism and the Negro: A Round-Table Discussion," *Commentary* 37 (March 1964): 25–42. Also see "Letters from Readers" in the August issue.

11. Ibid., 25.

12. Ibid., 26. Podhoretz's statement reiterated some of the ideas in an article by David Danzig, "The Meaning of Negro Strategy," *Commentary* 37 (February 1964): 41–46.

13. "Liberalism and the Negro," 31.

14. Ibid.

15. Ibid., 39.

16. That the speech was written by Goodwin and Moynihan is indicated in Daniel Patrick Moynihan, *Family and Nation* (New York: Harcourt Brace Jovanovich, 1986), 30. At Johnson's direction the speech was read to several prominent civil rights leaders. According to Moynihan, "Each in turn was quite transported by propositions that a year later each, save one, would quite reject" (30). The unnamed civil rights leaders who "cleared" the speech were Martin Luther King, Whitney Young, and Roy Wilkins; Allen J. Matusow, *The Unraveling of America: A History of Liberalism in the 1960s* (New York: HarperTorchbooks, 1986), 196.

17. Johnson's Howard University address is reprinted in Rainwater and Yancey, *The Moynihan Report and the Politics of Controversy*, 125–32 (emphasis added). The speech was drafted by Richard N. Goodwin and Daniel Patrick Moynihan, though it would appear that Moynihan was the chief architect, judging from a paper that he delivered at a *Daedalus* conference only a month earlier. Moynihan began the paper by noting that the civil rights revolution was entering "a new phase," representing a shift from issues of liberty to issues of equality. He also predicted that this shift would result in an attenuation of liberal support. Finally, after a series of theoretical gyra-

tions, he focused on the problems in the black family that, he held, were preventing lower-class blacks from taking advantage of expanding opportunities. "Employment, Income, and the Negro Family," *Daedalus* 94 (Fall 1965): 745–70.

18. Eli Ginzberg, *The Negro Potential* (New York: Columbia University Press, 1956), 7. Later Ginzberg writes: "The habits, the values, and the goals that the child acquires provide the basis for his later accomplishments in school and at work. Because of his history, the American Negro is not prepared in the same way as the white population to take full advantage of the economic opportunities that exist. The Negro must alter many of his values before he will be able to cope effectively with his new situation" (93). Ginzberg also advanced the argument for universal as opposed to targeted social policy: "The best hope for the Negro's speedy and complete integration into American society lies in the continuation of a strong and virile economy in which his labor is needed and his skills and capabilities rewarded" (117).

19. Tom Wicker, "Johnson Pledges to Help Negroes to Full Equality," *New York Times*, June 5, 1965.

20. Moynihan ascribes the term to "the world of diplomacy" and has used it in his political sparring over the years. See the *Wall Street Journal*'s "Notable and Quotable" column, April 18, 1985; "'Loose Cannon' Moynihan on a Roll," the *Buffalo News*, July 4, 1993; and *Firing Line*, January 15, 1994.

21. According to the *Washington Evening Star* (June 5, 1965), Johnson was interrupted eighteen times by applause; Orr Kelly, "President Calls Partley 'To Fulfill Civil Rights': 14,000 at Howard Give Him Ovation as Johnson Hails New Era for Negro," *Washington Evening Star*, June 5, 1965. In his retrospective account Moynihan makes a point of "the stunning ovation" that Johnson received at the conclusion of his speech, as if this placed a stamp of black approval on the speech; "The President and the Negro: The Moment Lost," *Commentary* 43 (February 1967): 34.

22. The conference transcript is published in a two-volume series of *Daedalus* in Fall 1965 and Winter 1966. The quoted excerpt is found in vol. 2, 288–89.

23. "Review of the Week," *New York Times*, June 6, 1965.

24. Quoted in Rainwater and Yancey, *The Moynihan Report and the Politics of Controversy*, 135.

25. Ibid., 59. It should have been obvious that the burgeoning welfare rolls were an artifact of two factors: the migration of young blacks to cities in the North and West, and the liberalization of eligibility as a response to rising black protest.

26. Daniel Patrick Moynihan, "The Negro Family: The Case for National Action," in Rainwater and Yancey, *The Moynihan Report and the Politics of Controversy*, 76.

27. Christopher Jencks, "The Moynihan Report," in Rainwater and Yancey, *The Moynihan Report and the Politics of Controversy*, 443 (emphasis added).

28. Herbert J. Gans, "The Negro Family: Reflections on the Moynihan Report," in Rainwater and Yancey, *The Moynihan Report and the Politics of Controversy*, 450.

29. As Rainwater and Yancey write, "The controversy was, then, a kind of lucky break for the administration since it served to distract from and conceal the fact that the Administration was not really ready to assume the independent role it had reached for at Howard University"; ibid., 294.

30. At the very outset of his study, Gutman writes, "This volume . . . was stimulated by the bitter public and academic controversy surrounding Daniel P. Moynihan's *The Negro Family in America: The Case for National Action* (1965)"; Herbert G. Gutman, *The Black Family in Slavery and Freedom, 1750–1925* (New York: Pantheon, 1976), xvii. The controversy also stimulated a plethora of studies in all of the social sciences on race, poverty, and the family.

31. Moynihan, "The President and the Negro: The Moment Lost," *Commentary* 43 (February 1967): 31.

32. Ibid., 32 (emphasis in original).

33. Ibid.

34. Ibid., 34.

35. Michael B. Katz, *The Undeserving Poor* (New York: Pantheon, 1989), 24. Elsewhere Katz writes that "the furor over Moynihan's report, in fact, drove black families off the agenda of social science for nearly two decades. Similar attacks discredited the culture of poverty"; "The Urban 'Underclass' as a Metaphor of Social Transformation," in *The "Underclass" Debate*, ed. Michael B. Katz (Princeton, N.J.: Princeton University Press, 1993), 13.

36. William Julius Wilson, *The Truly Disadvantaged* (Chicago: University of Chicago Press, 1987), 4.

37. Joyce A. Ladner, *The Death of White Sociology* (New York: Vintage Books, 1973).

38. Moynihan, *Family and Nation*, 42. Soon after the publication of *The Declining Significance of Race*, Nathan Glazer also commented: "These are not things that haven't been said before. It is the first time that a black social scientist has said them with such strength"; quoted in Hollie West, "Getting Ahead and the Man Behind the Class-Race Furor," *Washington Post* (January 1, 1979).

39. These ideas pervade Moynihan's writing, but are clearly articulated in "Employment, Income, and the Ordeal of the Negro Family," *Daedalus* 94 (Fall 1965): esp. 753–54.

40. Daniel Patrick Moynihan, transcript of the American Academy Conference on the Negro American, May 14–16, 1965, *Daedalus* 95 (Winter 1966): 288 (emphasis in original).

41. This statement is based on the fact that in a chapter titled "The Urban Underclass," published three years before *The Truly Disadvantaged*, Wilson indicated that "this chapter is based on a larger study, *The Hidden Agenda: Race, Social Dislocations, and Public Policy in America*, to be published by the University of Chicago Press"; in *Minority Report: What Has Happened to Blacks, Hispanics, American Indians, and Other Minorities in the Eighties*, ed. Leslie Dunbar (New York: Pantheon, 1984), 75. The same notation is found in Wilson's chapter on "The Urban Underclass in Advanced Industrial Society," in *The New Urban Reality*, ed. Paul E. Peterson (Washington, D.C.: Brookings Institution, 1985), 129.

42. William Julius Wilson, *The Truly Disadvantaged*, 155.

43. William Julius Wilson, *New York Times*, March 24, 1990, and March 17, 1992. See also his article "Race-Neutral Programs and the Democratic Coalition," *American Prospect*, no. 1 (Spring 1990): 74–81. Also see Kenneth Tollett's reply and Wilson's rejoinder in the subsequent issue.

44. This reference to Wilson was made by President Clinton in a speech to black ministers in Memphis on November 13, 1993, and cited in a profile on Wilson in *People* magazine (January 17, 1974, 81). According to one journalist: "Throughout the Presidential campaign, he [Clinton] quoted Wilson's work at every turn. '*The Truly Disadvantaged* made me see the problems of race and poverty and the inner city in a different light,' he said recently. 'It reinforced my conviction that we have to find broad-based economic solutions to a lot of our country's challenges.'" Gretchen Reynolds, "The Rising Significance of Race," *Chicago* 41 (December 1992): 82.

45. Reynolds, "The Rising Significance of Race," 81.

46. Alvin Ward Gouldner, *The Coming Crisis of Western Sociology* (New York: Basic Books, 1970), 29 (emphasis in original).

47. In 1978, Wilson's *Declining Significance of Race* was awarded the American Sociological Association's Sydney S. Spivak Award in intergroup relations. It is worth noting that this award was condemned by the Association of Black Sociologists in a resolution that complained that Wilson's book "obscures the problem of the persistent oppression of blacks" (quoted in Hollie West, "Getting Ahead and the Man Behind the Class-Race Furor"). Among Wilson's recent laurels was being named as a member of the President's Committee for the National Medal of Science. He was also selected as the 1994 winner of the Frank E. Seidman Distinguished Award in Political Economy. Robert Solow, MIT economist and former Nobel Prize winner, who served on the selection committee, commented: "If anyone is a successor to Gunnar Myrdal in the study of black society in the U.S., it's Bill Wilson"; "W. J. Wilson Awarded Seidman Prize," *Footnotes* (American Sociological Association), October 1994, 5. Indeed, if *An American Dilemma*

was the "exemplar study" of the pre–civil rights era, it is safe to say that *The Declining Significance of Race* and *The Truly Disadvantaged* are the exemplar works of the post–civil rights era.

48. These two issues were originally published in liberal-left journals: "Nihilism in Black America" in *Dissent* 38 (Spring 1991), and "Beyond Affirmative Action: Equality and Identity" in *American Prospect*, no. 9 (Spring 1992).

49. West, *Race Matters*, 1.

50. Ibid., 2.

51. Ibid., 12 (emphasis in original).

52. Ibid., 12–13.

53. Ibid., 15.

54. Ibid., 17.

55. Ibid., 36.

56. Ibid., 37.

57. Moynihan, "The Negro Family: The Case for National Action," 93.

58. West, *Race Matters*, 12.

59. Ibid., 18.

60. Ibid., 19.

61. Ibid.

62. Ibid.

63. Ibid., 20.

64. Ibid., 14.

65. Ibid., 46.

66. "Excerpts from Clinton's Speech to Black Ministers," *New York Times*, November 14, 1993. This speech also had the imprint of William Julius Wilson, who had dined at the White House the previous week. In an op-ed piece in the *Washington Post*, E. J. Dionne linked Wilson's ideas with Clinton's Memphis speech. To quote Dionne: "Clinton, as a good Wilson student, was thus insistent in his speech that if you couldn't address the plight of the African American poor without talking about moral values and personal responsibility, then neither could you expect worthy values to flourish in the absence of jobs"; "Clinton's Bully Pulpit," *Washington Post*, November 16, 1993.

67. Wilson's position is reported in Steven A. Holmes, "Mulling the Idea of Affirmative Action for Poor Whites," *New York Times*, August 18, 1991.

68. West, *Race Matters*, 64.

69. Ibid., 57.

70. W. E. B. Du Bois, "The Propaganda of History," in *Black Reconstruction* (New York: Harcourt, Brace, 1935), 714.

71. Aldon Morris, *The Origins of the Civil Rights Movement* (New York: Free Press, 1984), 288.

WHITE WORKERS, NEW DEMOCRATS, AND AFFIRMATIVE ACTION

David Roediger

■

W ITHOUT A CONSTITUTIONALLY structured programme of deep and
extensive affirmative action," African National Congress legal
theorist Albie Sachs wrote in 1991, "a Bill of Rights in South Africa is
meaningless." Sachs added:

> Affirmative action by its nature involves the disturbance of in-
> herited rights. It is redistributory rather than conservative in
> character. . . . In the historical conditions of South Africa, affir-
> mative action is not merely the correction of certain perceived
> structural injustices. It becomes the major instrument in the tran-
> sitional period after a democratic government has been installed,
> for converting a racist oppressive society into a democratic and
> just one.

Incorporating such logic into its policy documents, the ANC has at
times drawn optimistically on a tradition and a language of affirmative
action developed largely in the United States. Thus, the draft constitution promised to use race-specific initiatives to eliminate discrimination in "form and substance."[1] Meanwhile, in the United States, much
of liberalism and part of the left has come to see affirmative policies designed specifically to remedy the effects of racism as electoral liabilities,
perhaps suitable in moral discourses but not in political ones. That the

current* Republican calls for an end to affirmative action have provoked so much "review" and such belated defense of the policy by the Clinton administration is therefore unsurprising. Not only has a vigorous political defense of the principles and politics of affirmative action never been undertaken by Democratic leaders, but the "new Democrats" of the Clinton administration have developed their electoral strategies largely around claims to be uniquely well attuned to voters "fed up" with race- and gender-specific policies.

Irony abounds in the U.S.–South Africa comparison. In a United States in which, theoretically and demographically at least, thoroughgoing affirmative action could substantially improve employment opportunities for a large percentage of the nonwhite population, the demand is seen as utopian and unworkable. In South Africa, where the white population is so small that opening "white" jobs to affirmative action hiring could at best benefit an important, but small, layer of the nonwhite population, the demand is seen as promising and central.²

The relative justice of moral claims to redress by the oppressed cannot account for current differences in attitude toward affirmative action and other race-specific initiatives in the United States and in South Africa. It is true that the Nationalist governments in South Africa have implemented what amounts to a huge and more-or-less explicit pro-Afrikaaner affirmative action program for decades But it is likewise true that, as legal scholar Cheryl Harris brilliantly puts it, the U.S. government and private industry have recognized and forwarded a "property interest in whiteness." Federal relief for victims of the midwestern floods of 1993, Garry Wills quipped at the time, might well have been called an "affirmative action program" for flood plain dwellers. But, he continued, such relief differed in one important particular from affirmative action designed to remedy inequalities: the government did not cause the flooding, as it did, in large part, the racial and gender oppression.³

The dynamics of electoral politics do powerfully help to account for

---

* This article was written in the spring of 1994. Political demagoguery around affirmative action has since then proliferated at such a pace as to ensure that any rewriting of it will be dated by the time of publication. I have therefore kept its text largely intact and have maintained its focus on the logic of "new Democrats" where race is concerned.

the different places of affirmative action in the South African and U.S. contexts. In the former case, demanding affirmative action for nonwhites before a largely nonwhite electorate has considerable potential benefits. In the latter case, demanding affirmative action for nonwhites before an overwhelmingly white electorate is seen as having considerable potential costs. In such a situation, new Democrats and social democrats, neoliberals and pragmatists, leadership councils and followership counsels have seemed to have hardheaded, vote-counting logic very much on their sides in arguing that the downplaying of race-specific initiatives is not only the strategy most likely to yield general social progress but also most apt to win reforms that benefit the black and Latino poor.

The article challenges such a view, one which, with the success of the Clinton strategy of abjuring antiracist appeals in the 1992 elections, and the Republican success in "using" race in 1994, threatens to make the abandonment of egalitarian race-specific initiatives a hallmark of liberal political common sense. The article insists that an emphasis on short-term vote-counting has caused us to leave unexamined historical precedents, as well as the present vagaries and future implications of what is being argued by those who oppose race-specific initiatives. My focus will lie especially on the slippery place the white working class occupies in neoliberal discussions of race.

Leading Clinton strategists, I argue, have portrayed white workers as so obsessed with race as to be unable to enter into coalition politics unless issues of racial justice are removed from the agenda. They have offered a confused analysis of the race-thinking of such workers, sometimes hinting that the workers are unfortunately backward and at other times suggesting that they are uncommonly shrewd. But however confused, this analysis has allowed the Clinton administration to move away from both race and class politics. Rather than appealing to civil rights constituencies and to labor, in the highly diluted forms that the old liberalism favored, new Democrats profess the necessity of appealing to white workers, who are, in their view, defined much more by the adjective than by the noun. In so doing, the historical reflections that close the article argue, neoliberals lead us to a misapprehension of the relationship between whiteness and class that is bound to be disastrous.

When neoliberalism explains why we in the United States cannot have initiatives such as those proposed by the ANC, the usual suspects are rounded up. It is the fault of white workers or, no, check that, I mean black workers, or, no, the "black underclass." Although there is considerable talk about the "declining significance of race" inside neoliberalism, such talk relates to economics, not politics, and certainly not to any supposed decline in the depth of racism among white workers. Properly speaking, the arguments of William J. Wilson and others for race's declining significance center on the relative weight of race and class in structuring black poverty.* Race has anything but a declining significance *politically* for commentators like Stanley Greenberg, Thomas and Mary Edsall, Paul Starr, or Wilson himself. It is, they argue, the *potency* of race-thinking among white voters, and especially among white working-class and ethnic voters, that necessitates the downplaying of race-specific initiatives.[4] Jesse Helms's use of an ad that encouraged every white voter who ever got turned down for anything to blame affirmative action to help win a 1990 North Carolina Senate election is seen as both evidence of the "virulence of race" and of the necessity to shift debate to other issues.[5] An adoring *New York Times* reviewer rightly perceives that the Edsalls argue that "race not class—dominates the domestic political agenda." Greenberg, a Yale political scientist turned Clinton pollster-adviser, is more precise in locating the race-thinking of white *working-class* "Reagan Democrats" as a key to modern politics. He argues that

---

* Wilson's most recent work on the "new poverty" moves to a more equivocal position even on this score. There is, he argues, widespread "employer discrimination" against black men and this discrimination is "sharply" increasing. Such bias results not only from "underclass" habits and values emphasized in Wilson's earlier work, but also from employer preferences for "an expanding immigrant and female labor force." Moreover, cultural-racial conflicts matter enormously. Young black workers who "express bitterness and resentment about their poor employment prospects" foster the "perception that black men are undesirable workers." The tendency of "socially isolated inner city residents" to "enjoy a movie in a communal spirit" precipitates "white flight." Given these emphases, Terry Williams's admiring commentary on Wilson's recent analysis—a commentary which holds that in effect Wilson has set the "new poverty" in a "race-class nexus" and illuminated a "new racism" as well—seems apt. See William Julius Wilson, "The New Urban Poverty and the Problem of Race," and Terry Williams, "Moving Beyond the Academy," both in *Michigan Quarterly Review* 33 (Spring 1994): 253, 262, and 292–93.

among these vital voters, African Americans "constitute the explanation for nearly everything that has gone wrong" so that "virtually all progressive symbols and themes have been redefined in racial and pejorative terms."[6]

But as soon as the Edsalls approvingly quote Greenberg on working-class white Reagan Democrats, they shift focus to explain that the "significant worsening of social dysfunction of the bottom third of the black community" since 1966 *conditioned* changes in white working-class attitudes.[7] The shift is a significant one. Pegging of white working-class discontent to perceptions of black social degradation enables neoliberal opponents of affirmative action to avoid the question of whether working whites really were victimized massively by "reverse discrimination," a troublesome issue on which opponents of "strong" affirmative action have taken a welter of conflicting positions. On the one hand, many commentators, neoliberal and otherwise, have striven to see affirmative action as an upper-middle-class, suburban, liberal assault on white, often ethnic, urban workers who paid for the new policies. On the other hand, critics have wanted to emphasize, evidence to the contrary notwithstanding, that only upper- and middle-class blacks significantly benefited from affirmative action, which can supposedly offer little help to the ghetto "underclass" and working poor. Moreover, from Barry Gross's 1978 attack on affirmative action to Theda Skocpol's lukewarm 1994 defense, the policy has been portrayed as much more successful in reaching university admissions staffs than employers hiring for good working-class jobs. However much these inconsistencies are rooted in an objectively complex and changing situation, they embarrass neoconservative and neoliberal indictments of affirmative action, not the least by implying that when the bottom of white society loses, the top of black society gains—a situation that hardly argues that race-specific initiatives are outmoded.[8]

But the Edsalls deftly sidestep this issue. Black underclass dysfunction, they maintain, not only causes black economic misery but "assaults efforts to eliminate prejudice" among whites and "crush[es] recognition of the achievements of liberalism." Moreover, in effusing recently over Paul Sniderman and Thomas Piazza's *The Scar of Race*, Thomas Byrne Edsall has come around to the view that the history of affirmative action has been one of rank injustice to white workers and students. His earlier coauthored work portrayed instead tragically conflicting claims at play in affirmative action, but now employed black workers as well as the so-called underclass can come in for their share of race-specific blame for liberalism's plight.[9] A studied lack of clarity leaves open the question of whether white workers are reacting as racists or acting as apt observers of black social pathology and preferential treatment. But that very question is fraught with powerful implications for political strategy.

The Edsalls discredit race-specific initiatives largely by discussing policies that are in fact *not* race-specific but are typed that way by white voters. In fact, almost no positive race-specific policies exist. Affirmative action procedures cover white women, veterans, and others. Such procedures potentially benefit a large majority of the population and of the working class, and should be defended in such terms. If we avoid neoliberal formulations that implicitly identify the "worker" as both white and male, affirmative action is far less race-specific than such negative neoliberal-supported policies as expanded capital punishment, the demonization of crack cocaine in sentencing guidelines, and the suspension of constitutional guarantees in federal housing projects. Welfare, including Aid to Families with Dependent Children, is both race-neutral and much utilized by whites.[10] Nonetheless, in a recent Mississippi gubernatorial election, the successful Republican candidate, Kirk Fordice, concluded a highly effective TV spot assailing welfare with a still picture of a black mother and her kids. He invited whites literally to vote against black people, but within the context of a race-neutral, not a race-specific, policy.[11]

As Greenberg's quote suggests, a far more consequential issue than that of whether policies are "race-specific" or "universal" is how those policies come *to be seen* in "racial and pejorative" terms. Thus, welfare and job-training programs become "nonwhite." The tremendous benefits of Federal Housing Administration loans, home-mortgage tax deductions, and federal subsidy of highway construction of new suburbs meanwhile are typed, as George Lipsitz has recently demonstrated, as race-neutral, despite their accruing overwhelmingly to the white middle class. Indeed, those policies are not seen as welfare at all. Although the Edsalls often offer very perceptive commentary on racial "coding" in U.S. politics, their strategy is mute on how to prevent the process of racial typing from recurring and stigmatizing new rounds of "universal" reforms the new Democrats sometimes advocate.[12] Because of existing inequalities of race, some new benefits will clearly be utilized at different levels across racial lines. Race neutrality, in other words, does not work in the long run even on its own terms. Both white racism and black poverty need to be confronted as problems, or the cycle Greenberg identifies will repeat itself.

Whatever its many weaknesses, the strategy of labor and civil rights unity around a program of economic reforms articulated by Bayard Rustin in the mid-1960s was begun as a serious effort to mobilize a constituency based on class interest. The racial discourse of neoliberalism disguises the fact that neoliberalism lacks such an agenda. It has undertaken no significant initiatives to create a legal and political climate in which the labor movement can be rebuilt, for example. After identifying the white working class as a key voting bloc, it offers very little programmatically to workers and working-class organizations. Compare, for example, the expenditure of political energy and pork on the passage, over fierce labor opposition, of the corporate-sponsored North American Free Trade Agreement (NAFTA) with the meager mobilization of legislative support for the striker replacement bill by the Clinton administration. Writers on race and politics in recent America mirror this tendency to treat labor organizations as irrelevant. The AFL-CIO receives three glancing mentions in the Edsalls' detailed and deeply historical treatment of the Democratic Party in *Chain Reaction*. Andrew Hacker's *Two Nations* manages to do without discussion of trade unions even in a long chapter on "equity in employment."[13]

This absence of attention to class and to class politics is tied intimately to the racial politics of neoliberalism, or, perhaps more precisely, to its pretended transcendence of racial politics. We are too ready to assume that the removal of "racial" demands clears political space for class mobilizations. But much of the logic of neoliberalism runs just the other way. Because white workers serve as alternately (and often, simultaneously) the backward masses and the honest observers of black social pathology, there is every political reason for new Democrats to take seriously their views as whites and very little reason to consider their demands as workers.

Greenberg's strategy in developing polling data to guide the right and center of the Democratic Party in developing a strategy to build coalitions "no longer bedeviled by race" perfectly illustrates the tendency to remove the "workers" from considerations of "white workers." As his recent book shows, Greenberg chose to concentrate his 1985 and 1989 efforts on understanding why the all-white largely working-class constituencies of Macomb County, Michigan, had turned to supporting Ronald Reagan's presidential candidacies, why they had not returned to the Democrats in the 1988 Bush–Dukakis race, and on how they might be won back by Clinton in 1992. Greenberg's data came largely from "focus groups," which he insisted had to be "homogenous" so that they would tell the hard truth about their alienation. The homogeneity is racial and so are the truths in which Greenberg is interested. In 1985, 40 percent of households in Macomb County were union households, with the highly integrated United Auto Workers the leading organization. But homogenous focus groups did not convene based on union affiliations and class position. Macomb Countians were brought together as white residents, not as auto workers. Greenberg gloried that Clinton showed that he understood the concerns reported by these white identity politics-based focus groups, in a brilliant Cleveland speech. That speech, to the Democratic Leadership Council (DLC), was picketed by Jesse Jackson and others who protested the DLC's support for NAFTA, a treaty bitterly opposed by the UAW.[14]

Neoliberalism's appeals to the white working class have largely focused on issues that are ostensibly class-neutral, but are highly charged in racial terms: being "tough" enough to criticize hip-hop and black parenting, "ending welfare as we know it," implementing and expanding the death penalty, "three-strikes-and-you're-out" incarceration, justification of NAFTA as an insurance policy against Mexican immigration, and so on. If white workers can be won on these issues, no class agenda is required. Still less is a mobilization around the specific interests of white women workers necessary. Moreover, despite the apologies of Deirdre English and others who have praised the current administration for being "as liberal as it's going to get" in the rightist popular climate in the United States, it is clear that Clinton's search for positions that are impenetrable to Republican appeals to whiteness sometimes take him to the right of the general population on racialized policy issues. Thus, a recent *Time*/CNN poll had but 42 percent of Americans favoring capping welfare when recipients continue to have children. But Clinton supports both state's rights to engage in such capping and the logic of the "reform" itself in the same issue of *Time* that features the poll.[15]

Racial appeals to white workers also resonate with white upper- and middle-class suburban voters, who may well be the real prize being pursued in many invocations of the need to attend to the racial views of white workers. In a fascinating closing section of *Chain Reaction*, the Edsalls suddenly depart from an analysis predicated on the centrality of "Reagan Democrats" and argue for the increasing weight of the "white suburbs," analyzed overwhelmingly in race, rather than class terms, to the future of U.S. politics. In this section, the white working class moves from the center to the margins of neoliberal political analysis with such astonishing ease as to suggest that Reagan Democrats (and Southern "bubbas") have been courted by new Democrats not so much as constituencies in their own rights but as groups whose putative demands and foibles could reposition the party to appeal to middle-class suburban white voters nationally. Indeed, the 1985 Democratic National Committee study on key constituencies that informs much of the Edsalls' analysis is quite suggestive in laying the basis for an effortless transition from white working-class to middle-class concerns. It characterizes the grievances of white ethnics and southern moderates as centering on the belief that "the Democratic Party has not stood with them as they moved from the working to the middle class."[16]

But if the short-term question of whether we should buy an Edsall is rather easily answered in the negative, the larger one of how we should conceptualize race and class in current U.S. politics remains vital. I do not propose to answer that question in the brief balance of this paper, beyond offering the opinion that radical South Africans who argue that the way to nonracialism is through race have much to teach us. What I would like to do is to suggest, arguing largely from history, three broad generalizations that might help us toward such a reconceptualization, especially where white workers are concerned. These generalizations suggest that even in its Rustin-inspired, social democratic variant, and certainly in its current neoliberal one, race neutrality is a problematic strategy, which leads away from meaningful mobilizations against class inequality.

The first generalization is that the choice between race and class approaches to U.S. working-class history and to current politics is a false one. Fixation on such a choice obscures the fact that people of color form and have always formed a large and dynamic sector of the U.S. working class, so that, for example, what Du Bois calls the general strike of the slaves during the Civil War is somehow seen as lying outside labor history. Moreover, the class consciousness of white workers has long been and is today fully understandable only in the content of race. As I have argued in *The Wages of Whiteness* and *Towards the Abolition of Whiteness*, white workers have created racialized class identities by reflecting not only on their roles as the producers and the exploited, but also in reference to their positions as nonslaves, and as refusers of "nigger work."[17] In the present, as Greenberg remarks in one of his few comments on the United States that reach the standard of his fine earlier work on South Africa, for many working whites "not being black is what constitutes being middle class; not living with blacks is what makes a neighborhood a decent place to live." David Halle's careful ethnographic study of New Jersey chemical workers sharply confirms Greenberg's point. Halle's white subjects sometimes describe nonunion, nonworking-class white neighbors as "workingmen" or "middle class" like themselves. Their black union brothers are cast as aliens, outsiders, and intruders.[18] One might fairly ask, in such a situation, how class issues could be raised without a discussion of race.

Halle's observation leads to a second, related generalization. While, as Barbara Fields carefully notes, common class and union experience can at times act as a "solvent" of some of "the grosser illusions of racialism," race can also dilute, dissolve, and even outlast the impact of class experiences. Historically, radical class organizations in the United States have often unlearned the lessons of interracial unity forged in class struggle. The examples of dramatic turns away from nonracialism even after experience in common struggle are many, dramatic, and tragic in U.S. history: the National Labor Union and the Knights of Labor (both of which flirted with support for mass deportation of black workers in their later stages), the early AFL and, most notably, Tom Watson and much of the Populist movement.[19] Nor does shared grief necessarily generate unity across racial lines. Katherine Newman's fine recent study of industrial decline provides another revealing New Jersey example of the disfiguring impact of racial ideology on class experience. Newman reports that one response of white workers in Elizabeth who have suffered through capital flight, runaway shops, and loss of jobs is to blame laws that force employers to hire black and Latino workers, supposedly thereby making profitable American industry impossible.[20]

The third generalization is the most unfamiliar and difficult. It holds that the whiteness of white workers is so complex and conflicted as to profoundly complicate both simplistic variants of the neoliberal perception of white workers—that is, seeing white workers as simply racists on the one hand, and as simply observers of alleged social pathologies of the inner cities on the other. As Michael Omi and Howard Winant have recently observed, white views on race are quite heterogeneous:

> There are all sorts of [white] people out there, many who have committed themselves to integrated neighborhoods, churches and schools, recognized the overlaps between racism, sexism, homophobia, and anti-Semitism, and generally struggled to resist the temptations of racial privilege. White identities remain uneven and contested: white workers, even white ethnics, are not uniformly "Reagan Democrats."

Moreover, beyond differences of opinion among whites, there are important strains and contradictions within the racial consciousness of individual whites that lend weight to Omi and Winant's conclusion that the "volatility of contemporary white identities, not their consolidation, is what must be emphasized."[21] White identity, as Eric Lott, Stuart Hall, and others have brilliantly shown, is compounded of hatred *and* attraction toward nonwhite cultures, of repulsion *and* desire, of "love" *and* theft. African-Americanness in particular has historically symbolized the terrifying limit of possible working-class degradation, especially among poor whites in the South and among darker and poorer European immigrant groups. At the same time, it has symbolized an alternative to regimented labor, a refusal to endlessly delay gratification, and a preservation of ties with land and tradition.[22]

This doubleness, the secret to the popularity of the minstrel stage, makes whites notoriously unreliable observers of so-called social pathology among African Americans and of supposed preferential treatment toward nonwhites. During slavery a good deal of white labor literature maintained that slaves led more leisurely and secure lives than white workers.[23] During the Jim Crow era, polling data showed a large majority of white southerners, and a majority of whites nationally, believing that blacks had as easy a time as whites in making a living. As David Alan Horowitz's enormously sympathetic account of white southerners' reaction to the pre–affirmative action phase of the civil rights movement puts it, integration was seen even then by many whites in the South "as providing license for blacks to eat in gourmet restaurants, to sleep in elaborate hotels."[24]

A concrete example humanizes these often quite tortured perceptions. In the 1930s a Federal Writers Project interviewer in Bridgeport, Connecticut, heard this from a Slovak-American woman:

I always tell my children not [to] play with the nigger-people's children, but they always play with them just the same. I tell them that the nigger children are dirty and that they will get sick if they play. I tell them they could find some other friends that are Slovaks just the same. This place now is all spoiled, and all the people live like pigs because the niggers they come and live here with the decent white people and they want to raise up their children with our children. If we had some place for the children to play I'm sure that the white children they would not play with the nigger children. . . . All people are alike—that's what God says—but just the same it's no good to make our children play with the nigger children because they are too dirty.

The informant continued:

. . . the nigger people can stay up to 3 o'clock in the morning playing and dancing and they don't have to worry about going to

work. . . . We [white] poor people can't even have a good time
one time a week. . . . The nigger people have a holiday every day
in the week.[25]

Here proximity to the oppression of African Americans—Slovaks suffered consistently under the stereotype of being a dirty people—produces
not solidarity but a poignant mixture of attraction, guilt, disdain, and de-
spising.[26] Absent a politics that challenges white supremacy and indeed
critiques whiteness as well—which is to say, given a continued neoliberal
recognition of the property right of whiteness—it is the disdain and de-
spising in such a mixture which will consistently predominate politically,
if not culturally.

Two decades ago the London-based theorist Ambalavaner Sivanandan wrote that "the white working-class must, in recovering its class
instinct, its sense of oppression, both from technological alienation
and a white-oriented culture, arrive at a consciousness of racial oppression."[27] In this view a critique of whiteness is *both* the precondition and
the result of *both* class and antiracist struggles. To peg political strategies on such a challenging dialectical formulation is difficult but, I think,
necessary. One element of such strategies should include an attempt to
take advantage of what Cheryl Harris has called the "destabilizing" character of affirmative action—its tendency to call into sharp question
"the illusion that the original or current distribution of power, property
and resources is the result of 'right' or 'merit'" and to demand "a new
and different sense of social responsibility in a society that defines
individualism as the highest good and the 'market value' of the individual as the just and true assessment." Fully knowing, with Harris,
that affirmative action lacks "any magical capacity to create cross-
racial solidarity with the white working class against class exploitation,"
we should nonetheless champion it both out of a sense of justice and
as part of a long process in which whites may lose the privileges, burdens, and illusions associated with their racial identity. To capitulate
to race neutrality is to abandon white workers to their own worst impulses and their society's. It is to close, rather than open, space for class
politics.

NOTES

1. Albie Sachs, "Towards a Bill of Rights for a Democratic South Africa," *Journal of African Law* 35 (1991): 21, 29, and ANC Constitutional Commission, *Discussion Document: Constitutional Principles and Structures for a Democratic South Africa* (Bellsville, South Africa: University of the Western Cape, 1991). Cheryl I. Harris's "Whiteness as Property," *Harvard Law Review* 106, no. 8 (June 1993): 1789–90, alerted me to these sources. Thanks to help and criticism from Jean Allman, John Wright, David Noble, Lary May, Leola Johnson, Jean O'Brien-Kehoe, Lisa Disch, Carol Miller, and Sundiata Cha-Jua, this is a better essay on revision than on the first draft. Tom Sabatini's and Patrick Huber's research assistance along with Wahneema Lubiano's remarkable generosity in providing materials and apt editing sped its completion.

2. A. Leon Higginbotham, "Racism in American and South African Courts: Similarities and Differences," *New York University Law Review* 65 (June 1990): 479–588; "Affirmative Action—Time for a Class Approach," *African Communist* (Third Quarter 1993): 4–6. See also the special section on affirmative action in South Africa in *Die Suid-Afrikaan* 44 (May–June 1993), particularly Vincent T. Maphai, "One Phrase, Two Distinct Concepts," 6–9, which reflects on the U.S. example, and Linda Loxton, "Empowering the People," 23–24.

3. Harris, "Whiteness as Property," 1713; conversation with Wills (July 15, 1994).

4. Wilson's most influential works are *The Declining Significance of Race* (Chicago: University of Chicago Press, 1980) and *The Truly Disadvantaged: The Inner City, The Underclass, and Public Policy* (Chicago: University of Chicago Press, 1987). See also Thomas Byrne Edsall with Mary D. Edsall, *Chain Reaction: The Impact of Race, Rights, and Taxes on American Politics* (New York and London: Norton, 1992); Paul Starr, "Civil Reconstruction: What to Do Without Affirmative Action," *American Prospect* 9 (Spring 1992); Theda Skocpol, "Sustainable Social Policy: Fighting Poverty Without Poverty Programs," *American Prospect* 2 (Summer 1990), and Skocpol, "The Choice," *American Prospect* 10 (Summer 1992): 86–90. Useful commentary on what Stephen Steinberg has called the "liberal retreat from race" includes Michael Omi and Howard Winant, *Racial Formation in the United States from the 1960s to the 1990s* (New York and London: Routledge, 1994), 147–59; Winant, *Racial Conditions: Politics, Theory, Comparisons* (Minneapolis: University of Minnesota Press, 1994), 75–76 and 90–92; Steinberg, "The Liberal Retreat from Race," *New Politics* 5 (Summer 1994): 30–51. Conservatives (neo- and otherwise) also continue a relentless attack on affirmative action. Timur Kuran's remarkable "Seeds of Racial Explo-

sion," *Society* 30 (September–October 1993): 55–67, aptly embodies the apocalyptic tone of the right-wing critique. For a good illustration of how blurred is the line between neoliberalism and conservatism on these matters, see Barry R. Gross, "The Intolerable Costs of Affirmative Action," *Reconstruction* 2 (1994): 58–63.

5. Edsall, *Chain Reaction*, 256–57.

6. David Oshinsky, "Review of *Chain Reaction*," *New York Times Book Review* 96 (October 20, 1991): 1; Stanley B. Greenberg, *Report on Democratic Defection* (Washington, D.C.: The Analysis Group, 1985), as cited in Edsall, *Chain Reaction*, 182.

7. Thomas Byrne Edsall with Mary D. Edsall, "Race," *Atlantic Monthly* 267 (May 1991): 56.

8. Barry R. Gross, *Discrimination in Reverse: Is Turnabout Fair Play?* (New York: New York University Press, 1978), 31; Theda Skocpol, "The Choice," 89; James E. Jones, Jr., "The Rise and Fall of Affirmative Action," in Herbert Hill and James Jones, Jr., *Race in America: The Struggle for Equality* (Madison, Wis.: University of Wisconsin Press, 1993), 354 and passim; Edsall, *Chain Reaction*, 186–87; Cornel West, *Race Matters* (Boston: Beacon Press, 1993), 64; Shelby Steele, *The Content of Our Character* (New York: St. Martin's Press, 1990); Jim Sleeper, *The Closest of Strangers: Liberalism and the Politics of Race in New York* (New York: Norton, 1990), 172–77; Wilson, *Truly Disadvantaged*, 115; Gertrude Ezorsky, *Racism and Justice: The Case for Affirmative Action* (Ithaca, N.Y.: Cornell University Press, 1991), 63–65; Stephen Steinberg and Jerome Culp, in "Critiques of Stephen Carter's Reflections of an Affirmative Action," *Reconstruction* 1 (1992): 116, 124. On class and the benefits of affirmative action, see Adolph Reed, Jr., "Assault on Affirmative Action," *Progressive* 59 (June 1995): 20.

9. Edsall, "Race," 56; on affirmative action, cf. Edsall, *Chain Reaction*, 122–29, 186–91, with Thomas Byrne Edsall, "Clinton, So Far," *New York Review of Books* (October 7, 1993), 6–7. Paul M. Sniderman and Thomas Piazza, *The Scar of Race* (Cambridge, Mass.: Harvard University Press, 1993), argue that Nathan Glazer's fear that affirmative action would bring "an increasing divisiveness on the basis of race . . . a spreading resentment among the disfavored groups against the favored ones" has materialized, with neoracism being largely the result of affirmative action rather than a source of opposition to it. Cf. Glazer, *Affirmative Discrimination* (New York: Basic Books, 1975), 220, and Sniderman and Piazza, *The Scar of Race*.

10. Andrew Hacker, *Two Nations: Black and White, Separate, Hostile, Unequal* (New York: Scribner's, 1992). 84–92. Theda Skocpol, "The New Urban Poverty and U.S. Social Policy," *Michigan Quarterly Review* 33 (Spring 1994): 278–79, is susceptible to misreading on this score, referring as it does to AFDC as an outstanding example of "targeted antipoverty policies [which are] part of the problem, not part of the solution" in the context of

a polemic against "policies narrowly targeted on the black poor." The confusion arises because Skocpol uses "targeted" at times to refer to race-based policies and at times to refer to antipoverty policies, both of which she regards as far more problematic than "universal social policies." See also Linda Gordon, "How 'Welfare' Became a Dirty Word," *Chronicle of Higher Education*, July 20, 1994, B-1 and B-2; Gordon, "Welfare Reform: A History Lesson," *Dissent*, Summer 1994, 323–28; and Jill Quadagno, *The Color of Welfare: How Racism Undermined the War on Poverty* (New York and Oxford: Oxford University Press, 1994), esp. 172–73. On the history of the decline of "race-specific" policies, see Gary Orfield, "Race the Liberal Agenda: The Loss of the Integrationist Dream, 1965–1974," in *The Politics of Social Policy in the United States*, ed. Margaret Weir, Ann Shola Orloff, and Theda Skocpol (Princeton: Princeton University Press, 1988), 313–56.

11. Edsall, *Chain Reaction*, 289.

12. George Lipsitz, "The Possessive Investment in Whiteness: Racialized Social Democracy and the 'White' Problem in American Studies," *American Quarterly* 47 (September 1995): 369–87; Edsall, "Clinton, So Far," 6–7; Edsall, *Chain Reaction*, 198–214.

13. Edsall, *Chain Reaction*, 87, 203–4. Rustin's strategy and rationale are outlined in "From Protest to Politics: The Future of the Civil Rights Movement," *Commentary* 39 (February 1965): 25–31; see also Rustin, *Down the Line: The Collected Writings of Bayard Rustin* (Chicago: Quadrangle Books 1971), and Margaret Weir, *Politics and Jobs: The Boundaries of Employment Policy in the United States* (Princeton: Princeton University Press, 1992), 95–96; on Hacker, see Roediger, "The Racial Crisis of American Liberalism," in *Towards the Abolition of Whiteness: Essays on Race, Politics, and Working Class History* (New York and London: Verso, 1994), 122. Earl Black and Merle Black, *The Vital South: How Presidents Are Elected* (Cambridge, Mass., and London: Harvard University Press, 1992), likewise ignore organized labor, labor issues, and indeed workers as a social category.

14. Stanley B. Greenberg, *Middle Class Dreams: The Politics and Power of the New American Majority* (New York: Times Books, 1995), 13, 22–54, 215–22, 263–64, 284–85. Greenberg discussed the logic of the composition of the Macomb County focus groups in an interview on C-SPAN's *Booknotes* program in a discussion of *Middle Class Dreams* (1995).

15. Omi and Winant, *Racial Formation*, 147–57, provide acute criticism of Clinton's "handling" of race, but Edsall's praises on this score in "Clinton, So Far," 6–7, are equally revealing. English cited in "Clinton and the Left," *Nation* 258 (June 13, 1994): 818, and *Time* 143 (June 20, 1994): 26, 28–29. For recent figures on race and the death penalty in the United States, see Michael Ross, "A Matter of Life and Death," *Socialist Review* (London) 93 (July–August, 1994): 17–19.

16. Edsall, *Chain Reaction*, 183, 227–32. See also Omi and Winant, *Racial For-*

mation, 150. Clearly, many such "middle-class" voters hold working-class jobs. Neoliberalism both validates suburbanized workers' identification as middle-class and closes possibilities for political action by whites mobilizing as workers.

17. Du Bois, *Black Reconstruction in America, 1860–1880* (New York: Atheneum, 1992, [1935]), 55, 727; Roediger, *The Wages of Whiteness: Race and the Making of the American Working Class* (New York and London: Verso, 1991), 65–92 and 144–45; Roediger, *Abolition of Whiteness*, 61–68; Edsall, *Chain Reaction*, 343–43.

18. Greenberg, as quoted in Edsall, *Chain Reaction*, 182; David Halle, *America's Working Man: Work, Home, and Politics Among Blue-Collar Property Owners* (Chicago: University of Chicago Press, 1984), 202–3.

19. Fields, "Ideology and Race in American History," in *Region, Race, and Reconstruction*, ed. J. Morgan Kousser and James M. McPherson (New York: Oxford University Press, 1982), 159; Roediger, *Abolition of Whiteness*, 62–63.

20. Katherine Newman, *Falling from Grace: The Experience of Downward Mobility in the American Middle Class* (New York: Free Press, 1988), 193–96.

21. Omi and Winant, "Response to Stanley Aronowitz's 'The Situation of the Left in the United States,'" *Socialist Review* (London) 93 (1994): 131.

22. Eric Lott, *Love and Theft: Blackface Minstrelsy and the American Working Class* (New York and Oxford: Oxford University Press, 1993); Lott, "White Like Me: Racial Cross-Dressing and the Construction of American Whiteness," in *Cultures of United States Imperialism*, ed. Amy Kaplan and Donald E. Pease (Durham, N.C., and London: Duke University Press, 1993), 474–95; Hall, "What Is This Black in Black Popular Culture?" *Social Justice* 20 (Spring–Summer 1993): 104–14.

23. Roediger, *Wages of Whiteness*, 76–77, 115–31.

24. Stetson Kennedy, *Southern Exposure* (Garden City, N.Y.: Doubleday, 1946), 67, citing a 1945 National Opinion Research Center poll; Horowitz, "White Southerners' Alienation and Civil Rights: The Response to Corporate Liberalism, 1956–1965," *Journal of Southern History* 54 (May 1988): 184. It is therefore especially distressing that such a committed scholar-activist as Mark Naison regards the spread of "affirmative action 'horror stories'" in white "folk culture" as a convincing argument against affirmative action. See Naison, "Jared Taylor's America: Black Man's Heaven, White Man's Hell," *Reconstruction* 2 (1994): 64–65.

25. As cited in Ivan Greenberg's impressive "Class Culture and Generational Change: Immigrant Families in Two Connecticut Industrial Cities During the 1930s" (Ph.D. diss., City University of New York, 1990), 76–77.

26. See Stanley Lieberson, *A Piece of the Pie: Blacks and White Immigrants Since 1880* (Berkeley, Calif.: University of California Press, 1980), 25, 349.

27. Ambalavaner Sivanandan, *A Different Hunger: Writings on Black Resistance* (London: Pluto Press, 1982 [1974]), 96. On the "destabilizing" character of affirmative action, see Harris, "Whiteness as Property," 1778–79. See also Kimberlé Crenshaw, "Race, Reform, and Retrenchment: Transformation and Legitimation in Antidiscrimination Law," *Harvard Law Review* 101 (1988), 1361–62.

TALES OF TWO JUDGES

Joyce Karlin in People v. Soon Ja Du;
Lance Ito in People v. O. J. Simpson

∎

Neil Gotanda

INTRODUCTION

I WOULD LIKE TO BEGIN two California race stories with paired assertions: Asian Americans are not white; Asian Americans are not black. What I seek in my paper is to problematize the seeming simplicity of these assertions through an examination of Judge Joyce Karlin's sentencing colloquy—the judicial statement made to explain a criminal sentence. Examining this text from a highly publicized criminal trial suggests the crucial role of the state in the production of race. The second part of this essay examines the position of Judge Lance Ito in the O. J. Simpson trial and demonstrates another dimension of racial construction.

People v. Soon Ja Du preceded the Rodney King incident and attracted widespread local attention but little national coverage. Du Soon Ja, a fifty-one-year-old Korean immigrant, mother, and store owner, shot and killed Latasha Harlins, a fifteen-year-old African-American girl in a dispute over a bottle of orange juice. As in the Rodney King incident, a security video camera captured the events: one can see the confrontation, a brief struggle with blows, Harlins turning to leave, and Du shooting Harlins from behind, killing her instantly. This tape was played repeatedly after the incident, after the sentence, and during the Los Angeles uprisings.

The incident generated anger and apprehension in the African-American and Korean-American communities. But it was the extremely lenient sentence—probation with no jail time—by the white trial judge that elevated the shooting, trial, and sentence into a shorthand summary of resentment and outrage at the judicial system's treatment of African Americans.

Current black–Asian race relations in the national consciousness are characterized by forms which, while available in the past, have never before achieved a pervasive presence and acceptance. These new forms threaten to displace the traditional bipolar class structuring of race— white subordination of African Americans. In place of bipolarism are more complex, tiered, *stratified* racial relations.

My interpretation of racial stratification is not a simple stepladder, but is highly textured across a range of social, economic, and cultural privi- legings. Racial stratification for Asian Americans has taken place most rapidly through the elaboration of an older stereotype into a new cultural construction, the model minority. The origin of this construction can be dated with precision—January 1966, with the publication of an article in the *New York Times Magazine* titled "Success Story: Japanese-American Style." This date is, not accidentally, less than two years after passage of the Civil Rights Act of 1964. In three decades, the Asian-American model-minority construction has been elaborated and naturalized into a self-evident truth. The state, through the legal system, is a significant arena in which the model minority has been constructed and deployed.

Turning to the text itself, my examination of Karlin's language reveals three racial elaborations: the first is one of blackness—a demonization of the victim, Latasha Harlins; second is Asianness—Du Soon Ja as a mem- ber of the Korean model minority; and third, Judge Karlin's position of whiteness. The demonization of the victim and valorization of the defen- dant occur as Harlins and Du are posed against each other.

BLACKNESS: KARLIN'S DEMONIZING
OF LATASHA HARLINS

Judge Karlin differentiates between the defendant Du and the victim Har- lins by humanizing Du but "demonizing" Harlins through harmful stereotypes. She draws upon existing "racial identities," i.e., socially developed attributes ascribed to those identified as African-American or Korean-American or Asian-American, which are either assumed to apply to Latasha Harlins and Du Soon Ja, or are at odds with the specific descriptions of them from the court of appeals. I am not trying to deny there exists gang activity among African Americans. What I call a stereotype is the universalization of the notion of a criminal menace from African-American youth into a powerful image that can be assigned to Latasha Harlins in the face of factual evidence which directly contradicts that universalized image. Further, these images need not necessarily be "demonic" or universally harmful. This section explores the implications of "benign" or "favorable" stereotypical images. There are a number of opposing stereotypes loosely connected to Du and to Harlins. In that process Latasha Harlins is criminalized while Du is favorably portrayed.

Karlin describes Du as a fifty-one-year-old woman who is a victim of circumstances, including gang terror and a gun altered by unknown thieves. Further, Du was present on the day of the killing only because of her maternal loyalty to her son, to shield her son from the repeated robberies, and "to save him one day of fear." And Karlin is generally sympathetic to the hardships faced by innocent shopkeepers who are under frequent attack.

Judge Karlin portrays defendant Du through reproduction of the Korean-shopkeeper "innocent victim" stereotype. This is a race-ing even though Karlin is ostensibly praising Du and other Korean shopkeepers. As discussed below, this "model minority" stereotype includes ominous dimensions of racial subordination. In the colloquy Du is a hard worker and has no criminal record. Further, gangs terrorize Du's hardworking and noncriminal family while they operate the store. The actual killing was the result of the assault by Harlins upon Du and the modification of the revolver by unknown thieves who had rendered the revolver "defective." Judge Karlin does not mention the choice by Du and her family to operate a store in a racially particularized neighborhood. The appeals court noted that the Du family sold one business and chose to purchase this business in a "bad neighborhood."[1] Had Karlin recognized a "consenting shopkeeper" instead of an "innocent shopkeeper," Karlin could then have allowed an inference that Du understood some of the dangers of operating a small business in a poor neighborhood. Du's use of the revolver would take on a more calculated character. Instead of Du as the innocent victim of a "defective" revolver, her use of the revolver was part of the difficult and sometimes harsh environment in which the Du family had chosen to work. I am not suggesting that self-defense, including armed self-defense, is inappropriate. At issue here is Judge Karlin's understanding of the context for the use of firearms and how Karlin has characterized Du Soon Ja's use of the weapon as completely without fault.

By contrast, Karlin portrays Latasha Harlins as a criminal. Harlins is described as having likely committed a criminal assault upon Du after an act of shoplifting. Harlins is an example of shoplifters who attack shopkeepers after being caught in the act. Further, Karlin associates Harlins with gang theft and terror; and Harlins is the person who caused Du to commit a criminal act when Du had previously led a crime-free life.

Judge Karlin also stereotypes Harlins through continued references to gangs and gang terror. These references to gangs are not an allegation that Harlins was herself a gang member. The use of stereotypes with Harlins is indirect and involves linking Harlins to a racial group identity an audience already knows and of which it is already afraid. Judge Karlin's portrayal of Harlins therefore operates within the context of an existing social consciousness of "gangness." That is, street gangs exist in society and in addition to being a serious social problem are imagined to be pervasive. The actual prevalence of gangs is much more restricted than is popularly presented or imagined in the television, news, or police attribution of a "gang-related incident." The popular imagination has constructed gangness so that it is now present in all African-American youth. (See, for example, the discussion in the appellate opinion that quotes defendant Du as testifying that she told her son that "gang members in America" . . . "wear some pants and some jackets . . . wear light sneakers, wear a cap or a hairband, headband . . . have some kind of satchel and wear some thick jackets . . . [B]e careful with those jackets sticking out."[2]) In line with images in popular culture, Karlin constructs and imagines members of these street gangs as violent criminals, dealing drugs and engaging in theft. She further connects "gangness" with African Americans, ignoring the widespread prevalence of gangs comprised largely of Asians. Judge Karlin emphasizes her understanding of "gangness" and the threat it represents by using the word "terror" three times in her colloquy: "victimized and terrorized by gang members"; "the very real terror experienced by the Du family"; "repeated robberies and terrorism in the same store."

Judge Karlin's omission of any humanizing information about Harlins also works to demonize her. Karlin might have done well to note a number of facts related by the court of appeals about Latasha Harlins:

> The probation report also reveals that Latasha had suffered many painful experiences during her life, including the violent death of her mother. Latasha lived with her extended family (her grandmother, younger brother and sister, aunt, uncle and niece) in what the probation officer described as "a clean, attractively furnished three-bedroom apartment" in South Central Los Angeles. Latasha had been an honor student at Bret Hart Junior High School, from which she had graduated the previous spring. Although she was making only average grades in high school, she had promised that she would bring her grades up to her former standard. Latasha was involved in activities at a youth center as an assistant cheerleader, member of the drill team and a summer junior camp counselor. She was a good athlete and an active church member.[3]

The absence of these observations from Karlin's comments, their presence in the probation report, and their inclusion by the opinion of the court of appeals, suggest that these facts may not have been overlooked by Karlin but actively judged by her to be unworthy of mention. They may also have been omitted because of their racial content—that African-American churches and social clubs have a lower value on the scale of racial balancing.

ASIANNESS: KARLIN'S CONSTRUCTION
OF A MODEL-MINORITY REPRESENTATION
OF DU SOON JA

The individualized racial characterizations by Karlin of Du and Harlins coincide with and reproduce the image and structure of Koreans and other Asian Americans as a "model minority." Karlin emphasizes Du's model-minority status through an emphasis upon the race and class nature of the "innocent shopkeeper." Karlin understands, and expects others to understand, that Du is a *Korean* shopkeeper.

The shopkeeper stereotype is a complex one with a substantial history. There are references at the beginning of the century to the hapless Chinese laundryman, and the villainous Japanese antique dealer.[4] In the legal curriculum the most famous case involving a person of Asian ancestry is the 1886 U.S. Supreme Court decision in *Yick Wo v. Hopkins*, involving a San Francisco ordinance discriminatorily applied to Chinese laundries.[5]

The "middleman minority" cited in the work of Edna Bonacich emphasizes groups that have successfully occupied various economic and social niches between larger social groupings. Those groups have often been shopkeepers and operators of small commercial enterprises.[6] In the modern context the image of the Korean grocery-store owner has become the dominant media image of an Asian American.[7] Sales transactions between Korean grocers and African-American patrons are now exemplary of all social interaction between Asians and African Americans. At a 1993 statewide California meeting of civil rights activists, the question of reissuing liquor-store licenses to Korean grocers in the face of African-American opposition to the perceived proliferation of liquor stores was presented as a significant civil rights issue. The actions of Korean grocers are exemplary of all Asian-American cultures. Consider the endlessly repeated story of Korean cultural reluctance to touch strangers, resulting in hostile encounters when money is offered and change returned.

Judge Karlin characterizes Du Soon Ja as a successful shopkeeper and by implication presents the Korean community as a successful model minority. This presentation thus provides Judge Karlin with an ideological framework to both distance herself from Latasha Harlins individually, and also more generally to absolve nonblacks, especially those in the highest tier of the three-tiered system of the model minority of any social responsibility for the effects of racial subordination upon African Americans.

By contrast, Harlins was closely tied to criminal conduct and gang terror. As noted earlier, Harlins' personal background as an honor student in junior high school and an active participant in her church and social groups was omitted by Judge Karlin. These omissions invited the inference that Harlins, an African American living in a poor neighborhood, was a participant in a crime and welfare subculture who did not have any middle-class aspirations to education and economic success.

WHITENESS: KARLIN

Besides the racialization of Harlins into a criminal and Du into a model minority shopkeeper, Karlin can also be seen as writing from a position of whiteness. I find four dimensions in Karlin's colloquy—subject position, racial transparency, legal color blindness, and racial paternalism—which, taken together, strongly reflect such whiteness. Note that my claim of whiteness will not be derived from Judge Karlin's being racially classified as white. Rather, this is an interpretation based upon contextual structures of whiteness.

The first derives from Karlin's creating distanced "otherness" through the demonizing of Latasha Harlins and the model-minority Koreanness of Du Soon Ja. This differentiated otherness creates and reproduces a racialized context. As author of the colloquy, Karlin's position of nonblackness and non-Koreanness is the superordinate position in the racial hierarchy—the position of whiteness, a position that can acknowledge otherness.

A second dimension has been described by Barbara Flagg (a white law professor):

> The most striking characteristic of whites' consciousness of whiteness is that most of the time we don't have any. I call this the transparency phenomenon: the tendency of whites not to

think about whiteness, or about norms, behaviors, experiences, or perspectives that are white specific.

Karlin demonstrates this white racial transparency in her colloquy as she is completely unaware of her exercise of racial authority in reproducing racial constructions.

The third dimension of whiteness is seen in Karlin's measured use of color blindness. The sentencing colloquy is structured around an opening and closing in which she specifically recognizes and lectures to the African-American and Korean-American communities. In her actual sentencing comments, however, Karlin makes no explicit reference to "African-American" or "Korean." This omission underscores her use of the technique of legal color blindness that then frees her to use encoded racial references.

Finally, a fourth dimension of whiteness structures the opening and closing paragraphs when she drops the posture of judicial impartiality. As described by *Los Angeles Times* writer Itabari Njeri:

> During the sentencing, Judge Joyce A. Karlin, like a schoolmarm admonishing a potentially rowdy room of children, lectured the African American community as to what their behavior should be in response to her choice of probation instead of jail time. . . : Be quiet, go home, and stay quiet.

This manifestation of unself-conscious maternalism within admonitions directed to the Korean and African-American communities reinforces the other three dimensions of Karlin's whiteness.

THE POLITICAL COST AND SIGNIFICANCE OF THE MODEL MINORITY

I will turn next to a brief examination of the significance and political costs of "the model minority." The standard response of Asian-American academics has been to discredit in some fashion the idea that Asian Americans have "made it." Ron Takaki, for example, has argued:

In their celebration of this "model minority" thesis media pundits have exaggerated Asian American "success." . . . Actually, in terms of personal incomes, Asian Americans have not reached equality. While many Asian Americans are doing well, others find themselves mired in poverty: they include Southeast Asian refugees such as the Hmong and Mien as well as immigrant workers trapped in Chinatowns.

Takaki suggests that recognition of past common struggles, especially labor struggles, can provide a common bond with other oppressed groups. However, as a basis for building new racial coalitions, this recognition has been of limited value. Besides practical difficulties, that analysis reproduces bipolar racial politics. It points to racial class solidarity but ignores class differences. On one side is white supremacy and the white establishment; on the other are ranged various people of color. As analysis, this is inadequate.

Instead, I suggest a closer look at the model minority construction. As often happens with stereotypes, it is important to recognize the half-truths in this construction. Karlin's colloquy not only reflects the "myth of the model minority" but it also reinscribes it by ascribing to the generic racial Korean such class privileges as shopkeeper status, the social worth of the strong Asian family, and the moral worth of being law-abiding citizens—all of these at the expense of the demonized Latasha Harlins. An examination of the elements of the model minority as reproduced by Judge Karlin suggests the parameters of the Asian-American racial category, a set of parameters which indicate that real racialized class privileges have accrued to the Asian-American racial category.

Briefly, let me explain how I use the term "racial category." I refer to that dimension of race in which the racial category is the reification of other economic and social relations of subordination. An accessible historical example comes from the early colonial history of slavery, in the 1600s. Early efforts in the New World to legitimate slavery initially used "Negro" as descriptive. It was only in the early 1700s that the term "Negro" became the reification of enslaveability, so that the Negro racial category was itself, without further elaboration, the justification for enslavement and subordination. Today this use of race as a reification of privileging is occurring in a crudely stratified context, in which white occupies the preferred position and black the subordinate position, but with distinct, intermediate positions for yellow and brown.

In traditional economic-discrimination terms, for example, this might mean that when a Vietnamese American moves into a white neighborhood, the property values go down, but they don't go as far down as they might have for an African American. Or, as another example, employment discrimination does not completely exclude all racial groups, but the glass ceiling limiting advancement is placed higher for a Chinese American than it is for an African American.

These more complex class dimensions to the Asian-American racial category also suggest the limitations of the model-minority construction. The model minority has operated to caricature and to hinder analysis of racial stratification The model minority is a denial of the working-class history of Asian Americans: Filipino farmworkers, or Japanese on Hawaiian sugar plantations. It also denies our presence as workers today: in hotels and restaurants or women in garment sweatshops. None of these Asian Americans exist—either in historical media memory or in popular consciousness. Even the caricatures have changed. The Chinese coolie laborer, while a stereotype, encompassed a clear working-class reference. That historical memory, as far as the general U.S. public is concerned, has been erased by the model-minority image. The Korean grocer has become the fulcrum of Asian black racial relations.

I have a set of nested categories to illustrate this problem. All Asian Americans are not Korean. All Koreans are not shopkeepers. All Korean shopkeepers do not run grocery stores; and all Korean grocery-store operators do not own stores in South Central Los Angeles or in Harlem. Nevertheless, the Korean grocer and African-American customer has become a defining paradigm for encounters between Asian Americans and African Americans.

LANCE ITO AND THE O. J. SIMPSON TRIAL

In this next section I will examine the role of Judge Lance Ito in the O. J. Simpson trial and illustrate another dimension of the model minority—

how the "model minority" can caricature even an accomplished and intelligent Asian-American jurist.

In contrasting the O. J. Simpson murder trial with the Latasha Harlins trial, we find a curious racial scramble of the participants. The defendant is a black male, the victim is a white female, and the judge is a Japanese-American male. Almost every aspect of the Simpson trial has been the subject of comment. The actions of Judge Ito have been criticized; however, the racial position of Ito has been unexplored. In this reading of Ito's conduct of the trial, his criticized actions are comprehensible and noteworthy.

BLACKNESS AND WHITENESS IN THE O. J. TRIAL

There have been endless commentaries about black and white in the Simpson trial and verdict, most centering upon the defendant, the victims, and the jury. The violent and volatile nature of Los Angeles racial politics was obvious but ignored in the glitzy atmosphere that overtook the trial in the national media. Race in Los Angeles is made in the streets of Koreatown, Pico-Rivera, East L.A., and South Central, populated by Koreans, Salvadoreans, Mexicans, and African Americans. Racial violence and racial divisions were very much on the minds of most Los Angeles residents before and during the Simpson trial.

Ito's selection as judge was not surprising. Either a Latino or an Asian could occupy a symbolic intermediate position—a judge to mediate between black and white while avoiding any signal that the judicial system was taking sides. Because of the pool of experienced Asian and Latino judges, this choice could be a symbolic choice without necessarily succumbing to blatant tokenism.

Ito's judicial work on earlier trials was widely respected. A model-minority judge could play the racial role of intermediary and look good for the television cameras. Ito's role as racial intermediary was narrow—to preside without antagonizing race relations. What emerged during the trial, however, were additional racial conditions. Ito was to be a model-minority intermediary, not a mediator. And Ito was to be a color-blind model minority, without a racial identity of his own. The loudest and most outspoken attacks upon Ito came as his actions operated either to assert his own racialized identity as a Japanese American or when he acted as an independent racial mediator in the public "shadow trial" rather than simply presiding over the courtroom trial.

NEITHER BLACK NOR WHITE:
ITO AS JAPANESE AMERICAN

The first attacks came after the announcement that Ito had conducted an interview for television broadcast with the well-established local news anchor Tritia Toyota. In the interview, Ito was talking about his parents and the Internment. Upon reflection, I concluded that Ito had decided to take advantage of his moment in the media spotlight to play his own "race card" and talk about the Japanese-American concentration camps.

The print media reaction was extraordinarily sharp and angry. In the *Los Angeles Times* there were six news and editorial items over two days. Judge Ito had become "Judge Ego," he was a "hypocrite" denounced by law and by the *Times* itself in an editorial. Leading the nastiness was Howard Rosenberg, the *Times*'s principal television critic.

In the television interview Ito had presented himself as a Japanese American pointing to our particular history of racial justice and injustice. There had been neither anger nor smugness. Ito had been polite and understated in his interview with a senior news anchor. Yet for the keepers of media orthodoxy, this interview was unacceptable. Ito had broken important unspoken rules.

A couple of years ago, when talking about the hysterical reaction of New York media to the Asian-American protests about the Broadway musical *Miss Saigon*, I labeled this media reaction the "Miss Saigon Syndrome." When any model-minority Asian American steps out of line and complains about our racial situation, he risks being slapped down.

There were two unspoken racial codes that Judge Ito violated: being a good media "model minority" and being a "good judge" who is to referee the black–white racial conflict in the courtroom.

Rosenberg's commentary embodied race-baiting of Ito in a very modern form—color blindness. Throughout his article, he denied any Japanese-American substance to Ito, rendering Ito without race. While Bill Boyarsky, another *Los Angeles Times* columnist, devoted half of his piece to Ito's family story of incarceration in a relocation camp, Rosenberg ignored Ito's Japanese-American family background—the entire subject of Ito's television interview. The only exception was a nasty little cross-ethnic dig: Rosenberg says, "There's an ancient Japanese word that describes anti-polluter Ito's decision to appear on Channel 2 this week and merge himself with the polluters: chutzpah." After imposing a color-blind position upon Ito, Rosenberg himself invokes an acceptable ethnicity— Jewish—to denounce an unacceptable ethnicity—Japanese American.

Rosenberg suggests that Ito should have done his interview on the MacNeil/Lehrer show. Ito should have appeared with two gray-haired white males, who speak in low, ponderous tones and haven't the slightest idea about race in Los Angeles. Tritia Toyota, a television news veteran, was unacceptable because she is Japanese American.

Rosenberg's denunciation of Toyota was also revealing. Rosenberg spends almost as much time criticizing her work as he does complaining of Ito. At first that puzzled me, until I realized that Toyota had herself violated an unspoken rule of TV racial politics. She had conspired with Ito to reveal her own Japanese-Americanness. Rosenberg correctly understood that Ito and Toyota talking about the camps gave both of them personal histories.

Rosenberg even denied the validity of an Asian-American stereotype. He complained that Toyota was "worshipful" when she noted that Ito's parents "must be very proud of you." Rosenberg found fault with the close family ties that are one of the strong points in the model-minority stereotype.

In the subsequent months of the trial Ito set forth an understated yet consistent message of Japanese-American identity. His few public appearances were primarily at Asian-American events, including a panel in Los Angeles's Little Tokyo on the concentration-camp experience.

I think that the media response, led by the *Los Angeles Times*, was an implicit effort to limit Ito's racial role to that of a raceless model-minority intermediary between black and white. Ito was to have no real public identity. The proper place for a model minority is in the background. By constructing the television image of Japanese Americans discussing Japanese-American issues, Ito had raised racial issues other than black versus white. In the fever pitch of the Simpson trial, that was distracting and unacceptable.

ITO AS RACIAL MEDIATOR

Also unacceptable were Ito's efforts to mediate between black and white in local Los Angeles racial politics. Early in the trial, Ito signaled through his criticisms of the mass media that he would not play directly to the national press. Instead, his actions can be seen as working on a local level to prevent the perception that the judicial system was once again working against an African-American defendant.

To that end, Ito used a judicial approach that he had followed in the past—let the lawyers run their own case. That meant that as judge he would not dominate the courtroom so as to limit either the prosecution or the defense. Without live televised broadcasts, a labored and ponderous legal presentation would bore only a jury.

In the Los Angeles context, however, allowing both sides to present at their own pace meant that there could be no claims that a racist judicial system had prevented an African-American defendant from presenting his own case. Similarly, there could be no claim that the court had tilted against the prosecution and in favor of an African-American sports hero so as to prevent another violent uprising by African Americans.

The result was sometimes tedious television, but few charges of a racist judicial system. Instead, the attacks centered on Ito as having a trial that was "out of control," and that he was an ineffectual judge. These charges surfaced at different moments—when Ito was asserting his individual racial identity, and when he was acting as racial mediator.

The Los Angeles Times criticism of the Ito-Toyota interviews suggests Ito failed in properly playing his judicial role. One op-ed article, by Robert C. Fellmeth, a former prosecutor and University of San Diego law professor, lionized the two-fisted, macho judge. "The image of a friendly, human, vulnerable, folksy Will Rogers type of OK guy is fine for the next-door neighbor; not for this job. This is not someone we are supposed to like, this is someone we are supposed to respect." Fellmeth doesn't want to hear anything about Ito's "past, his values, his dreams."

But advocates of macho judging can't really mean that a judge should not have a past or values. Such a person would be inhuman and unacceptable to anyone as a judge. Fellmeth is for some reason objecting to Ito's Japanese-American past and to Ito's Japanese-American values.

Why would a Japanese-American past be a problem? Because Ito was introducing another racial dimension into the judicial justice mix. And the court-watchers and the lawyers didn't want to hear about new complications.

There has evolved an unwritten set of rules for black-white racial issues in our courts. An example were statements early in the trial by lead defense attorney Johnnie Cochran, himself an African American who has added to Simpson's all-white defense team. With a straight face and little comment from reporters, Cochran objected to the prosecutors' adding Christopher Darden, an experienced African-American prosecutor, to their legal team. The emerging black-white racial rules allowed Cochran to carry out this type of black-white courtroom racial maneuvering.

Ito's Japanese-American interview threatened those very tentative understandings. As long as Ito appeared to be color-blind and without "values or history," he was safely hidden behind his judicial robes and the invisibility of the black-white racial framework was maintained. For Ito openly to present a racial position different from the accepted black and white models was a threat to existing racial understandings.

The macho-judge vision of the judiciary reflects a traditional white understanding of how a judge deals with racial politics in the courtroom. A macho judge simply commands order and discipline upon unruly racial subjects.

In the context of Los Angeles there is no one in a position to demand or to command racial discipline. Such efforts would have exacerbated the already tense politics. Later in the trial this sentiment was stated clearly by Attorney Harland Braun, who represented police officer Ted Briseno in the Rodney King trials. "Most of the people who are criticizing Ito weren't here for the Latasha Harlins case or the first Rodney King trial. They weren't here when 53 people were killed in a riot. No one is criticizing Ito for giving O. J. Simpson an unfair trial. . . . The reason is he is patient, and that's important if you're in a city sitting on a powder keg."

Other mediating moments came when Ito allowed the infamous Mark Fuhrman tapes to be played in court and when defendant Simpson was allowed to make a public statement. Both of those occurred with the jury absent from the courtroom. Ito allowed them for public discussion, not for jury consideration.

The Mark Fuhrman tapes portrayed a police officer holding racist views and having carried out unlawful actions in uniform. Their admissibility was legally questionable, and ultimately only a few short statements were played for the jury. As an issue of criminal-law evidence, they are of little note. Their importance, however, was as part of the public discussion in Los Angeles of the conduct and misconduct of the police department. The Rodney King trial had centered on police conduct, and the Mark Fuhrman tapes were a powerful contribution to the ongoing debate.

Ito's playing of the significant excerpts from the tapes in open court but without the jury present suggests that he was intervening in the public debate over the Los Angeles Police Department. Since Ito had apparently decided that almost none of the tapes were to be used in the trial, they were for community use, not for the courtroom trial.

Similarly, allowing Simpson to make statements with the jury absent suggests that Ito was giving Simpson a moment for public comment and discussion, not giving Simpson access to the jury. These were two examples of community racial mediation. They should be seen as efforts to address local racial politics, not as an "out of control" courtroom.

CONCLUSION

As I stated at the beginning, Asian Americans are not white and are not black. The law, media, education—all participate in racial construction. I have examined two vastly different variations of the model-minority construction. The objects of those racial constructions were situated in sharply different social positions. Yet in both circumstances the model-minority construction operated upon lives and helped to determine courses of action. To the extent that we allow the model-minority construction to determine our actions—either directly or as reaction—we limit our own political possibilities, we limit our own imaginations.

APPENDIX

Text of remarks by Los Angeles Superior Court Judge Joyce A. Karlin in the sentencing of Soon Ja Du.

One thing I think both sides will agree on is that nothing I can do, nothing the judicial system can do, nothing will lessen the loss suffered by Latasha Harlins' family and friends. But the parties involved in this case and anyone truly interested in what caused this case can make sure that something positive comes out of this tragedy by having Latasha Harlins' death mark a beginning rather than an end—a beginning of a greater understanding and acceptance between two groups, some of whose members have until now demonstrated intolerance and bigotry toward one another.

Latasha's death should be a catalyst to force members of the African American and Korean communities to confront an intolerable situation by creating constructive solutions. Through that process, a greater understanding and acceptance will hopefully result so that similar tragedies will not be repeated.

Statements by the district attorney, (which) suggest that imposing less than the maximum sentence will send a message that a black child's life is not worthy of protection, (are) dangerous rhetoric, which serves no purpose other than to pour gasoline on a fire.

This is not a time for revenge, and my job is not to exact revenge for those who demand it.

There are those in this community who have publicly demanded in the name of justice that the maximum sentence be imposed in this case.

But it is my opinion that justice is never served when public opinion, prejudice, revenge or unwarranted sympathy are considered by a sentencing court in resolving a case.

In imposing sentence I must first consider the objectives of sentencing a defendant:

1. To protect society.
2. To punish the defendant for committing a crime.
3. To encourage the defendant to lead a law-abiding life.

4. To deter others.
5. To isolate the defendant so she can't commit other crimes.
6. To secure restitution for the victim.
7. To seek uniformity in sentencing.

The question becomes, are any of these sentencing objectives achieved by Mrs. Du being remanded to state prison?

Let us start with the last objective first: uniformity in sentencing. According to statistics gathered for the Superior Courts of California, sentences imposed on defendants convicted of voluntary manslaughter last year ranged from probation with no jail time to incarceration in state prison for several years.

Because of the unique nature of each crime of voluntary manslaughter, and by that I mean the uniquely different factual situations resulting in that crime, uniformity in sentencing is virtually impossible to achieve.

Which, then, of the other sentencing objectives lead to the conclusion that state prison is warranted?

Does society need Mrs. Du to be incarcerated in order to be protected? I think not.

Is state prison needed in order to encourage the defendant to lead a law-abiding life or isolate her so she cannot commit other crimes? I think not.

Is state prison needed to punish Mrs. Du? Perhaps.

There is, in this case, a presumption against probation because a firearm was used.

In order to overcome that presumption, the court must find this to be an unusual case, as that term is defined by law.

There are three reasons that I find this is an unusual case:

First, the basis for the presumption against probation is technically present. But it doesn't really apply. The statute is aimed at criminals who arm themselves when they go out and commit other crimes. It is not aimed at shopkeepers who lawfully possess firearms for their own protection.

Second, the defendant has no recent record, in fact, no record at any time of committing similar crimes or crimes of violence.

Third, the defendant participated in the crime under circumstances of great provocation, coercion and duress. Therefore, this is, in my opinion, an unusual case that overcomes the statutory presumption against probation.

Should the defendant be placed on probation?

One of the questions a sentencing court is required to ask in answering that question is "whether the crime was committed because of unusual circumstances, such as great provocation." I find that it was.

I must also determine the vulnerability of the victim in deciding whether probation is appropriate. Although Latasha Harlins was not armed with a weapon at the time of her death, she had used her fists as weapons just seconds before she was shot.

The district attorney argues that Latasha was justified in her assault on Mrs. Du. Our courts are filled with cases which suggest otherwise.

Our courts are filled with defendants who are charged with assault resulting in great bodily injury as a result of attacks on shopkeepers, including shopkeepers who have accused them of shoplifting.

Had Latasha Harlins not been shot and had the incident which preceded the shooting been reported, it is my opinion that the district attorney would have relied on the videotape and Mrs. Du's testimony to make a determination whether to file charges against Latasha.

Other questions I am required to address in determining whether probation is appropriate are "whether the carrying out of the crime suggested criminal sophistication and whether the defendant will be a danger to others if she is not imprisoned."

Having observed Mrs. Du on videotape at the time the crime was committed and having observed Mrs. Du during this trial, I cannot conclude that there was any degree of criminal sophistication in her offense. Nor can I conclude that she is a danger to others if she is not incarcerated.

Mrs. Du is a (51)-year-old woman with no criminal history and no history of violence. But for the unusual circumstances in this case, including the Du family's history of being victimized and terrorized by gang members, Mrs. Du would not be here today. Nor do I believe Mrs. Du would be here today if the gun she grabbed for protection had not been altered. This was a gun that had been stolen from the Du family and returned to them shortly before the shooting.

The court has been presented with no evidence, and I have no reason to believe that Mrs. Du knew that the gun had been altered in such a way as to—in effect—make it an automatic weapon with a hairpin trigger.

Ordinarily a .38 revolver is one of the safest guns in the world. It cannot go off accidentally. And a woman Mrs. Du's size would have to decide consciously to pull the trigger and to exert considerable strength to do so.

But that was not true of the gun used to shoot Latasha Harlins. I have serious questions in my mind whether this crime would have been committed at all but for a defective gun.

The district attorney would have this court ignore the very real terror experienced by the Du family before the shooting, and the fear Mrs. Du experienced as she worked by herself the day of the shooting. But there are things I cannot ignore. And I cannot ignore the reason Mrs. Du was working at the store that day. She went to work that Saturday to save her son from having to work. Mrs. Du's son had begged his parents to close the store. He was afraid because he had been the victim of repeated robberies and terrorism in that same store.

On the day of the shooting Mrs. Du volunteered to cover for her son to save him one day of fear.

Did Mrs. Du react inappropriately to Latasha? Absolutely.

Was Mrs. Du's over-reaction understandable? I think so.

If probation is not appropriate, and state prison time is warranted, then a short prison term would be an injustice. If Mrs. Du should be sent to prison because she is a danger to others or is likely to re-offend, then I could not justify imposing a short prison term.

But it is my opinion that Mrs. Du is not a danger to the community and it is my opinion that she will not re-offend. She led a crime free life until Latasha Harlins walked into her store and there is no reason to believe that this is the beginning of a life of crime for Mrs. Du. But if I am wrong, Mrs. Du will face severe consequences.

For all of these reasons it is hereby adjudged that: on her conviction for voluntary manslaughter, Mrs. Du is sentenced to the midterm of 6 years in state prison. On the personal use of a firearm enhancement, the defendant is sentenced to the midterm of 4 years, to run consecutive to the 6 years for a total of 10 years. Execution of this sentence is suspended.

Mrs. Du is placed on formal probation for five years on the following terms and conditions:

Mrs. Du is to perform 400 hours of community service. I strongly recommend that for the maximum impact on Mrs. Du and for the community, this service should be in connection with efforts to various groups to unite the Korean and African American communities.

Mrs. Du is to pay $500 to the restitution fine [sic] and pay full restitution to the victim's immediate family for all out of court expenses for Latasha Harlins' funeral and any medical expenses related to Latasha Harlins' death.

Mrs. Du is to obey all laws and orders of the probation department and the court.

If I am wrong about Mrs. Du and she re-offends, then she will go to state prison for 10 years.

NOTES

1. Appeal at 828.
2. Appeal at 826. n. 5.
3. Appeal at 829 n 7.
4. Stuart Creighton Miller, *The Unwelcome Immigrant: The American Image of the Chinese, 1785–1882* (Berkeley: University of California Press, 1969), and John Kuo Wei Tchen, "Modernizing White Patriarchy: Re-Viewing D.W. Griffith's *Broken Blossoms*," in *Moving the Image: Independent Asian Pacific American Media Arts*, ed. Russell Leong (Los Angeles: UCLA Asian American Studies Center and Visual Communications, 1991), 133. See

also John W. Dower, *War Without Mercy: Race and Power in the Pacific War* (New York: Pantheon, 1986), 147–80; Dennis M. Ogawa, *From Japs to Japanese: An Evolution of Japanese American Stereotypes* (Berkeley: McCutchan Publishing, 1971).

5. 118 U.S. 360 (1886).

6. Edna Bonacich, *The Economic Basis of Ethnic Solidarity: Small Business in the Japanese American Community* (Berkeley: University of California Press, 1980); Edna Bonacich and Ivan Light, *Immigrant Entrepreneurs: Koreans in Los Angeles, 1965–1982* (Berkeley: University of California Press, 1988); Edna Bonacich, ed., *Global Production: The Apparel Industry in the Pacific Rim* (Philadelphia: Temple University Press, 1994).

7. More recently, the *Los Angeles Times Magazine* presented a photo with accompanying text of Korean grocers and African-American patrons. *Los Angeles Times Magazine*, October 17, 1993. Photograph by Chang W. Lee, article by John W. Lee, "Counter Culture: In Los Angeles, Korean-American Stores Are Sometimes the Flash Point of Racial Animosity—But They Are Also the Proving Ground For Tolerance."

RACIAL DUALISM
AT CENTURY'S END

Howard Winant

■

RACIAL DUALISM

RACE MATTERS: whether we in the United States—and in many other countries as well—wish this to be the case or not. The United States: what is it? A nation built on the soil of conquest, battened on the theft of human beings. Yet it is not only this. The United States was also created out of the doctrine of natural rights, whose restrictive application was continually eroded by the struggles of the excluded: first the European "others," and then the other "others" down to our own day. Throughout U.S. history, racial conflicts continually shaped and reshaped the categories into which identities—all identities—were classified. The racial struggles at the heart of U.S. society, the racial *projects* whose clash and clangor leap off the pages of today's headlines as they have for centuries, have created the politics and culture of today.

Race matters: yet race today is as problematic a concept as ever. Over the last few decades the way we in the United States think of race has changed once again, as so often in the past. I shall argue in this essay that we are now in a period of *universal racial dualism*.

Once U.S. society was a nearly monolithic racial hierarchy, in which everyone knew "his" place; under racial dualism, however, everyone's racial identity is problematized. "How does it feel to be a problem?" Du Bois reported being asked (Du Bois 1989 [1903]). The racial dualism he discerned was, of course, that of black people, who (he argued) were forced to live simultaneously in two worlds. His insight, which at the beginning of the twentieth century addressed black experience in a society of all-encompassing white supremacy, continues to apply, but the situation he analyzed has now become considerably more complicated. Today the racial anxiety, uncertainty, conflict, and tension expressed by the term "racial dualism" affect everyone in the United States, albeit in different ways.

Monolithic white supremacy is over, yet in a more concealed way, white power and privilege live on. The overt politics of racial subordination has been destroyed, yet it is still very possible to "play the racial card" in the political arena. Blacks and other racially defined minorities are no longer subject to legal segregation, but they have not been relieved of the burdens of discrimination, even by laws supposedly intended to do so. Whites are no longer the official "ruling race," yet they still enjoy many of the privileges descended from the time when they were.

The old recipes for racial equality, which involved creation of a "color-blind" society, have been transformed into formulas for the maintenance of racial inequality. The old programs for eliminating white racial privilege are now accused of creating nonwhite racial privilege. The welfare state, once seen as the instrument for overcoming poverty and social injustice, is now accused of fomenting these very ills.

What racial dualism means today is that there are now, so to speak, two ways of looking at race, where previously there was only one. In the past, let's say the pre–World War II era, everyone agreed that racial subordination existed; the debate was about whether it was justified. Theodore Bilbo and Thurgood Marshall—to pick two emblematic figures—shared the same paradigm, perhaps disagreeing politically and morally, perhaps even representing the forces of evil and good respectively, but nevertheless looking at the same social world.

But today agreement about the continuing existence of racial subordination has vanished. The meaning of race has been deeply problematized. Indeed, the very idea that "race matters" is something which today must be argued, something which is not self-evident. This in itself attests to the transformation which racial dualism has undergone from the time of *The Souls of Black Folk* to our own time.

On the one hand, the world Du Bois analyzed is still very much with us. We live in a racialized society, a society in which racial meaning is engraved upon all our experiences. Racial identity shapes not only "life-chances," but social life, taste, place of residence. Indeed, the meaning of race, the racial interpretation of everyday life and of the larger culture, polity, and economy, has been so finely tuned for so long, and has become so ingrained, that it is now "second nature," a "common sense" that rarely requires acknowledgement.

As our racial antennae are tuned and retuned, race becomes "naturalized." As an element of "human nature," race partakes of the same degree of reality today—so it seems—as it did at the end of the nineteenth century when biologistic theories of race held sway and eugenics was advocated by supposedly enlightened and progressive thinkers. Indeed, if race is so much a part of "common sense"; if it is so involved in the production of person, culture, state, and nation; if racial identity is so recognizable, so palpable, so immediately obvious, then in practical terms at least, it becomes "real." The sociological dictum that if people "define situations as real, they are real in their consequences," has its truth (Thomas and Thomas 1928, 572).

On the other hand, though, this "reality" is a rank illusion. It is patently inadequate, if not wholly false, to understand human experience, individual or collective, in racial terms. Indeed, it is difficult even to specify the meaning of race beyond the most superficial notions. When we seek to delineate the principles underlying racial categorization, we encounter tremendous obstacles. Not only ordinary individuals, but even specialists—say, anthropologists or sociologists or geneticists—cannot present a convincing rationale for distinguishing among human groups by physical characteristics. Our "second nature," our "common sense" about race, it turns out, is deeply uncertain, almost mythical.

Consider: in the United States, hybridity is universal; most blacks have "white blood," and tens of millions of whites have "black blood." Latinos, Native Americans, Asian Americans, and blacks, as well as whites, have centuries-long histories of contact with one another; colonial rule, enslavement, and migration have dubious merits, but they are all effective "race-mixers" (Davis 1991, Forbes 1988). Of course, even to speak in these terms, of "blood," "mixture," or "hybridity," even to use such categories as "Asian American," "Latino," or "white," one must enter deeply into the complexities of racial discourse. Such language reveals at once the sociohistorical imbeddedness of all racial ideas. For these are merely current North American designations, and hardly unproblematic ones at that. They are not in any sense "true" or original self-descriptions of the human groups they name. Nor could any language be found which would avoid such a situation.

Race matters, then, in a second sense: it matters not only as a means of rendering the social world intelligible, but simultaneously as a way of making it opaque and mysterious. Race is not only real, but also illusory. Not only is it common sense; it is also common nonsense. Not only does it establish our identity; it also denies us our identity. Not only does it allocate resources, power, and privilege; it also provides means for challenging that allocation. Race not only naturalizes, but also socializes. The ineluctably contradictory character of race provides the context in which racial dualism—or the "color-line," as Du Bois designated it—has developed as "the problem of the 20th century."

RACIAL DUALISM AS HISTORY

The racial dynamics of conquest, of colonization, and of enslavement placed an indelible stamp on U.S. society. *Racialization* (Omi and Winant 1994, Roediger, 1991) affected every individual and group, locating all in the hierarchy of the developing *Herrenvolk* democracy (Takaki 1993, van den Berghe 1967, Roediger 1991). The *Herrenvolk*, of course, were the white men of a certain standing or class, the only ones deemed worthy of full citizenship rights.

For centuries white supremacy went almost entirely unquestioned in the political mainstream. This fact established the overall contours, as well as the particular political and cultural legacies, of racial subordination and resistance. It eliminated or at best severely limited the political terrain upon which racially defined groups could mobilize within civil society, thus constituting these groups as "outsiders." It denied the existence of commonalities among whites and nonwhites—such as shared economic activities and statuses, shared rights as citizens, even on occasion shared humanity—thus constructing race, at least in principle, in terms of all-embracing social difference.

Not only did racialization tend to minimize differences among people considered white, but it also homogenized distinctions among those whose difference with whites was considered the only crucial component of their identities. Over time, then, this "white versus other" concept of difference created not fixed and unchanging racial identities—for these are always in flux—but the potentiality, the social structure, indeed the necessity, of universally racialized identities in the United States. Elsewhere, Omi and I have described this process (drawing on Gramsci 1971), as *racial war of maneuver*: a conflict between disenfranchised and systematically subordinated groups and a dictatorial and comprehensively dominant power (Omi and Winant 1994). In a war of maneuver, the principal efforts of the subordinated are devoted to self-preservation and resistance. They are anathematized; they lack social standing or political rights. In respect to social action, their options are generally reduced: to withdrawal into exclusive (and excluded) communities, to subversion (Bhabha 1994), and occasionally, to armed revolt.

In a schematic account of the type developed here, there is an inevitable tendency to render the dynamics of racial oppression as more homogeneous than they actually were. But of course racial war of maneuver is not static, not frozen. At various moments, for example under the impact of the Haitian revolution or the pressures of abolitionism, and in the interregnum of Reconstruction, the power of white supremacy waxed or waned considerably. Its component parts—its ideology and instrumentalities—evolved and changed over time. Furthermore, what is true of oppression is true for resistance: both everyday, small-scale forms of opposition (Scott 1985), and large-scale challenge such as armed revolt and institution-building among free blacks, varied significantly with the conditions of racial war of maneuver. Nor should the account of racial war of maneuver be confined to black-white dynamics alone. Efforts to subordinate Native American nations (Cornell 1988, Rogin 1975), Mexicans (Montejano 1987), and Asians (Okihiro 1994, Takaki 1990) through warfare, expropriation of land, exclusion, denial of political rights, and superexploitation, all fit into the general pattern of racial war of maneuver. Regional and temporal variations in these conflicts (Almaguer 1994) do not diminish the general applicability of this concept. Although I cannot detail these processes here, I have discussed them elsewhere (Winant 1994), and they have been extensively treated by others (Du Bois 1935, Foner 1988, Williamson 1986, Takaki 1993).

Paradoxically, white institutionalization of racial difference; white refusal to grant such basic democratic rights as citizenship, access to the legal system, and the vote; and white resistance to the participation by racially defined minorities in civil society, permitted—and indeed demanded—the organization and consolidation of excluded communities of color. Because it had so comprehensively externalized its racial "others," racial war of maneuver helped constitute their resistance and opposition. It set the stage for its own destruction because, over centuries, whites forced nonwhites to draw on their own profound cultural and political resources, to suppress their differences, and to unite outside the high walls of a supposedly democratic society whose rights and privileges were systematically restricted on the basis of race.

Racial war of maneuver can be linked to the racial dualism discerned by Du Bois. If in the present we have no trouble understanding *racism* as a relation with both macro- and microsocial dimensions, as something that necessarily operates at both the institutional and social structural levels on the one hand, and at the levels of identity and experience on the other (Omi and Winant 1994), it is not anachronistic to discern that dynamic in earlier historical moments. What for whites was a fierce and pathological rejection of the possibility that they might harbor traits identified with various racial others, was for nonwhites a quasi-terroristic requirement that they anticipate and strive to protect themselves against the "violence of representation" (Armstrong and Tennenhouse 1989), not to mention the physical violence, directed against them by members of the ruling race. Psychohistorical approaches to U.S. racial dynamics have long investigated these processes (Drinnon 1985, Rogin 1975, Williamson 1986).

Thus, racial dualism was in part an adaptation, a resistance strategy of the oppressed, the excluded, the terrorized, under the conditions of racial war of maneuver. This recognition is clearly present in Du Bois, although by the time of *Souls* the seeds of the breakdown of this centuries' racial regime are already germinating; indeed, Du Bois himself is the chief cultivator of those seeds, the key agitator for a very different strategic orientation, racial *war of position*.

In the United States, a racial war of position came into being gradually in the twentieth century, taking full shape only in the years following World War II. Gramsci explains war of position as political and cultural conflict, undertaken under conditions in which subordinated groups have attained some foothold, some rights, within civil society; thus, they have the leverage, the ability to press some claims on their rulers and on the state (Omi and Winant 1994). Du Bois was the crucial early theorist of the transition to racial war of position, as well as the key strategist of black movement politics in that transition. His conflicts with Booker T. Washington, and later with Marcus Garvey, can be understood in terms of his commitment to politics, his ceaseless struggle for black access to civil society—in other words, his effort to create a racial war of position. Like Horatio at the bridge, Du Bois stands between the old and the new racial orders, fighting tenaciously at the cusp of historical transition. Among modern theorists and activists, the only figure to whom he can be compared is Marx, who also ushered in almost singlehandedly a new way of thinking about the world, and who, like Du Bois, made his new manner of thought into a distinct kind of political practice.

RACIAL DUALISM AS POLITICS

Once a foothold in civil society was achieved, it was only a matter of time until full-scale political struggle over race emerged. The sources of the modern black movement have been extensively analyzed (Morris 1984, Branch 1988, Carson 1981, Zinn 1985, Omi and Winant 1994, Kluger 1977, Grant, 1968) and need not detain us here. For present purposes the important thing is that the movement transformed the American political universe, creating new organizations, new collective identities, and new political norms, challenging past racial practices and stereotypes, and ushering in a wave of democratizing social reform. This "great transfor-

affected blacks, but soon touched Latinos, Asian
Americans as well, permitted the entry of millions
members into the political process. It set off the
inism, a new anti-imperialist and antiwar move-
gay and disability rights, and even for environmental protection. The black movement deeply affected whites as well,
challenging often unconscious beliefs in white supremacy, and demanding
new and more respectful forms of behavior in relation to nonwhites.

In transforming the meaning of race and the contours of racial politics, the movement shifted the rules of participation and the organizing
principles of American politics itself. It made identity, difference, the
"personal," and language itself political issues in very new ways.

Once racial politics had taken the form of war of position, once basic
political rights had been achieved, racial dualism ceased to be an exclusively black or minority response to white supremacy. The "normalizing"
quality of white (and male) identity, which in the past had tended to render whiteness "transparent" and to equate it with U.S. nationality itself,
as in the phrase "a white man's country," necessarily experienced a certain
erosion as nonwhites and women acquired a significant degree of admission into mainstream institutions, and began to exercise their voices
and rights from inside, rather than from outside, the terrain of democratic
politics.

By the mid-1960s, popular support for the main principles of the
"civil rights revolution" had been secured, and legislation passed. An alternative viewpoint to the exclusionary framework of racial war of maneuver, to the archaic principles of overt white supremacy, had been
institutionalized; and in legal terms (or in respect to what Max Weber
would call "formal rationality") something that could be described as
"equality" had developed.

But no more than that. Substantive equality had not been achieved.
White supremacy had not been vanquished. Indeed, as soon as civil rights
legislation and "equal opportunity" policies were initiated, they started to
erode under reactionary pressures. Because a significant breach had been
opened in the armor of white supremacy, it was not expedient for the
forces of "racial reaction" (Omi and Winant 1994) to seek a return to

overtly exclusionary policies. Instead, they sought to reinterpret the movement's victories, to strip it of its more radical implications, to rearticulate its vision of a substantively egalitarian society in conservative and individualistic terms. "Equality" has had many meanings since the nation was founded; it was hardly unprecedented to redefine it in terms of formal and legal standing rather than in terms of redistribution of resources, compensation for past wrongs, or forceful efforts to reshape the material conditions of minorities. In retrospect, we can see that to have undertaken these measures would have involved as revolutionary a change as the Reconstruction measures did (Du Bois 1935, Foner 1988), for it would have required not only the dismantling of segregated neighborhoods, workplaces, and schools, but the transformation of the status of white workers as well. Substantive equality would have meant massive redistribution of resources; it would have clashed with fundamental capitalist class interests; such dramatic social change was never even on the table.

The seeds of racial reaction were thus already present in the ideological choices available in the 1960s: moderate tendencies that espoused integration and "color-blind" racial policies, and radical positions that advocated black (or brown, or red, or yellow) power, in other words racial nationalism. While each of these positions had something to recommend it, neither was sustainable by itself, and no synthesis between them seemed possible. Integrationist views held open the possibility of a class-based alliance between minority and white poor and working people, a position that Martin Luther King, Jr., was espousing in the last year of his life (Garrow 1988). In ideological terms, though, integrationism tended to erode the specifically racial dimension of the movement that had spawned it, for it sought to create institutions in which race would not play so central a part. Nationalist perspectives had the opposite problem: though they could assert the irreducibility of racial differences, they lacked the ideological equipment to forge alliances across racial lines, particularly with whites. The few groups that possessed the ability to walk the line between racial nationalism and radical multiracial class politics—such as the Black Panther Party—were undone by repression and by their precarious hold on an impoverished and volatile membership.

Thus the rise to power of neoconservatism, which inherited and rearticulated the "moderate" tendencies that emerged from the movement. Indeed, already in the mid-1960s such voices were heard decrying the tendency toward "positive discrimination" (M. Gordon 1964); by the mid-1970s a leading neoconservative could produce an influential tract entitled *Affirmative Discrimination* (Glazer 1975), and an important intervention of 1978 claimed that race was "declining in significance" (Wilson 1978).

Among ordinary whites similar fragmentations occurred: reacting to perceived losses in their racially privileged status but unable to identify with the more radical successors to the movement; unable in the aftermath of the civil rights era to espouse white supremacy but excluded and condemned by a racial politics that paid little attention to class, most whites came to support a conservative and individualistic form of egalitarianism, advocating a supposedly "color-blind" (but actually deeply race-conscious) political position. This was the *white* "politics of difference." This synthesis acquired particular force as job losses and stagnating income cut deeply into whites' sense of security. It gathered strength as the lower strata of the black and Latino communities were plunged into deeper poverty by massive cutbacks in welfare-state programs, education, and federal assistance to the cities; when the inevitable moral panics about crime, drugs, drive-by shootings, and teenage pregnancy ensued, they fueled the white flight to the right. In a thoroughly corporate culture, no countervailing arguments (against corporate greed and deindustrialization, for example) acquired so much as a foothold in the mainstream political discourse.

Meanwhile blacks, as well as other racially defined minority groups, were convulsed by new conflicts over group identity. Class divisions and various strains of resurgent cultural nationalism disrupted the black community and drove some blacks, both elite and "everyday" folks, in strongly conservative directions. Latinos, Native Americans, and Asian Americans experienced different, but parallel, schisms. Even those whose "whiteness" retains problematic elements, such as Arab Americans and Jews, were newly confronted by conflicts over where their political and moral allegiances lay in the post–civil rights era.

These examples need not be extended further. The point is clear: a new racial paradigm, tension-ridden, uncertain, an unstable, came into being. This paradigm combined the pre–World War II inheritance of white supremacy, which survived in significant measure, with the legacy of the 1960s movements—themselves based on a centuries-long tradition of resistance to conquest, enslavement, and racial oppression.

So, all the social practices that enforced black racial dualism in 1903 continue today: the segregation of minority (and particularly black) communities (Massey and Denton 1993), the discriminatory and regressive allocation of underemployment, undereducation, and other forms of substantive inequality to members of these communities, and the general cultural subordination that accompanies white supremacy.

Nevertheless, we are not in 1903. Massive transformations have occurred in the U.S. racial order, particularly over the last half-century. From the mid-1950s to the early 1970s, an important wave of racial reform swept across the land, altering not only racial policy but also racial identity, redrawing the American political and cultural map, refueling oppositional currents that had lain dormant in the United States for decades, such as feminism and anti-imperialism. Strictly speaking, of course, this was not a "new" movement at all, but rather an upwelling of oppositional forces that abided, that had their origins in the earliest moments of conquest and enslavement, and that were linked to the most epochal struggles of oppressed peoples across the globe for emancipation and justice.

From the 1960s to the present, then, not only black people, but the nation at large, have been riven by a throughgoing and deep-seated struggle: *the antagonistic coexistence, the contradiction, of the two great forces of white supremacy on the one hand, and of the movement for racial and indeed broader social justice on the other.* It is this convulsion, this contradiction, that constitutes racial dualism at century's end.

I anticipate various objections to the line of argument that race no longer operates as a simple signifier—as it largely did in Du Bois's day— absolutely locating one in a certain largely homogeneous community or another. Was white supremacy ever truly that monolithic? Did not Du Bois's narrative already expose its delusions of absolute racial difference? And hasn't "the movement" accomplished at least this much: that it has made possible a greater "crossing over," a greater cultural hybridization, a

:ness of the presence of "others" who are also subjects, who
.hts, who can act politically, etc.? Furthermore, isn't the des-
"duality" suspect for various reasons? Does it not privilege
whites, for instance, by suggesting that there are whites and there are "the
others"? In racial terms, shouldn't I be talking about "pluralism" rather
than dualism?

And what about the other dimensions of politics and identity? What
about gender and class? These dynamics shape politics and culture today
in ways very different from the manner in which Du Bois—feminist and
socialist though he was—encountered them nearly a century ago. Even if
we think about their impact on racial identity and politics, on the problematic theme of racial dualism today, they appear to play a fragmenting
role: pointing to many fissures, not just two.

Without question there are weaknesses in my use of the racial-
dualism framework in a revised, contemporary form. Although I think
these objections can all be answered, for now, I want simply to stress the
effectiveness of this approach in illuminating the charged and con-
tentious sociohistorical context in which racial politics are framed in the
U.S. at century's end. I have shown how the concept helps us understand
the peculiar and contradictory character of large-scale, macrolevel racial
politics at century's end. I should like now to apply it to small-scale, mi-
crolevel racial politics.

RACIAL DUALISM AS IDENTITY

As the civil rights legacy was drawn and quartered—beginning in the late
1960s and with ever-greater success in the following two decades—the
tugging and hauling, the escalating contestation over the meaning of
race, resulted in ever-more conflicting and contradictory notions of racial
identity. The significance of race ("declining" or increasing?), the interpretation of racial equality ("color-blind" or color-conscious?), the institutionalization of racial justice ("reverse discrimination" or affirmative
action?), and the very categories—black, white, Latino/Hispanic, Asian
American, and Native American—employed to classify racial groups
were all called into question as they emerged from the civil rights

"victory" of the mid-1960s. These racial signifiers are all ambiguous or contradictory today. We cannot escape the racial labels U.S. society comprehensively assigns to all within it; this has been the fate of "Americans" since Europeans arrived on these shores. Yet less than ever can we identify unproblematically or unselfconsciously with these designations, for they are riven—as we ourselves are fissured—to an unprecedented extent by the conflicts and contradictions posed by the political struggles of the past decades.

How do these conflicts and contradictions shape the various racial identities available today? Without hoping to be anything more than schematic, I will now offer some observations on the racial "politics of identity" at century's end. As the entire argument I have presented here should suggest, I do not share the denunciatory attitude toward "identity politics" so evident on both right and left today (Newfield 1993, Gitlin 1993). In my view, the matrices of identity are ineluctably political, for they involve interests, desire, antagonisms, etc., in constant interplay with broad social structures. To explore these matters more fully would go beyond the present article's scope.

Still, the critics do have one thing right: if any of my account here rings true, there can be no "straightforward" identity politics. Our awareness of the pervasiveness of racial dualism today should serve to check claims of unmediated authenticity, whether hegemonic or subaltern. Appeals to "traditional values," to the national culture, to canonized texts that exemplify hegemonic claims, must therefore be treated with the extreme suspicion that awareness of standpoint demands. Subaltern claims, as expressed for example through invocation of supposedly direct experiences of oppression—of the form "As a black person I know X . . . ," or "As a woman I know X . . ." (where X is an undifferentiated generalization about blacks' or women's experience)—are also suspect.

With these guidelines in mind, let us briefly explore the terrain of the racial politics of identity, focusing our attention on the operations of racial dualism today.

BLACK RACIAL DUALISM: First, thirty years after the ambiguous victory of the civil rights movement, what does it mean to be "black"? The decline of the organized black movement in the 1970s, and the wholesale assaults against the welfare state initiated by Ronald Reagan during the 1980s, sharply increased divisions along class and gender lines in the black community. The divergent experiences of the black middle class and the black poor—experiences far more distant from each other than they were in the days of official segregation—make a unitary racial identity seem a distant dream indeed. A whole other set of divisions has emerged around gender, such that black men's and women's experiences probably diverge more significantly today than at any other moment since the time of slavery. Consequently, a coherent black politics that could reach across class and gender lines seems remote.

Divisions of class have meant that in the upper strata of the black community a portion of the ideal of substantive equality has indeed been achieved, though in the United States no black person can ever believe her- or himself to be beyond the reach of white supremacy (Cose 1993, Graham 1995, Williams 1991). Meanwhile the desolation of the poor increases steadily, fueled in part by the very claim that equality (formal equality, that is) has been attained, that we are now a "color-blind" society, etc. Such rhetoric attributes black poverty to defects in black motivation (Murray 1984, Kaus 1992), intelligence (Herrnstein and Murray 1994), or family structure (L. Gordon 1994), a strategy of victim-blaming that often takes aim not only at "underclass" blacks but at low-income black women in particular. Additionally, opportunity structures for blacks are changing by class and gender in unprecedented ways (Carnoy 1994, Hacker 1992).

The significance of a divided black community, and hence identity, is complex, even contradictory. On the one hand, the emergence of diverse and even conflicting voices in the black community is welcome, for it reflects real changes in the direction of mobility and democratization. On the other hand, the persistence of glaring racial inequality—that is, of an ongoing dimension of white supremacy and racism that pervades the entire society—demands a level of concerted action that division and discord tend to preclude. Racial dualism at century's end.

OTHER "OTHERS": In the 1990s, what does it mean to be "yellow" or "brown"? Before the success of civil rights (and particularly immigration) reforms in the mid-1960s, racialized groups of Asian and Latin American origin experienced very high levels of exclusion and intolerance. After 1965 these communities began to grow rapidly. Previously isolated in enclaves based on language and national origin, Koreans, Filipinos, Japanese, and Chinese underwent a substantial racialization process from the late 1960s onward, emerging as "Asian Americans" (Espiritu 1992). Accompanying these shifts was significant upward mobility for some—though by no means all—sectors of Asian America.

Similar shifts overtook Mexicans, Puerto Ricans, Central Americans, and even Cubans as the "Latino" and "Hispanic" categories were popularized (Moore and Pachon 1985). For example, the destruction of formal segregation in Texas had a profound impact on Mexican Americans there (Montejano 1987). Segregation of Latinos in the upper and middle economic strata decreased rapidly across the country (far more rapidly than that of comparable black income earners) (Massey and Denton 1993), and some Latino groups achieved or consolidated solid middle-class status (notably Cubans and to some extent Dominicans). The Mexican, Puerto Rican, and Central American barrios, however, continued to be plagued by immigrant-bashing and high levels of poverty that could only be seen as racially organized (Moore and Pinderhughes 1993).

Thus, for both Asian Americans and Latinos, contemporary racial identity is fraught with contradictions. Apart from long-standing antagonisms between particular groups—for example, Cubans and Puerto Ricans, or Koreans and Japanese—significant class- and gender-based conflicts exist as well. Tendencies among long-established residents to disparage and sometimes exploit immigrants who are "fresh off the boat," or for group ties to attenuate as social mobility increases, suggest the centrality of class in immigrant life (Portes and Bach 1985; Takaki 1990). The liberating possibilities encountered by immigrating women, and their greater proclivity to settle in the United States rather than to return to their countries of origin, suggest the centrality of gender in immigrant life (Grasmuck and Pessar 1991).

Not unlike blacks, Asian Americans and Latinos often find themselves caught between the past and the future. Old forms of racism have resurfaced to confront them, as in the renewed enthusiasm for immigrant-bashing and the recurrent waves of anti-Japanese and anti-Chinese paranoia. Discrimination has resurfaced, sometimes in new ways, as in controversies over Asian admissions to elite universities (Takagi 1993). Nonetheless, at the same time, the newly panethnicized identities of Asian Americans and Latinos have brought them face-to-face with challenges that were quite distinct from anything faced in the past. Some examples of these challenges are the dubious gift of neoconservative support (Asians as the "model minority," for example), the antagonism of blacks (Kim 1993, Omi and Winant 1993, Miles 1992), and the tendencies toward dilution of specific ethnic or national identity in a racialized category created by a combination of "lumping" and political exigency. Often more successful and accepted than in the past, but subject to new antagonisms and new doubts about their status, Asian Americans and Latinos experience a distinct racial dualism today.

For reasons of space I am going to slight Native Americans here, but there is ample evidence to believe that in the postwar period Indian nations as well came face-to-face with a racially dualistic situation. Here, too, the old logic of despoliation still applied: environmental destruction and land rape, appalling poverty, and cultural assault continued to take their toll. Still, a new, activist, and often economically and politically savvy Native America could also be glimpsed. Today, Indians have developed techniques for fighting in the courts, for asserting treaty rights, and indeed for regaining a modicum of economic and political control over their tribal destinies that would have been unthinkable a generation ago (Nagel 1995, Cornell 1988).

WHITE RACIAL DUALISM: In the post–civil rights period, what did it mean to be white? During the epoch of racial war of maneuver, in which exclusion was the predominant status assigned to racially identified minorities, white identity (and particularly white male identity) was "normalized"; "otherness" was elsewhere: among people "of color" and to some extent among women. All these were marked by their identities, but under conditions of virtually unchallenged white supremacy, white men were not. Once "white egalitarianism" (Saxton 1990) had been established as the political price elites had to pay to secure mass electoral support, *Herrenvolk* Republicanism (Roediger 1991) became the organizing principle of nineteenth-century United States politics and culture. Only whites (only white men) were full citizens; only they were fully formed *individuals*. In terms of race and gender their identities were, so to speak, transparent, which is what we mean by the term "normalized."

Of course, for a long time many whites partook of an ethnic "otherness" that placed them in an ambiguous relationship with both established WASP elites and with racially defined minorities. But by the 1960s white ethnicity was in serious decline. Large-scale European immigration had become a thing of the past; while urban ethnic enclaves continued to exist in many major cities, suburbanization and gentrification had taken their toll. Communal forms of white ethnic identity had been eroded by outmarriage, and by heterogeneous contact in schools, workplaces, neighborhoods, and religious settings (Alba 1990, Waters 1990).

Nor were alternative collective identities, other forms of solidarity, readily available to whites. Class-based identities had always been weak in the United States, and were particularly debilitated in the wake of the red-baiting period of the late 1940s and '50s, the same moment in which the black movement was gathering strength. What remained was the "imagined community" (Anderson 1983) of white racial nationalism (Walters 1987): the United States as a "white man's country." It was this ideological construct of whiteness, already deeply problematic in a thoroughly modernized, advanced industrial society, that the black movement confronted in the post–World War II period.

Detached from the previous generations' ethnic ties, unable to see themselves as part of a potentially majoritarian working class with larger social justice interests, and unable to revert to the discredited white supremacy of an earlier period, most whites were ripe for conversion to neoconservative racial ideology after the civil rights "victory" in the mid-1960s. Efforts on the part of Martin Luther King, Jr., Bayard Rustin, and even the Black Panther Party to forge multiracial alliances for large-scale redistributive policies and other forms of substantive social justice never had a serious chance in the national political arena.

Instead, neoconservative and new right politicians, initiated by the Wallace campaigns of the mid-1960s, appealed to white workers on the basis of their residual commitments to racial "status honor" (Edsall 1992). Wallace, and Nixon in his "southern strategy," invoked the powerful remnants of white supremacy and white privilege. Since white identities could no longer be overtly depicted as superior, they were now presented in "coded" fashion as a beleaguered American individualism, as the hallmarks of a noble tradition now unfairly put upon by unworthy challengers, as the "silent majority," etc. The racial reaction begun by Wallace and consummated by Reagan, which resurrected twentieth-century Republicanism from the oblivion to which the New Deal had supposedly consigned it, was thus a fairly direct descendant of the "white labor republicanism" (Roediger 1991, Saxton 1990) that had shaped the U.S. working class along racial lines more than a century earlier.

In this fashion from the late 1960s on, white identity was reinterpreted and rearticulated in a dualistic fashion: on the one hand egalitarian, on the other hand privileged; on the one hand individualistic and "color-blind," on the other hand "normalized" and white. With Reagan's election in 1980, the process reached its peak. A class policy of regressive redistribution was adopted; working-class incomes, stagnant since the mid-1970s, continued to drop in real terms as profits soared. Neoconservative racial ideology—with its commitment to formal racial equality and its professions of "color blindness"—now proved particularly useful: it served to organize and rationalize white working-class resentments against declining living standards. To hear Reagan, Bush, Gramm et al. tell it, the problems faced by white workers did not derive from corporate hunger for ever-greater profits, from deindustrialization and the "downsizing" of workforces; rather their troubles emanated from the welfare state, which expropriated the taxes of the productive citizens who "played by the rules" and "went to work each day" in order to subsidize unproductive and parasitic welfare queens and career criminals "who didn't want to work."

Nowhere was this new framework of the white "politics of difference" more clearly on display than in the reaction to affirmative action policies of all sorts (in hiring, university admissions, federal contracting, etc.). Assaults on these policies, which have been developing since their introduction as tentative and quite limited efforts at racial redistribution

(Johnson 1967), are currently at hysterical levels. These attacks are clearly designed to effect ideological shifts rather than to shift resources in any meaningful way. They represent whiteness as *disadvantage*, something that has few precedents in U.S. racial history (Gallagher 1994). This imaginary white disadvantage—for which there is almost no evidence at the empirical level—has achieved widespread popular credence, and provides the cultural and political "glue" that holds together a wide variety of reactionary racial politics.

To summarize: today, the politics of white identity is undergoing a profound political crisis. The destruction of the communal bases of white ethnicity is far advanced, yet whiteness remains a significant source of "status honor." White privilege—a relic of centuries of *Herrenvolk* democracy—has been called into question in the post–civil rights period. Far from being destroyed, however, the white "politics of difference" is now being trumpeted as an ideology of victimization. The situation would be farcical if it weren't so dangerous, reflecting venerable white anxieties and fortifying the drift to the right which, now as in the past, is highly conducive to race-baiting. Today's "color-blind" white supremacy, then, embodies the racial duality of contemporary white identity.

It is not the case, however, that whites have unequivocally or unanimously embraced the right, though certainly the ideological effects of neoconservatism have been profound, particularly on economically vulnerable whites. Although undoubtedly a minority among whites, there are still millions who have resisted the siren song of neoconservatism, recognizing that the claim of "color blindness" masks a continuing current of white supremacy and racism.

Why? What enables *any* whites to adhere to the objective of substantive social justice, rather than its merely formal illusions? And how deep does this commitment run? We know little about the sources of white antiracism today. Yet few themes on the domestic political horizon are more important.

Without becoming entirely speculative, it is possible to identify a few elements of white experience that have potential antiracist dimensions. Feminism and gay liberation have developed critiques of discrimination that are intimately related to the experiences of racially defined minorities. Furthermore, these struggles can trace their origins back to the black struggles of the nineteenth century as well as those of the 1960s. Millions of white lives have been changed by these movements. Other forms of radical political experience also taught basic antiracist lessons, despite various political and ideological limitations. Here I am thinking of the great industrial organizing drives of the 1930s, the various Communist currents, new left and antiwar activities during the 1960s, the farmworkers' movement, the solidarity movements with Central America in the 1970s and '80s, and above all, the civil rights movement, in which many thousands of whites were involved.

These political struggles exercised a moral influence on whites, just as they did on national politics; that influence has perhaps waned under decades of assault from the right, but it has proved far more difficult to eradicate than its opponents expected. Beyond its fundamentally ethical character, it draws upon various material interests as well (I recognize that this distinction is not an absolute one). Among these is the difficulty of uniting all whites under conservative banners: Jews in particular (whose "whiteness" continues to exhibit fissures and cultural contradictions) (Sacks 1994) still adhere disproportionately to social and political liberalism for reasons that have been extensively analyzed. Arab Americans, paradoxically, are in much the same position. Other sources of white antiracism may be located in religious institutions, the academy, and popular cultural forms, although none of these is free of ambiguity and contradiction.

In short, the problematic and volatile quality of contemporary white identities, not their consolidation, is evident at all levels of U.S. society, from the most casual conversation to the contortions and contradictions of national politics. This volatility provides ongoing evidence of racial dualism among whites.

TOWARD RADICAL DEMOCRACY

As U.S. politics plunges to the right, as the aspirations of the activists and adherents of the 1960s movements are forsaken, as indeed the legacy of those struggles is twisted and tortured into service as an *obstacle* to the achievement of real social and racial justice, the attempt to imagine a greater and more robust democracy, racially inclusive as well as substantively egalitarian, seems almost utopian. Still, I submit that it is precisely that task which most cries out for thought and action today. Those who wish to halt the gallop to the right need to be able to envision a convincing political alternative, if the cause of racial justice, and indeed of radical democracy, is ever to resume its advance.

Without presumption—for this task is more than the work of an article—I would like to suggest that the recognition of widespread racial dualism in U.S. politics and culture at century's end suggests certain principles that can be applied to this work of imagination.

To acknowledge racial dualism is to understand the malleability and flexibility of all identities, especially racial ones. One of the recognitions hard-won by the movements of the 1960s—not only the racially based ones, but all the so-called new social movements across the globe—was that identity is a political construct. Not carved in stone, not "sutured" (Mouffe and Laclau 1985), our concepts of ourselves can be dramatically altered by new movements, new articulations of the possible. It may yet turn out that the greatest achievement of the 1960s movements, sparked by the black movement, was not the political reforms they accomplished, but the new possibilities for racial identity they engendered, not just for black people, but for everyone.

The right wing has in a certain sense understood the challenge of "reimagining" race, for it has clearly articulated a particular vision of the meaning of race in a conservative democratic society. This is the concept of "color blindness." Undeniably, this vision has a certain appeal, not only as a cover for the perpetuation of white supremacy but as a plausible reinvention of fundamental elements of national ideology: individualism, an "opportunity, not entitlement" society, etc.

But this vision also has profound weaknesses, even beyond its disingenuousness. It is authoritarian, repressive, relentlessly homogeneous. It allows little space for the further development of racially based institutions and cultural representations—"difference"—whose vitality has persevered and ramified for centuries. "Color blindness"—let us imagine it to be a genuine antiracism for a moment—assumes that if we refuse to recognize racial difference it will disappear; it assumes that racial distinctions are inherently invidious. But this is not a convincing claim: race, and racial identity, are not merely produced by racism, as neoconservatives (as well as some on the left) might claim. They are also means of self-representation, autonomous signification, and cultural (and thus social and political) practice.

All the evidence suggests that once created and institutionalized, once having evolved over many centuries, racial difference is a permanent, though flexible, attribute of human society (Winant 1994). Racial categories can neither be liquidated ("color blindness"), nor reified as unchanging features of human nature (biologistic racism). Somewhat paradoxically, then, the permanence of race coexists with the necessarily contingent and contextual character of racial identity and racial difference. Racial dualism at century's end.

Beyond these inadequacies in neoconservative racial ideology lie the intersections between issues of race and those of class and gender. Neoconservatism rationalizes the regressive redistribution of income, not only along racial but also along class lines. As the gap between wealth and poverty increases, its consequences become more severe, not only for racially defined minorities, but also for whites. Thus far, it has proved quite effective to scapegoat impoverished minority strata as the cause of white underemployment and stagnating income levels. We can observe this strategy—which is a classical one—being extended further and further as its inadequacies become more obvious. For example, the gathering assault on affirmative action policies suggests that not only impoverished ghetto and barrio residents, but also working- and middle-class minorities, are now to be blamed for the white working class's failure to thrive.

It is also quite striking how much the "imagined community" of a supposedly color-blind nation also depends on the reassertion of maleness and heterosexuality. For example, the current effort to restigmatize illegitimacy (Murray 1993), explicitly tries to move beyond the traditional assault on minority (and particularly black) women's supposed promiscuity and hyperfertility, to stigmatize low-income white women as well. The attack on affirmative action clearly directs fire not only at racially defined minorities but at women, and gay rights are also growing more vulnerable.

Neoconservative scapegoating thus has perverse consequences for many whites as well as for racially defined minorities. It holds down white income levels and props up unemployment. It stigmatizes women and gays, white as well as nonwhite. And despite its "color-blind" facade, it depends on rigid concepts of racial, gender, and sexual identities that accord less and less with the authoritarian and repressive morality (Republican "family values") it seeks to enforce.

Scapegoating flourishes in large part because a radical democratic challenge to its fundamental premises has been silenced and marginalized. But must this be the case? Without presuming to write a prescription for a new antiracist political program, it is possible to identify some of the elements such a politics might encompass, based on the analysis of contemporary racial dualism presented here.

Radical democracy must compete with authoritarianism of all sorts to articulate a more open and flexible vision of politics. First, any radical democratic politics *must acknowledge and accept the uncertainty and fragility of social and cultural identities* (Przeworski 1986, Lechner 1988)—racial identities particularly—and the fears that threats to these identities can produce. This is necessary to avoid the temptations of neoconservatism evident not only on the right, but even on the left (Sleeper 1990). A more effective approach would be informed by an awareness of the pervasiveness of racial dualism at century's end. It would evoke the ethical dimensions of identity politics (West 1991, Lechner 1988), and ask to what extent we permit ourselves to know the racialized other, both outside us and within us.

When the instabilities inherent in both minority and majority identities are acknowledged, the door to coalition politics—closed since the defection to the right of the civil rights "moderates" in the mid-1960s—can be reopened. In many different settings, from school boards and city councils to ethnic studies programs, from feminist politics (often split along racial or ethnic lines) (Caraway 1991, Frankenburg 1993) to environmental issues (Bullard 1993), the absence or weakness of transracial political alliances plays into the hands of the right. And more often than not, what obstructs the formation of these alliances is the inability to get beyond either rigid denials of racial difference, or rigid conceptions of racial identity (or both). For whites, such conceptions usually involve defenses—often covert or even unconscious—of outmoded ideas of racial privilege. For members of racially defined minority groups, such conceptions usually involve appeals to flawed notions of racial or ethnic authenticity.

Our dire political situation demands that we reinvent coalition politics, not as an alternative to the "politics of difference," but as a supplement to it. A radical democratic politics would permit *both plural and singular* organizational projects, both multiracial and particular types of initiatives. There is room for the kinds of antiracist alliances now emerging in different parts of the country, *alongside* exclusively black or Indian or Chicano organizations. Indeed, these terms are no longer adequate: many types of "black" (Afro-Caribbean, Haitian, as well as Afro-American) distinctions must be both recognized and mobilized today. Chicano (Hispano), Puertorriqueño (Nuyorican), as well as Latino and Hispanic identifications exist, and coexist, among us.

And what about whites? It is crucial that antiracist whites take part in multiracial political activity if there is to be any effective challenge to the right. The organizations that currently do this work are few but vital: groups like the Children's Defense Fund, the Southern Poverty Law Center, and the Northwest Alliance, to name but a few. At this point it is difficult to see whites mobilizing independently *qua* whites in an antiracist fashion, for the legacy of white supremacy and the attachment to privilege is still too strong. But the time may come when this becomes a possibility, in the context of a stronger multiracial movement for radical democracy.

The account of racial dualism offered here seeks to open up political possibilities that have been shut down; I know full well that some of these ideas will be criticized as utopian, vague, and impractical. But precisely because the times are so tough, it is vital that we examine the contingency and multiplicity of our own identities. No individual belongs to "just" one socially constructed category: each has his or her multiple racial, gender, class-based, national identities, and that's just a start of the list. Nor are these categories uniform or stable; we are Whitmanesque, we contain multitudes. To recognize our many selves is to understand the vast social construction that is not only the individual, but history itself, the present as history. A radical democratic politics must invite us to comprehend this.

To understand the fragility of our identities can be profoundly disconcerting, especially in the absence of a political and moral vision in which the individual and the group can see themselves as included, supported, and contributing to the construction of a better society. To counter the authoritarian interpretation of fear and uncertainty, to resist the imposition of exclusive and repressive models of order, a radical democratic politics must acknowledge those very fears and uncertainties, while at the same time offering a way to accept and interpret these emotions publicly and collectively. Racial dualism can be something desirable. Not through repression, but through knowledge of the differences *within* ourselves can we achieve the solidarity with others which, though necessarily partial, is essential for the creation of a more just and free world.

NOTE

An earlier version of this paper was presented at the Race Matters Conference at Princeton University in May 1993. Thanks to Wahneema Lubiano for comments.

WORKS CITED

Alba, Richard D. *Ethnic Identity: The Transformation of White America.* New Haven: Yale University Press, 1990.

Almaguer, Tomas. *Racial Faultlines: The Historical Origins of White Supremacy in California.* Berkeley: University of California Press, 1994.

Anderson, Benedict. *Imagined Communities: Reflections on the Origins and Spread of Nationalism.* Rev. ed. New York: Verso, 1991 (1983).

Armstrong, Nancy, and William Tennenhouse. *The Violence of Representation: Literature and the History of Violence.* New York: Routledge, 1989.

Bhabha, Homi K. *The Location of Culture.* New York: Routledge 1994.

Branch, Taylor. *Parting the Waters: America in the King Years, 1954–1963.* New York: Simon & Schuster, 1988.

Bullard, Robert. *Confronting Environmental Racism: Voices from the Grassroots.* Boston: South End, 1993.

Caraway, Nancie. *Segregated Sisterhood: Racism and the Politics of American Feminism.* Knoxville: University of Tennessee Press, 1991.

Carnoy, Martin. *Faded Dreams: The Politics and Economics of Race in America.* New York: Cambridge University Press, 1994.

Carson, Clayborn. *In Struggle: SNCC and the Black Awakening of the 1960s.* Cambridge, Mass.: Harvard University Press, 1981.

Cornell, Stephen. *The Return of the Native: American Indian Political Resurgence.* New York: Oxford University Press, 1988.

Cose, Ellis. *The Rage of a Privileged Class.* New York: HarperCollins, 1993.

Davis, F. James. *Who Is Black? One Nation's Definition.* University Park: Pennsylvania State University Press, 1991.

Drinnon, Richard. *Facing West: The Metaphysics of Indian Hating and Empire Building.* Minneapolis: University of Minnesota Press, 1985.

Du Bois, W. E. B. *Black Reconstruction in America: An Essay Toward a History of the Part Which Black Folk Played in the Attempt to Reconstruct Democracy in America, 1860–1880.* New York: Atheneum, 1977 (1935).

———. *The Souls of Black Folk.* New York: Penguin, 1989 (1903).

Edsall, Thomas Byrne, with Mary Edsall. *Chain Reaction: The Impact of Race, Rights, and Taxes on American Politics.* Rev. ed. New York: Norton, 1992.

Espiritu, Yen Le. *Asian American Panethnicity: Bridging Institutions and Identities.* Philadelphia: Temple University Press, 1992.

Foner, Eric. *Reconstruction: America's Unfinished Revolution, 1863–1877.* New York: Harper & Row, 1988.

Forbes, Jack D. *Black Africans and Native Americans: Color, Race, and Caste in the Evolution of Red-Black Peoples.* New York: Basil Blackwell, 1988.

Frankenburg, Ruth. *White Women, Race Matters: The Social Construction of Whiteness.* Minneapolis: University of Minnesota Press, 1993.

Gallagher, Charles. "White Reconstruction in the University." *Socialist Review* 94 (1994): 1–2.

Garrow, David J. *Bearing the Cross: Martin Luther King Jr. and the Southern Christian Leadership Conference.* New York: Vintage, 1988.

Gitlin, Todd. "From Universality to Difference: Notes on the Fragmentation of the Idea of the Left." *Contention* 2, no. 2 (Winter 1993).

Glazer, Nathan. *Affirmative Discrimination: Ethnic Inequality and Public Policy.* New York: Basic Books, 1975.

Gordon, Linda. *Pitied but Not Entitled: Single Mothers and the History of Welfare.* New York: Free Press, 1994.

Gordon, Milton M. *Assimilation in American Life: The Role of Race, Religion, and National Origin.* New York: Oxford University Press, 1964.

Graham, Lawrence Otis. *Member of the Club: Reflections on Life in a Racially Polarized World.* New York: HarperCollins, 1995.

Gramsci, Antoni. *Selections from the Prison Notebooks.* Edited by Geoffrey Nowell-Smith and Quintin Hoare. New York: International Publishers, 1971.

Grant, Joanne, ed. *Black Protest: History, Documents, and Analyses, 1619 to the Present.* New York: Fawcett, 1968.

Grasmuck, Sherri, and Patricia R. Pessar. *Between Two Islands: Dominican International Migration.* Berkeley: University of California Press, 1991.

Hacker, Andrew. *Two Nations: Black and White, Separate, Hostile, Unequal.* New York: Scribners, 1992.

Hernnstein, Richard, and Charles Murray. *The Bell Curve: Intelligence and Class Structure in American Life.* New York: Free Press, 1994.

Johnson, Lyndon. "To Secure These Rights." In *The Moynihan Report and the Politics of Controversy,* edited by Lee Rainwater and William Yancey. Cambridge, Mass.: MIT Press, 1967.

Kaus, Mickey. *The End of Equality.* New York: Basic Books, 1992.

Kim, Elaine. "Home Is Where the Han Is." In *Reading Rodney King, Reading Urban Uprising,* edited by Robert Gooding-Williams. New York: Routledge, 1993.

Kluger, Richard. *Simple Justice: The History of Brown v. Board of Education and Black America's Struggle for Equality.* New York: Vintage, 1977.

Lechner, Norbert. *Los Patios Interiores de la Democracia: Subjetividad y Política.* Santiago: FLACSO, 1988.

Massey, Douglas, and Nancy Denton. *American Apartheid.* Cambridge, Mass.: Harvard University Press, 1993.

Miles, Jack. "Blacks vs. Browns." *Atlantic Monthly,* October 1992.

Montejano, David. *Anglos and Mexicans in the Making of Modern Texas, 1836–1986.* Austin: University of Texas Press, 1987.

Moore, Joan, and Harry Pachon. *Hispanics in the United States.* Englewood Cliffs, N.J.: Prentice-Hall, 1985.

Moore, Joan, and Raquel Pinderhughes. *In the Barrios: Latinos and the Underclass Debate.* New York: Russell Sage Foundation, 1993.

Morris, Aldon D. *The Origins of the Civil Rights Movement: Black Communities Organizing for Change.* New York: Free Press, 1984

Mouffe, Chantal, and Ernesto Laclau. *Hegemony and Socialist Strategy: Towards a Radical Democratic Politics.* London: Verso, 1985.

Murray, Charles. "The Other Underclass." *Wall Street Journal,* October 29, 1993.

———. *Losing Ground: American Social Policy, 1950–1980.* New York: Basic Books, 1984.

Nagel, Joanne. *American Indian Ethnic Renewal: Red Power and the Resurgence of Identity and Culture.* New York: Oxford University Press, 1995.

Newfield, Christopher. "What Was Political Correctness? Race, Right, and Managerial Democracy in the Humanities." *Critical Inquiry* 19, no. 2 (Winter 1993).

Okihiro, Gary. *Margins and Mainstreams: Asians in American History and Culture.* Seattle: University of Washington Press, 1994.

Omi, Michael, and Howard Winant. "The Los Angeles 'Race Riot' and Contemporary U.S. Politics." In *Reading Rodney King, Reading Urban Uprising*, edited by Robert Gooding-Williams. New York: Routledge, 1993.

———. *Racial Formation in the United States: From the 1960s to the 1990s*. 2nd ed. New York: Routledge, 1994.

Portes, Alejandro, and Robert L. Bach. *Latin Journey: Cuban and Mexican Immigrants in the United States*. Berkeley: University of California Press, 1985.

Przeworski, Adam. "Some Problems in the Study of the Transition to Democracy." In *Transitions from Authoritarian Rule: Comparative Perspectives*, edited by Guillermo O'Donnell et al. Baltimore: Johns Hopkins University Press, 1986.

Roediger, David R. *The Wages of Whiteness: Race and the Making of the American Working Class*. New York: Verso, 1991.

Rogin, Michael P. *Fathers and Children: Andrew Jackson and the Subjugation of the American Indian*. New York: Random House, 1975.

Sacks, Karin Brodkin. "How Did Jews Become White Folks?" In *Race*, edited by Steven Gregory and Roger Sanjek. New Brunswick: Rutgers University Press, 1994.

Saxton, Alexander. *The Rise and Fall of the White Republic: Class Politics and Mass Culture in Nineteenth-Century America*. New York: Verso, 1990.

Scott, James. *Weapons of the Weak: Everyday Forms of Peasant Resistance*. New Haven: Yale University Press, 1985.

Sleeper, Jim. *The Closest of Strangers: Liberalism and the Politics of Race in New York*. New York: Norton, 1990.

Takagi, Dana Y. *The Retreat from Race: Asian Admissions and Racial Politics*. New Brunswick: Rutgers University Press, 1993.

Takaki, Ronald I. *A Different Mirror: A History of Multicultural America*. Boston: Little, Brown, 1993.

———. *Strangers from a Distant Shore: A History of Asian Americans*. New York: Penguin, 1990.

Thomas, W. I., and Dorothy Swaine Thomas. *The Child in America*. New York: Knopf, 1928.

van den Berghe, Pierre. *Race and Racism: A Comparative Perspective*. New York: Wiley, 1967.

Walters, Ronald. "White Racial Nationalism in the United States." *Without Prejudice* I, no. 1 (Fall 1987).

Waters, Mary C. *Ethnic Options: Choosing Identities in America*. Berkeley: University of California Press, 1990.

West, Cornel. "Nihilism in Black America." *Dissent* (Spring 1991).

Williams, Lena. "When Blacks Shop, Bias Often Accompanies Sale." *New York Times*, April 30, 1991.

Williamson, Joel. *A Rage for Order: Black-White Relations in the American South Since Emancipation*. New York: Oxford University Press, 1986.

Wilson, William Julius. *The Declining Significance of Race: Blacks and Changing American Institutions*. Chicago: University of Chicago Press, 1978.

Winant, Howard. *Racial Conditions: Politics, Theory, Comparisons*. Minneapolis: University of Minnesota Press, 1994.

Zinn, Howard. *SNCC: The New Abolitionists*. Westport, Conn.: Greenwood, 1985 (1965).

"AIN'T NOTHIN' LIKE
THE REAL THING"

*Black Masculinity, Gay Sexuality,
and the Jargon of Authenticity*

■

Kendall Thomas

S OME YEARS AGO I found myself sitting with hundreds of other people
in the sanctuary of the Cathedral of St. John the Divine in New York
City, just a few blocks away from where I lived and worked in Morning-
side Heights, on the other side of Harlem. We had gathered to remember
and celebrate the life of a writer whose novels, plays, and essays are a powerful record of his historical moment.

During the ceremony, a number of prominent African Americans
from the literary world paid tribute to this man whose prophetic pen had
given us such pain and pleasure. They all praised James Baldwin as a son
of black Harlem who had faithfully borne witness to the suffering and
struggle of his people. This, of course, was Jimmy the "bug-eyed griot" (in
Amiri Baraka's words), the Baldwin of *Go Tell It on the Mountain*, *The
Amen Corner*, and *The Fire Next Time*. Not one of these speakers mentioned the "other" Jimmy, the Baldwin of *Giovanni's Room*, *Another Country*, and *Just Above My Head*, whose stories I had read as a confused
teenager in Oroville, California. As I sat in that cold, cavernous cathedral, the silence about this Baldwin cut me to the core, because I knew
that while Baldwin may have left America because he was black, he left
Harlem, the place he called "home," because he ·was gay. It was this
"other" unacknowledged Jimmy whose stories I had devoured by flashlight
under the bedsheets when I was supposed to be asleep. This Jimmy knew
that many held him in contempt as an "aging, lonely, sexually dubious . . .

unspeakably erratic freak."[1] It was in the words of this Jimmy and in "the heavy grace of God"[2] that I, like so many other confused teenagers, began to understand that those who called me "homo," "punk," or "sissy" did not really know, or care to know, my name. Reading Baldwin, I began to understand that I had another name. Somebody who lived somewhere in the south of France knew that name, and had written with deep insight and aching beauty about the experiences this name so imperfectly expressed. As Baldwin put it in a late interview, he had felt a "special responsibility" to serve as "a kind of witness" to "that phenomenon we call gay."[3]

In the years since Baldwin's death in 1987, his testimony as a witness to gay experience has become the target of a certain revisionist impeachment. One (but by no means the only) representative instance of this tendency is a recent review by Ekweume Michael Thelwell of James Campbell's *Talking at the Gates: A Life of James Baldwin*.[4] Thelwell launches a scathing attack on the Campbell biography by asserting that "certain writers—these days, mostly men and mostly white" find James Baldwin "a source of unending mystery and provocation."[5] Thelwell contrasts the "challenge" Baldwin poses for white readers with his reception among "most of us in the black world," for whom "Baldwin's life and career, though admittedly complex, are neither so ambiguous nor so troubling. . . ." (90). In Thelwell's account, *Talking at the Gates* belongs to a disturbing "new dispensation" of "'major,' 'corrective' new biographies by white men" of figures like Frederick Douglass, Paul Robeson, Martin Luther King, Jr., and Malcolm X, all of which have sought to "supplant the accounts of their lives left by the men themselves" (90). For Thelwell the chief characteristic Campbell's life of Baldwin shares with other recent biographical work on these "luminaries of the Afro-American experience" is its "spirit" of "intellectual appropriation, an assertion of literary and conceptual proprietorship. . . ." (90–91).

Now, there is more than a little irony in all this, since Thelwell betrays the very spirit of appropriation and proprietorship that he finds so objectionable in *Talking at the Gates*. I refer here to Thelwell's treatment of Baldwin's sexuality, to which the review first alludes in discussing the "virtues" of the Campbell biography. It is odd (to say the least) that the sole example Thelwell offers of the "thoughtful clarifications" for which

Talking at the Gates should be commended is Campbell's observation that "Baldwin was *essentially androgynous* rather than homosexual" (92) (my emphasis). As one progresses through the essay, Thelwell's favorable assessment of this purported "clarification" of Baldwin's biography seems all the more curious. On the very next page of the review, Thelwell mentions the discomfort that Baldwin's "openly admitted sexual orientation" provoked among some of "the more 'established' Negro leaders" (93). The image of Baldwin as androgyne becomes even more perplexing when one comes to Thelwell's assertion (in the final paragraphs of his essay) that "slender, gay James Baldwin taught a generation of us how to be black men in this country, and he gave us a language in which to engage the struggle" (113). Needless to say, these last two remarks about Baldwin's sexuality sit uneasily with Thelwell's earlier insistence on the writer's essential androgyny.

What is at stake here? One could argue that Thelwell has simply failed to say what he means. Perhaps he intends to argue that Baldwin was "essentially bisexual" rather than "essentially androgynous," and unwittingly confuses an expression for gender identity (androgyny) with a reference to sexual orientation (bisexuality). Indeed, this reading of Thelwell would comport with the known facts, at least of Baldwin's early erotic life. Unhappily, Thelwell's utter silence about the substantial body of work Baldwin produced on homoerotic themes (about which Campbell himself has a great deal to say) leads the mind to a less comfortable conclusion. Taken together, Thelwell's equivocations about Baldwin's sexuality and his evident indifference to Baldwin's writings on the subject suggest that something more is involved here than linguistic mistake or conceptual confusion. Stated bluntly, Thelwell's vision of a "neutered" Baldwin betrays a deep and disturbing ideological investment regarding the connections among masculinity, sexuality, and "authentic" black identity.

How is this claim to be understood? The beginnings of an answer to this question might take us to the dictionary. "Androgyne" is a compound noun that consists of the Greek words (respectively) for man and woman. In its "positive" meaning the word refers to an individual who embodies "a mixing of secondary masculine and feminine sexual characteristics";[6] in its "negative" sense, the word refers to someone who is neither a man nor a woman. Moreover, the term "androgyny" has historically been the semantic site of a vertiginous slippage. As Francette Pacteau has noted, the "sexually ambiguous" figure of the androgyne simultaneously possesses a "dual sexual identity" *and* a "non-sexual identity."[7]

Both of these "impossible referents"[8] appear to be at work in the Thelwell review, and they suggest two different but equally disturbing understandings of the "androgyny" thesis. To interpret Thelwell's remark as a claim that Baldwin possessed a "dual sexual identity" is to view it as making an underlying, unstated argument about masculinity and male homosexuality. One might infer from Thelwell's remarks that he takes gay identity to be at odds with the very idea of masculinity. In this conception, which has a long pedigree, the male homosexual is deemed to possess "a woman's soul confined by a man's body."[9] The ascription of an ambiguous "dual" sexual identity to Baldwin allows Thelwell to confer a degree of masculinity on the writer to which a homosexual (read "effeminized") man cannot, by definition, lay claim. Needless to say, this understanding of the relationship between masculine identity and gay male sexuality betrays a very narrow vision of both.

A second possible reading of the "androgyny" thesis would take Thelwell's remark as a claim that Baldwin was not "bisexual" but "asexual" in both personality and practice. The implicit assumption here appears to be that sexual identity can be read off from sexual activity. According to this logic, if we want to know who Baldwin was (sexually speaking), we need only determine what (sexually speaking) he did or did not do. Presumably, we are supposed to conclude that because Baldwin did not lead an active sexual life (a fantastication that does not square with the known facts), he could not have been homosexual.[10]

This latter interpretation is in many ways even more distressing than the first, since it does not merely introduce an element of ambiguity regarding Baldwin's erotic affinities, but excludes them altogether. For better or worse, we live in a world in which individual identities are constructed in and through constructs of gendered sexual difference. The very notion of human subjectivity has come to rest on the fictional foundation of a stable, unified sexuality into which we are all inserted at birth. To say in such a world that an individual is androgynous in this second, neutered sense is in effect to deny that s/he exists: the androgyne has no sexual identity, which means that s/he has no identity at all. Nobody can know the androgyne's name, because there is no name by which s/he can be called.

In any event, I am less interested here in what the "androgyny" thesis *means* than in what it *does*. As I have already noted, Thelwell begins his essay by arguing that "most of us in the black world" do not find Baldwin's "admittedly complex" life and literary legacy "ambiguous" or "troubling." Nevertheless, it is clear that Thelwell's review may be read as a cultural brief, which seeks to secure a place for Baldwin in the patriarchal pantheon of "luminaries of the Afro-American experience" (the names of black women are tellingly absent from this list). While "most of us in the black world" may not doubt the significance of James Baldwin's contributions to the struggle against white supremacy in the United States (indeed, throughout the world), the fact remains that some of "us" do: one can point to any number of African Americans for whom Baldwin's sexuality raises an irrebuttable presumption against his inclusion in the annals of black American freedom fighters. Seen in this light, Thelwell's characterization of Baldwin's sexuality serves as a preemptive identificatory strike. Thelwell is surely aware of the ugly homophobic history of Baldwin's reception in certain quarters of black America. Sadly, his defensive insistence that Baldwin was "essentially androgynous" betrays the degree to which the writer's sexuality poses an evidentiary embarrassment for Thelwell himself. In making the case that Baldwin "almost singlehandedly elevated the terms of our discourse on race" (113), Thelwell cannot resist the felt but false necessity to discount, indeed to deny, the sexual dimensions of Baldwin's life. In doing so Thelwell's essay reveals its reliance on the homophobic rule of racial recognition to which his defense of the "androgynous" Baldwin is meant to provide a response. I refer here to the heteronormative logic that conditions the ascription of "authentic" black identity on the repudiation of gay and lesbian sexualities. This jargon of racial authenticity insists, in the words of gangsta-rapper Ice Cube, that "true niggers ain't gay."[11]

Whatever its motivation, Thelwell's awkward answer to those who would "deracinate" Baldwin and reduce the writer to his sexuality is to "desexualize" Baldwin and reduce him to his race. To be sure, these two equally misguided moves are impelled by very different purposes: where Baldwin's detractors remark his sexuality in order to renounce him, Thelwell minimizes Baldwin's sexuality in order to "redeem" him. Ultimately, however, this is a distinction without a difference. For in the final instance, the Thelwell essay stands as yet another example of the symbolic violence that has been inflicted on the name of James Baldwin even by African-American intellectuals who count themselves among the writer's most passionate proponents. The disingenuous disavowal of Baldwin's sexuality implicit in the contention that he was "essentially androgynous" not only deforms the facts of Baldwin's life but dismembers the man himself. Thelwell manages to maneuver his way around the question of Baldwin's sexuality only by engaging in the very "mythmaking, denial and distortion" (93) of which he charges others. To paraphrase Thelwell, there is a "spirit" of "appropriation" and "proprietorship" behind the confident claim that, sexually speaking, James Baldwin was "essentially" not who and what he himself said he was: a man who slept with other men. Baldwin once remarked of his early years, "I did not have any human identity."[12] In divesting the writer's biography of its homoerotic substance, Thelwell dishonors the memory of Baldwin's struggle to resolve what for a time was "the most tormenting thing"[13] in his life: the recognition, as Baldwin put it in his diary, that "I am a homosexual."[14] Seen in this light, Thelwell's "redemption" of Baldwin's name exacts too brutally high a price.

I do not wish my own interest in the case of James Baldwin to be misunderstood. Despite his willingness to talk and write publicly about his sexuality, Baldwin held that, for him, "one's sexual preference is a private matter."[15] Indeed, reading Baldwin's public pronouncements on the subject of sexuality, one cannot help but be struck by their ambivalence. In this respect Baldwin falls short of the achievement of his fellow writer Audre Lorde, whose contemporaneous reflections on gay and lesbian sexualities not only reveal an intellectual rigor but an uncompromising existential confidence regarding the "right and responsibility" of black women "to love where we choose."[16] In the one interview in which he treated the question of gay and lesbian sexualities at some length, Baldwin insisted that his erotic life "had nothing to do with these labels."[17] For Baldwin, the difficulty with the term "gay" was that it "answers a false argument, a false accusation," namely, that "you have no right to be here, that you have to prove your right to be here. I'm saying I have nothing to prove. The world also belongs to me."[18] Moreover, Baldwin's own experience persuaded him that "homosexual" was not a "noun" but a "verb," whose infinitive form is "to love": "I loved a few people and they loved me."[19]

Finally, Baldwin once stated that for black gay men and lesbians "[t]he sexual question comes *after* the question of color: it's simply one more aspect of the danger in which all black people live."[20] "A black person who is a sexual conundrum to society is already, long before the question of sexuality comes into it, menaced and marked because he's black or she's black."[21] At the same time, however, Baldwin remained emphatic about the indivisibility in his life and work of race, on the one hand, and of sexuality, on the other: "The sexual question and the racial question have always been entwined, you know."[22] Baldwin refused to say that sexuality had been "the most important part" of what he was about. "But," he added, "it's indispensable."[23]

My point is this. While I agree with Thelwell that James Baldwin "taught a generation of us how to be black men in this country, and he gave us a language in which to engage the struggle" (113), that was not Baldwin's only lesson. For all its ambivalence, the example of "slender, gay" (113) James Baldwin taught some of us how to be gay men in, and of, black America. The life and work of James Baldwin thus give the lie to the notion that black and gay identity are hostile to one another at all points. They show, too, that while "[i]t is difficult to be despised,"[24] black gay men and lesbians must resist the demand (heard in some quarters) that we must choose between these two sources of the self and commit a kind of psychic suicide. Baldwin provides us with an exemplary instance of someone who refused to make this false, and ultimately fatal, choice. We find in James Baldwin a sometimes equivocal, but always articulate, response to the call that gay and lesbian African Americans who want to prove that they are "really" black must renounce their sexuality: "I'm saying I have nothing to prove."

A decade after Baldwin's death it seems clear that the jargon of racial authenticity is alive and well in African-American sexual politics. Indeed, recent events suggest that the jargon has gained a new force, whose effects underscore the continuing relevance and urgency of what James Baldwin tried to teach us about the politics of sexual and racial identity, and its limitations. My project here is to challenge the terms of this jargon and to indicate the direction a critical account of it might take. I believe that the jargon of racial authenticity has had debilitating consequences for black American sexual politics. My hypothesis, in brief, is that the homophobia and virulent masculinism that underwrite the politics of racial authenticity in the current conjuncture are best understood as the displaced expression of internalized racism. I mean to show that the jargon of racial authenticity is an ideological symptom of a sexual anguish and alienation within black America of almost epidemic proportions. I shall argue that the embodied experience of gay, lesbian, and bisexual African Americans stands as a challenge to contemporary antiracist politics to break the grip of an increasingly homophobic black identity politics, and accord the right to black sexual freedom a place on its agenda.

My point of entry here is a moment from *Tongues Untied*,[25] a remarkable video work by one of James Baldwin's most accomplished cultural descendants, the late gay black artist and activist Marlon Riggs. In one of the most powerful segments of *Tongues Untied*, Riggs offers an extended meditation on the vexed relation between race and sexuality in black gay experience. At one point in the narrative, a black nationalist remarks:

> They say, we're all on the same political boat. We should be brothers. But before I accept his kinship, political or otherwise, this is what I want to know. Where does his loyalty lie? . . . Priorities, that's what I want to know. Come the final throwdown, what is he first, black or gay?[26]

Riggs responds to this set of questions with another, which is framed in terms that warrant some analysis: "How do you choose one eye over another, this half of the brain over that? Or in words this brother might understand, which does he value most, his left nut or his right?"[27]

To my mind, the most striking feature of this rejoinder to what Riggs calls the "absurdity" of the black nationalist demand for a statement of "priorities" lies in its metaphorical register. Riggs rightly takes this question of politics of identity all the way down to body. Identity, in this image, is literally *refigured*. The narrative of *Tongues Untied* shifts the terms of the debate over "authentic" black identity to the flesh-and-blood bodies on which racial (and other) identities are inscribed. Riggs substitutes a materialist "language of the body," thus exposing the poverty of the abstract, etiolated language of racial authenticity that all too many nationalist ideologues have used to mask their indifference to, and even contempt for, real, actually existing black lives. *Tongues Untied* draws on the embodied experience of gay black men to insist that any serious discussion of African-American identity and its attendant politics must come to grips with the existential fact that "identity is fundamentally about desire and death."[28] The ethical challenge of *Tongues Untied* may thus be read as an aesthetic instance of a position to which Cornel West has given a more sustained theoretical formulation. As West (drawing interestingly enough on James Baldwin) so forcefully puts it:

> How you construct your identity is predicated on how you construct desire and how you conceive of death: desire for recognition; quest for visibility (Baldwin—*No Name in the Street; Nobody Knows My Name*); the sense of being acknowledged; a deep desire for association—what Edward Said would call affiliation. . . . But identity also has to do with death. We can't talk about identity without talking about death. That's what [a gay Puerto Rican] brother named Julio Rivera had to come to terms with: the fact that his identity had been constructed in such a way that xenophobes would put him to death. Or brother Youssef Hawkins in Bensonhurst. Or brother Yankel Rosenbaum in Crown Heights. Persons who construct their identities and desires often do it in such a way that they're willing to die for it—soldiers in the Middle East, for example—or under a national identity, that they're willing to kill others. And the rampant sexual violence in the lives of thousands of women who are attacked by men caught up in vicious patriarchal identities—this speaks to what we're talking about.[29]

This recasting of the terms of the identity debate from questions of ideology, identity, and consciousness to material matters of bodies, life, and death provides a vantage point for critical consideration of issues that have been submerged by the jargon of racial authenticity, and by the obsessive search for black "realness" of which it is a part. One of the most pressing problems in contemporary African-American life is the culture of violence, which has brought devastation to far too many among us. I have argued elsewhere that this threat of violence and death is a continuing thread in gay, lesbian, and African-American experience in this country.[30] Along with African Americans of every sexual orientation, gay, lesbian, bisexual, and transgendered Americans of all colors live with and under the knowledge that at any time, anywhere, we might be attacked for being gay or lesbian or bisexual, for being black, or for being both. Indeed, in the United States, the historical roots of the consistent conjunction of homophobic and racist violence are older than the nation itself.

To take but one example, the 1646 Calendar of Dutch Historical Manuscripts reports the trial, conviction, and sentence on Manhattan Island, New Netherland Colony, of one Jan Creoli, "a negro, [for] sodomy; second offense; this crime being condemned of God (Gen., c. 19; Levit., c. 18:22, 29) as an abomination, the prisoner is sentenced to be conveyed to the place of public execution, and there choked to death, and then burnt to ashes."[31] On the same date the Calendar records the punishment meted out to "Manuel Congo . . . on whom the above abominable crime was committed," who was "to be carried to the place where Creoli is to be executed, tied to a stake, and faggots piled around him, for justice sake, and to be flogged; sentence executed."[32]

I mention the story of Manuel Congo and Jan Creoli not because of some felt necessity to "prove" that gay and lesbian sexualities are part of the black experience in America. I invoke it rather to underscore the political uses to which the history of African-American sexuality has been put. According to the jargon of authenticity, black American history is an essentially heterosexual or, more precisely, heteronormative history. In its more strident cultural nationalist versions, this history holds that gay and lesbian sexuality is alien to the "African tradition" on which the proponents of racial authenticity stake so much of their authority. (We may leave to one side the evidentiary difficulties that the well-documented history of same-sex intimacy in Africa poses for this claim. The asserted absence of homoerotic practices in "traditional" African societies would certainly come as a surprise to the Igbo people in Nigeria, the Basotho in Lesotho, the Kwayama and Ovimbundu in Angola, the Zulu and Bantu in South Africa, the Bakongo in Zaire, the Nandi in Kenya, the Konso and Amhara in Ethiopia, the Ottoro in Nubia, the Fanti in Ghana, the Thonga in Zimbabwe, the Tanala and Bara in Madagascar, the Wolof in Senegal, or the Dinka and Nuer in what is now the Sudan.)[33] In the heteronormative history of the jargon, the bodies of gay and lesbian African Americans are figured (insofar as they figure at all) as the contaminated effect of the encounter between a polluting white supremacy and a once pure (i.e., purely heterosexual) black desire.

One of the most troubling features of the jargon of authenticity lies in its deliberate distortion and denial of the convergent histories of racist and homophobic violence, of which the story of Manuel Congo and Jan Creoli represents but one instance. The heteronormative historical optic of black authenticity has blinded its proponents to the "scaling of bodies"[34] that has consigned black Americans and gay and lesbian Americans to adjoining, and sometimes identical, quarters at the bottom of our social order. The critical point is this. The history of blackness in this country is in large measure a history of degraded bodies and denigrated experience. The suggestion that gay and lesbian sexualities have not been a target of white racism's demonization of black desire is, quite simply, false. As a historical matter, the jargon of authenticity's arrogant insistence that "true niggers ain't gay" belongs less to the history of black sexuality than it does to the history of cynical ignorance and blatant ideological fraud.*

The preceding discussion has focused at some length on the fictive character of the historical account of black sexualities that underwrites the jargon of authenticity. However, my main aim here is not to challenge

---

* To avoid misunderstanding, I should make it clear that I in no way mean to imply that violence, death, and degradation (and the often heroic response to them) represent the sum and substance of either black or queer life in the United States. I would say rather that it is precisely in the culture of black joy and queer pleasure that gay, lesbian, and African Americans have found some of the most effective political weapons with which to resist racist and homophobic domination.

that jargon's account of our historical past but to make the case for a fresh perspective on our political present. I hope by now to have shown that the richest resource for thinking about the state of black America at the dawn of the twenty-first century is not the metaphysical illusion of an authentic racial identity but a material interest in actual, embodied black existence. In the remaining pages of this essay I want to explore what the move from the politics of black authenticity to a more inclusive body politics might mean in the current conjuncture. My specific concern is to indicate a few of the concrete possibilities that an embodied "politics of location"[35] creates for strategic alliances within as well as across movements against racism and homophobia. I shall proceed by canvassing a number of recent episodes in which a progressive black politics would have been better served by the shift in perspective and practice I am urging here.

The first is the political controversy surrounding the airing of Marlon Riggs's *Tongues Untied. Tongues* was produced for broadcast as part of the P.O.V. series of the Public Broadcasting System (PBS). It was the subject of at least two ugly episodes. Some twenty of the fifty PBS stations in the nation's largest markets flatly refused to air the work, and the Federal Communications Commission received a number of formal complaints about the video, filed by conservative media advocacy groups. A few months later *Tongues Untied* became a flashpoint of contention when Pat Buchanan produced campaign commercials during his bid for the 1992 Republican presidential nomination that prominently featured images from the video depicting men dancing semiclothed. Shortly thereafter, legislation was introduced to abolish the National Endowment for the Arts (NEA), which had supported production of the video. Buchanan's charge that Bush's NEA had "glorified homosexuality" also figured in the president's decision to fire John Frohnmayer, head of the NEA.[36]

During the skirmishes for which *Tongues Untied* served as a site of intersection, African Americans remained largely silent about this cynical political deployment of black cultural representation. This silence stood in striking contrast to the charges of racism leveled by many African Americans when a series of prosecutions was initiated against the black rap group 2 Live Crew and individuals who marketed their album *As Nasty as They Wanna Be* because of its graphic sexual nature.[37] You will re-

call that in that case the misogynistic lyrics of 2 Live Crew, which celebrated the mutilation of black women's bodies, were defended by leading
scholars as an example of black cultural genius. No such cultural defenses
were forthcoming for Marlon Riggs, whose *Tongues Untied* had offered a
trenchant critique of the violence directed against black gay and lesbian
bodies.

Similarly, few black voices were raised during the campaign to protest
the radio and video airplay of "Boom Bye Bye," in which reggae rapper
Buju Banton warned "Faggots to run / Or get a bullet in the head":

Homeboys don't condone nasty men
They must die
Two men necking
Lying in a bed
Hugging each other
And caressing one another's legs
Get an automatic or an Uzi instead
Shoot them now, let us shoot them.[38]

It takes no great insight to see that Banton's murderous melodic call belongs to the same culture of violence that has filled this nation's hospitals,
morgues, and mortuaries with the bullet-ridden bodies of young black
men and women, and populated its prisons with the "homeboys" who
have maimed and killed them. Now, I would like to think that the perspective I have offered here might well have led greater numbers of
African Americans to engage the issues raised by these episodes. Again,
the ground of this engagement would not be an exclusionary identitarian
appeal to racial authenticity, but a more inclusive ethical apprehension of
the danger the culture of violence poses to black Americans of whatever
sexual orientation, and to gay and lesbian Americans of all colors.

To understand that antiracist and antihomophobic politics are informed by a common ethical interest is to create the possibility of coalition across difference. But that is not all. A politics of embodiment sees
homophobic violence or violence against women as part of the danger "in
which all black people live,"[39] and thus realizes (as Kimberlé Crenshaw

has recently argued) that black identity itself represents a process and product of coalition.[40] It is important in this connection to say a word about what for me is perhaps the most disturbing dimension of the jargon of authenticity in the present period. The discourse of authentic black identity has been increasingly accompanied by an authoritarian effort to impose its normative vision. The proponents of authenticity have fashioned a crude racialist litmus test to establish true "blackness," which African Americans for whom the organicist idea of a unitary racial identity is neither a necessary nor desirable predicate for progressive antiracist politics predictably fail to pass. In the name of an imagined unity, the politics of racial authenticity has thus given rise to an aggressive, antidemocratic impulse. This politics has obscured the inflection of, and the antagonisms *within*, racial identity produced by differences of ethnicity, class, gender, religion, sexuality, and the like.

Consider in this connection the policing of racial identity that informed the politics of the recent Million Man March in Washington, D.C. In the months leading up to the October 1995 March, black feminist as well as gay and lesbian activists questioned its militant masculinist thrust. They recalled the long and ugly record of sexist and homophobic statements by the chief organizer of the March, the Nation of Islam's Minister Louis Farrakhan, of which these menacing words from a 1990 speech are a characteristic example:

> Now brothers, in the Holy world you can't switch. [Farrakhan walks across the stage like an effeminate man] No, no no . . . in the Holy world you better hide that stuff 'cause if God made you for a woman, you can't go with a man . . . You know what the penalty of that is in the Holy land? Death . . . They don't play with that . . . [he laughs] Sister get to going with another sister— Both women [are decapitated].[41]

Given this history, critics of the March rightly contended that Farrakhan's call to black men to gather in Washington, D.C., for a demonstration of their "at-one-ment" could not be divorced from his previous homophobic pronouncements. In the matter of sexual diversity, Louis Farrakhan's authoritarian vision of the black public sphere seemed to differ only in its details from the "New Jack-Boot City" depicted in Buju Banton's "Boom Bye Bye."

These concerns about the authoritarian sexual politics behind the Million Man March were compounded when March organizers failed to respond to the reported remarks of one of its spokesmen, the renegade ex-Catholic priest, the Reverend George Stallings, Jr. During a radio program in which a journalist canvassed the objections to Farrakhan's leadership of the March, Stallings offered the following gay-baiting reply: "What kind of leader do you want? A milque-toast? Some sissy-faggot?"[42] Against this backdrop, gay and lesbian African Americans had every reason to view the Million Man March with suspicion.

Our suspicions were not allayed even when as staunch a progressive ally as Cornel West lent his support to the Million Man March. Writing in the *New York Times*, West justified his participation in the March on the grounds that it would "highlight black suffering."[43] "The demonstration," argued West, "is about the general invisibility of, and indifference to, black sadness, sorrow and social misery, and the disrespect and disregard in which blacks are held in America and abroad."[44] What West, Michael Dyson, and other progressive intellectuals never fully addressed was the demonstrated indifference, indeed the morbid delight, that the leader of the march has time and again expressed at the idea of inflicting "black suffering" on the bodies of gay and lesbian African Americans: for us, Louis Farrakhan embodies the very "Politics of Death" against which he had mobilized the million men who came to the Washington Mall. We simply could not ignore the fact that the affirmation of black manhood staged at the Million Man March seemed to *require* the denigration of gay and lesbian African Americans as an enabling condition for its own formation. To many gay and lesbian African Americans the Million Man March was yet another confirmation of our continued invisibility, exclusion, and exile beyond the boundaries of the black public sphere.

Nonetheless, for all its exertions, the rhetorical politics of racial authenticity cannot erase the fact that "blackness" is invariably "lived in the modality"[45] of sexuality and *vice versa:* this is because sexuality is always "racialized" and race always "sexuated." In this respect, the chief lesson I draw from recent work on the construction of racial and sexual identities is that the two depend on one another for their force and form. The search for independent, autonomous racial and sexual identities can never fully or finally succeed. To borrow from Nick Ashford and Valerie Simpson, then, we might say that there "Ain't nothin' *like* the real thing." In their refusal to accept the impossibility of a pure racial identity, the ideologists of black masculinism (not all of whom are men) prove nothing so much as the depths of their own racial and sexual alienation in the signifiers of authenticity. In the retreat to a heterosexist conception of black identity, the jargon of racial authenticity does not repudiate but instead reveals its reliance on the white supremacist logic from which it purports to declare its independence. The homophobic jargon of authenticity simply transposes racism's register into a darker, but no less destructive key. Ironically, the heteronormative vision of a unitary racial identity that would suppress sexual difference among African Americans does not exorcise the specter of white supremacy from the body of black America, but rather reincorporates white racism's phobic conceptions of black sexuality in the denigrated figure of the colored homosexual. In a classic case of strange bedfellows, the homophobic proponents of authenticity thus find themselves embraced in an odd alliance with the racist ideology to which they otherwise claim to be opposed.

Finally, the jargon of racial authenticity forecloses a recognition that what social theorist Benedict Anderson has said about the notion of a "nation" holds true as well for the unitary conception of a "race." That is, it blinds us to the fact that membership in a race, like membership in a national community, is "imagined." Most African Americans "will never know most of their fellow-members, meet them, or even hear of them, yet in the minds of each lives the image of their communion."[46] This is most emphatically not to say that the imagined racial subject comes into being in conditions of its own making. One would be remiss not to point out the institutional and ideological imperatives by which the notion of a racial community takes one form rather than another. It is to suggest that the authentically black self is in significant measure what political theorist William Connolly has called a "branded" or "entrenched" contingency.[47]

What this means, I think, is that the discourse of collective racial identity must, as a political matter, be understood and engaged as a technique or strategy. We may say here of race what James Baldwin once said of sexuality: it is not a noun but a verb. To view "blackness" as a contingent situated strategy is to see that a racial rhetoric that holds out the promise of liberation at one moment may become perilous to our survival down the road. Assertions of black identity that once served as an indispensable tool at one historical moment in the struggle for racial justice may now have become unwitting traps. Gay and lesbian African Americans have borne the heavy costs exacted by the rigid adherence to the illusory ideal of a unitary black identity. The exclusion of black gay men and lesbians from full, equal participation in African-American life has provided an epistemic standpoint for understanding and intervening in the politics of life and death. We know that the obsessive preoccupation with proof of racial authenticity deflects attention and energy away from the need to come to grips with the real, material challenges in whose resolution black Americans of both genders and all sexual identifications have an immediate and urgent interest. In the spirit of James Baldwin, black gay men and lesbians must continue to argue clearly and without compromise that they have nothing to prove. On the contrary, the burden of proof should be shifted onto those who instituted the jargon of authenticity to show its continued relevance to African-American life in the "the Age of Crack"[48] and Uzis and AIDS. Baldwin wrote in Notes of a Native Son that because he loved America "more than any other country in the world," he insisted on the right "to criticize her perpetually."[49] Our love for black America demands no less.

NOTES

A slightly different version of this essay appears in Representing Black Men, ed. Marcellus Blount and George P. Cunningham (New York: Routledge, 1996), 55–69.

1. James Baldwin, No Name in the Street (New York: Dell, 1972), 18.
2. James Baldwin, Giovanni's Room (New York: Dell, 1956), 223.
3. Richard Goldstein, "'Go the Way Your Blood Beats': An Interview with James Baldwin," reprinted in Lesbians, Gay Men, and the Law, ed. William B. Rubenstein (New York: New Press, 1993), 41.

4. James Campbell, *Talking at the Gates: A Life of James Baldwin* (New York: Penguin, 1991).

5. Ekwueme Michael Thelwell, "A Profit Is Not Without Honor," *Transition* 58 (1992): 90. All subsequent citations will appear in the text.

6. Francette Pacteau, "The Impossible Referent: Representations of the Androgyne," in *Formations of Fantasy*, ed. Victor Burgin, James Donald, and Cora Kaplan (New York: Methuen, 1986), 62.

7. Ibid.

8. Ibid.

9. David Halperin, *One Hundred Years of Homosexuality and Other Essays on Greek Love* (New York: Routledge, 1990), 23.

10. Or, presumably, heterosexual. It bears remarking that the terms of the opposition Thelwell draws explicitly ignore this logical entailment.

11. O'Shea Jackson (Ice Cube), "Horny Lil' Devil," *Death Certificate* (Priority Records, 1991).

12. Campbell, *Talking at the Gates*, 3.

13. Goldstein, "'Go the Way Your Blood Beats,'" 42.

14. Campbell, *Talking at the Gates*, 33. Although Thelwell does not cite it, the one possible textual warrant for his insistence that Baldwin was "androgynous" is the late essay "Here Be Dragons," which originally appeared in *Playboy* under the title "Freaks and the American Ideal of Manhood." (James Baldwin, "Here Be Dragons," in *The Price of the Ticket* [New York: St. Martin's/Marek, 1985].) Baldwin argues in this essay that "we are all androgynous, not only because we are all born of a woman impregnated by the seed of a man but because each of us, helplessly and forever, contains the other—male in female, female in male . . ." (ibid., 690). Throughout the article, however, Baldwin takes care not to conflate claims regarding gender politics with those about sexual identity and practice. This much is clear from the fact that, alongside the claim that androgyny is a generalized figure of the human condition, "Here Be Dragons" is replete with quite specific references by Baldwin to his sexual experiences with other men and to "how I found myself in the gay world" (ibid., 686). I am grateful to Cora Kaplan for drawing my attention to this text.

15. Goldstein, "'Go the Way Your Blood Beats,'" 44.

16. Audre Lorde, "Scratching the Surface: Some Notes on Barriers to Women and Loving," originally published in *The Black Scholar* 9, no. 7 (1978), reprinted in *Sister Outsider: Essays and Speeches* (Freedom, Calif.: Crossing, 1984), 52.

17. Richard Goldstein, "'Go the Way Your Blood Beats,'" 44.

18. Ibid., 45.

19. Ibid., 44.

20. Ibid., 42.

21. Ibid. As these remarks suggest, Baldwin's argument has to do with the chronology of black gay and lesbian experience, not the priority of black or gay lesbian identity.

22. Ibid.

23. Ibid., 41.

24. Ibid., 44.

25. *Tongues Untied*, prod. and dir. Marlon Riggs, 55 min., color, 1985, videocassette.

26. Ibid.

27. Ibid.

28. Cornel West, "Identity: A Matter of Life and Death," in *Prophetic Reflections: Notes on Race and Power in America* (Monroe, Mass.: Common Courage Press, 1993), 163.

29. Ibid., 163–64.

30. See my "Beyond the Privacy Principle," *Columbia Law Review* 92, no. 6 (October 1992): 1431–1516.

31. Jonathan Ned Katz, *Gay American History: Lesbians and Gay Men in the U.S.A.* (New York: Harper & Row, 1976), 22–23.

32. Ibid., 23. What is more, for reasons that I cannot delineate in detail here, it seems fairly clear that both homophobic violence and racist violence have a distinctly erotic component. (I might note parenthetically that if you are a black gay man or lesbian, you know, too, that this eroticized violence might come from the hands of someone who looks like your father, uncle, or brother.)

33. A useful summary can be found in William N. Eskridge, Jr., "A History of Same-Sex Marriage," *Virginia Law Review* 79, no. 7 (October 1993): 1419–1513.

34. Iris Marion Young, *Justice and the Politics of Difference* (Princeton, N.J.: Princeton University Press, 1990), 122.

35. The term is Adrienne Rich's. Adrienne Rich, "Notes Toward a Politics of Location," in *Blood, Bread, and Poetry* (New York: Norton: 1986), 210.

36. A useful documentary history of the recounted episodes may be found in Richard Bolton, ed., *Culture Wars: Documents from the Recent Controversies in the Arts* (New York: New Press, 1992).

37. In June 1990, lyrics in 2 Live Crew songs about sodomy and sexual intercourse were adjudged obscene by a federal district court. *Skywalker Records, Inc. v. Navarro*, 739 F. Supp. 578, 596 (S. D. Fla. 1990). A federal circuit court of appeals reversed this conviction in *Luke Records, Inc. v. Navarro*, 960 F. 2d 134 (11th Cir. 1992).

38. From the album *Boom Bye Bye*. Produced by Clifton "Specialist" Dillon and Bobby "Digital" Dixon. Distributed by VP Records (Jamaica, Queens, N.Y.), 1992.

39. Goldstein, "'Go the Way Your Blood Beats,'" 42.

40. Kimberlé Williams Crenshaw, "Mapping the Margins: Intersectionality, Identity Politics, and Violence Against Women of Color," in *Stanford Law Review* 43, no. 6 (1991), 1299.

41. Louis Farrakhan, *The Time and What Must Be Done* (videotape of a speech given on May 20, 1990, in Oakland, California, produced by The Final Call, Inc., Chicago, Illinois). The quoted remarks are taken from Ron Simmons, "Some Thoughts on the Challenges Facing Black Gay Intellectuals," in Essex Hemphill, ed., *Brother to Brother: New Writings by Black Gay Men* (Boston: Alyson Publications, 1991), 222.

42. Kevin McGruder, "Black Men Marching: You Don't Have to Be Loud to Be Strong," *City Sun*, September 13-19, 1995, 29.

43. Cornel West, "Why I'm Marching in Washington," *New York Times*, October 14, 1995.

44. Ibid.

45. Judith Butler, *Bodies That Matter: On the Discursive Limits of "Sex"* (New York: Routledge, 1993), 117.

46. Benedict Anderson, *Imagined Communities: Reflections on the Origin and Spread of Nationalism* (New York: Verso, 1983), 15.

47. William E. Connolly, *Identity/Difference: Democratic Negotiations of Political Paradox* (Ithaca, N.Y.: Cornell University Press, 1991), 176.

48. Eugene Rivers, "On the Responsibility of Intellectuals in the Age of Crack," *Boston Review* 3 (September-October 1992): 3-4.

49. James Baldwin, *Notes of a Native Son* (Boston: Beacon, 1984), 9.

LIVING AT THE CROSSROADS

Explorations in Race, Nationality, Sexuality, and Gender

■

Rhonda M. Williams

GRADUATION DAY, Afro-American Studies Program, 1991: I remind myself that there are ruptures in my being an out lesbian on campus. My colleagues and superiors know I'm a dyke, as do some, but clearly not all, of our students. Two of my former students—both campus activists, both proponents of a distinctly masculine cultural nationalism of the 1990s—launch into a tirade against queers. One young man worries about what to do about the fags, and suggests putting them (me?) on a spaceship bound for outer space. He also ruminates on the possibility of a few good gay-bashings. I am disarmed and afraid, and do not name my queerness. As I question their hostility toward lesbians and gays, our conversation lurches from pillar to post: they inform me that queers are a detriment to our race, that "they" are selfish, unnatural, anathema to the building of a strong black nation.[1] My question begins to crystallize: why is heterosexuality so central to these young men's notions of blackness?

A play day in the park, a few weeks prior: I am playing with our youngest son, the brown-skinned child of my partner Elizabeth and her former husband, a Senegalese national. We share the play area with several neighborhood white mothers and children who are having their weekly park rendezvous. I am at first puzzled when the mothers ignore my greetings and efforts to make eye contact; after all, we often have seen one another in the neighborhood. As their conversation turns to the difficulties of finding and keeping "good help," my confusion evaporates into clarity: these women believed I was Elizabeth's child-care provider, and as such, clearly not a candidate for inclusion in a peer-based and class-specific conversation about the shortage of quality nannies.

The above experiences served as distinctive markers in my ongoing effort to explore the nexus of race and sexual orientation. Together they provide the entry points for this essay, which begins with a "coming out" story. My focus is the dialogues that articulated heterosexuality's centrality to student understandings of "blackness," the racialization of sexual discourse, and the notion that homosexuality is a "white thing."[2] I argue that black queers interrupt a longing for a stigma-free black sexuality, a longing forged in the fires of racist ideology. This essay posits that racialized discourses lend a specificity to some African-American heterosexisms. For some African Americans, the issue is not simply sexual orientation, but "blackness" itself.

My days in the park inform the second part of the essay, preliminary musings on racialized readings of black-white lesbian relationships. Strangers often construe my lesbian relationship as other than it is. I suggest that current and historical contours of white supremacy inform the readings of Elizabeth's and my partnership. Although the particularities of their readings vary a bit from encounter to encounter, our day-to-day experiences provide living testimony to the interpretive legacy of white supremacy in a heterosexualized life world. Straight African Americans who know us as partners are sometimes accepting, sometimes openly troubled by my commitment to a white woman. It is the latter—my being viewed as a race traitor—that I address herein.

BEING SEEN

The University of Maryland is a formerly all-white public institution that now has a larger African-American population than most traditionally white universities. The black student population includes more than two thousand African Americans, who have created a host of academic, cultural, social, and political organizations. They are a varied lot, and joined on campus by more than sixty tenured and tenure-track black faculty and more than one thousand black staff and administrators.

There were few out gay and lesbian faculty in the spring of 1992; those who were out are white. I speculated that the absence of visible black lesbians and gays on campus bolstered those in the African-American community who harbor sexuality-based fears and hostilities. Such was the thinking behind my consenting to being named as a lesbian in the *Diamondback*, the student paper with the largest readership. This initial article (March 1992) described an upsurge in antigay activity on campus. Two members of the faculty and three students condemned the harassment and called for an administrative response.

In the wake of the *Diamondback* story, Shannon Murray, an editor for the *Eclipse* (one of our two black student papers), requested an interview for her Women's History Month feature story on three black professors. Shannon also interviewed several students for her article, straight and gay folk who spoke candidly about homophobia and heterosexism in black communities. Two black lesbians named the pain of rejection by their black peers; a young gay man lamented black heterosexism, but is quoted under an assumed name. Steve Palmer, then president of the campus chapter of the NAACP, cautioned black homosexuals:

> Homosexuals have a spiritual and moral problem that they have to deal with. I do not believe anyone should be physically bashed, but the Black community needs to take a stand on homosexuality and stop being shaped by white standards. (*Eclipse*, March 23, 1992)

Palmer's heterosexism is very much in keeping with contemporary cultural nationalist thinking on sexual orientation. His critique of homosexuality was moral, racialized, and informed by notions of sharp and fixed boundaries between black and white community standards and cultural norms. For Palmer, the black community should and does affirm a morality that precludes homosexuality. Whites, in sharp contrast, are more embracing of homosexuals. His problematic assertions notwithstanding, Palmer became a voice of authoritative blackness in the student dialogues. Subsequent editorials and articles frequently referenced his editorial.

My spring syllabus for "Introduction to Afro-American Studies" included a unit entitled "Black Families, Black Kin: Beyond the Discourse of Pathology" and a subsection on homophobia in black communities.

The lecture compared white racist narratives of black familial pathology to cultural nationalist discourse on black homosexuality. Whereas the former naturalizes the two-parent heterosexual family and stigmatizes black female-headed households, the latter normalizes and privileges heterosexuality at the expense of queerness. Several departmental staff and a professor attended the lecture in a show of solidarity. I presented, then challenged, the writings of Nathan and Julia Hare, Haki Madhubuti, Amiri Baraka, and Frances Cress Welsing.[3] These writers share a common nationalist perspective on black gays and lesbians: our behavior is both a consequence of one or more strains of white supremacy and a threat to kinship and family:

> Unlike the white male, the Black male does not arrive at the effeminate bisexual or homosexual stance from any deeply repressed sense of genetic weakness, inadequacy, or disgust, which I refer to as *primary effeminacy* (effeminacy that is self-derived and not imposed forcibly by others). Instead, the Black male arrives at this position *secondarily*, as the result of the imposed power and cruelty of the white male and the totality of the white supremacy social and political apparatus that has forced 20 generations of black males into submission. This pattern of imposed submission is reinforced through every institution within the white supremacy system, but especially in the fundamental social institution of the family or, in this case, the Black survival unit. (Welsing, 86)

Subsequent private conversations with students confirmed my suspicion that many students affirmed cultural nationalist sentiments. They were uncomfortable voicing such views in the classroom (in my presence?), but would speak their minds to one another. I learned through the grapevine the parameters of the debates. Some students again claimed that homosexuality *is* a "white thing," worthy of condemnation by those true to authentic blackness. Some reaffirmed biblical sanctions against homosexuality, others voiced resentment toward those white gay activists who draw comparisons between heterosexist and racist oppression. In sub-

sequent issues of both the *Eclipse* and the *Black Explosion*, the campus
community debated the issue. Each paper published letters and editorials
from those who condemned queers and from those who castigated heterosexism.

BEING BLACK

I take as a given the pervasiveness of racial representations in U.S. culture,
and indeed throughout the Western world. I understand these representations to be nonstatic, shifting, contested, gendered, and class-specific.[4]
Narratives of black pathology are one of racist culture's most enduring
legacies. These narratives are both gendered and fraught with representations of black sexuality. Thus, any discussion that engages popular notions
of black sexuality must reckon with racism's larger story of black dysfunction.

Western racist discourses routinely construct "blackness" as a problematic sign and ontological position. In so doing, the architects of cultural and (social) scientific racism historically have represented black
communities, black families, and black bodies as the bearers of stigma, disease, danger, violence, social pathology, and hypersexuality. In this part of
the essay, I am particularly interested in the racialized narratives that address black families and sexuality. Black families have long functioned as
markers in the public imagination: they generally signify and manifest a
morally problematic sexually agency, a cultural degeneracy. The conventional social scientific wisdom is clear: "the problem" is that so much
black sexuality and kinship formation transgresses the boundaries of married (and therefore healthy) heterosexuality.[5]

However, social managers and engineers do not have a monopoly on
the generation and propagation of deeply gendered familial tropes. In
their musings on the well-being of "the black nation," African-American
nationalists have long invoked family metaphors. Martin Delany—often
identified as the father of black nationalism—was among the earliest nationalists to embrace an explicitly patriarchal domestic ideal. Writing in
the nineteenth century, Delany believed that masculine authority was es-

sential for the well-being of the exiled black nation (Gilroy, 23–24). In what follows I will suggest that family tropes are vital today, and function in part to circulate specific notions of racial authenticity.

Today's African-American college students have come of age in a political culture that regularly recycles two signs of black dysfunction: antisocial black (male) criminality and (female) sexuality are the behavioral manifestations of contemporary black cultural chaos. Scholarly and journalistic treatises on the underclass anchor contemporary race talk, and speak the language that distinguishes the aberrant underclass from the striving middle class.[6] As long as they aver affirmative action and other race-based policies, the middle classes are potential (though suspect) members of the community of citizens. In sharp contrast, the behaviorally deviant underclass compels vigilant monitoring, discipline, and control.[7]

A recent magazine article retells the story of black families in trouble. The August 30, 1993, issue of *Newsweek* premiered a lengthy lamentation on the decline of marriage among African Americans. The authors of "Endangered Family" make much of noting the ubiquity of black family crisis: declining marriage rates and out-of-wedlock births are not restricted to the black poor. Across the board, African-American men and women are at odds with one another:

> Black men say black women are "Sapphires," trying to dominate, explains Harvard psychologist Alvin Poussaint, referring to the wife of Kingfish in "Amos 'n' Andy," who epitomized the bitchy, bossy black woman. But Boston anchorwoman Liz Walker believes that many black men mistake self-reliance for high-handedness. (*Newsweek*, 20)

The spectacle of a conflicted black heterosexuality saturates the magazine's pages, and the theme is familiar: there are too many female-headed households. Social scientists are left to weigh the relative importance of structural and cultural explanations. Author Michel Ingrassia summons the authority of empirical social science to trash the notion that female-headed families, whatever their "cause," are potentially viable and life-enhancing, as good as "the nuclear unit":

The evidence comes down solidly on the side of marriage. By every measure—economic, social, educational—the statistics conclude that two parents living together are better than one. (21)

Readers familiar with this narrative are not surprised to (re)learn that African-American women are the primary carriers of black familial pathology—makers of the homes that nurture violent black sons and daughters seemingly in rebellion against male power. In Valerie Martin's home in Washington, D.C., the signs of trouble are already apparent:

Latoyia, who's going into fifth grade, gets A's and B's, but this articulate girl who seems so calm at home was suspended three times last year for getting into fights. George . . . had to repeat first grade. He seems only mildly rambunctious, but Valerie says he's getting hard to discipline. (18)

Ms. Martin's three children have three different (and nameless) fathers. Her relationships with the fathers faltered when Latoyia's got bossy and George's started to "act stupid." Valerie's story is familiar and comforting to readers already attuned and receptive to cultural explanations of black distress: the welfare-dependent single mother embodies and reproduces heterosexual confusion in poor, urban African-American communities.

Ms. Martin has her counterparts among working black women not receiving AFDC. Here, to, we find single mothers, raising their children, struggling to make ends meet. Sylvia Berry works for wages outside the home, but the consequences for her son are nonetheless dire. Marcus was "stuck in solitary" while his mother worked: his home is a prison, because his neighborhood (the Shaw district, again in the nation's capital) is unsafe. Restless and bored, he played in school and earned low grades.

Black students read these stories—they bring them to me, offerings that, for them, personalize William J. Wilson's thesis of a crisis-ridden, aberrant underclass. Many Maryland undergraduates do not know this narrative's genealogy. They experience it as a new and powerful truth. Some read it as a call for a new movement, one that strives for black economic independence. For others these narratives are a comforting pallia-

tive, stories that help them differentiate themselves from the "others"—
the hated and feared African-American underclass. When compared to
the Martins and Berrys, most of their families emerge as shining examples
of domestic bliss. For yet another group these texts concretize a class-
specific missionary zeal—here are the lumpen folk to whom they can offer
the gift of racial uplift. Whatever the particular reading, many students
weave these stories into their customized brands of social conservatism.

Wahneema Lubiano discusses the power of these stories, the saliency
of the meanings deployed and circulated in the juxtaposition of welfare
and working mothers. Her analysis of the gendered pathology discourse
takes as an entry point the Clarence Thomas/Anita Hill hearings.

> . . . the flip side of the pathological welfare queen . . . is the black
> lady, the one whose disproportionate overachievement stands for
> black cultural strangeness and who ensures the underachieve-
> ment of "the black male" in the lower classes because "ours [the
> U.S.] is a society which presumes male leadership in private and
> public affairs." (Lubiano, 335—quotation from the *Moynihan Re-
> port*, 1965)

Lubiano catalogues the narratives mobilized by Hill's opponents: they
sought to discredit her professional status by invoking affirmative action,
and/or by casting her as the living embodiment of a spurned/lesbian womanhood. She is most compelling in her interpretation of the development
of black hostility to Hill:

> Blackness, as an abstraction, did battle for Thomas because few
> people actually belonging to the group "black" or "African-
> American" [here referred to by Lubiano as a taken-for-granted so-
> cial fact] would have gone to war on behalf of Thomas the corrupt
> judge, Thomas the bigot, Thomas the incompetent head of the
> EEOC. But for Thomas the black male victim of "Sapphire"—
> black female emasculation and betrayer of black men and carrier
> of black family pathology—well, the African American legions
> would and did rise to battle against her. Out of the ooze of his past
> record climbed Thomas, the *real black* thing. (345)

Lubiano's analysis presumes that many African Americans affirm the racialized and gendered narratives of black pathology. To the extent that she is right, Lubiano provides us a means to conceptualize the stakes in black reluctance to embrace gays and lesbians in our own communities.

In the ideologies of contemporary cultural nationalism, families are *the* sanctioned site for the reproduction of authentic racial ethnic culture. Healthy families are monogamous, dedicated to masculine authority, and affirm traditional gender roles; unwell families include sexually promiscuous adults and foster female dominance. Recalling "Endangered Family," women are the primary reproductive agents in this narrative, and their dysfunctional families spawn a crisis-ridden racial community populated by carriers of a disabled masculinity. However, redemption is possible:

> . . . the crisis of black masculinity can be fixed. It is to be repaired
> by instituting appropriate forms of masculine and male authority,
> intervening in the family to rebuild the race. (Gilroy, "Family Af-
> fair," 312)

Like Sapphire, black queers betray the quest for healthy black families, a regulated and normalized black sexuality. Whether viewed as the products of broken families or betrayers of family life together, black gays and lesbians are a potential anathema to straight African Americans whose resistance to racist narratives inspires them to "clean up" images of black sexuality. When these African Americans publicly reject homosexuality, they do so in a social context that persistently regenerates public images and discourses of sexual perversion and familial damage. For those seeking to sanitize and normalize popular perceptions of black sexuality, the public affirmations of queerness—a category marked with the stains of hypersexuality, promiscuity, and danger—can only serve to further the stigmatization of blackness.[8]

Racist narratives that pathologize our families and sexualities diminish heterosexual privilege within black communities. Black heterosexuality is constructed as unnatural, already beyond God's law and nature's logic. Accordingly, the redemption of African-American families requires the harnessing and disciplining of black sexual behavior. Hypersexual heterosexuals can, in principle, change or be changed. As noted above, the solution is a communal recommitment to the male-dominated and sexually restrained domestic unit. However, queerness is not so easily reigned in —indeed, it is a pathology that totally destabilizes the parameters of social life and thwarts the building of a strong black nation.

Many African Americans have expended copious amounts of energy resisting and transforming the discourses that pathologize heterosexual black families and kinship systems.[9] This essay questions the contours of that resistance: do they reify black families and sexualities, or historicize them as complex, diverse, and flexible? My contention is that many cultural nationalist projects reject this complexity. Thus, efforts to affirm "blackness" generate a contradictory narrative: although nationalists seek to remove stigma, they offer in its place a terrifyingly rigid and tyrannical notion of "family"—one that collaborates with and consents to normative and demonizing notions of race, community, and culture.

Insofar as they reinscribe rigid boundaries of blackness, cultural nationalist efforts to destigmatize display at least three noteworthy tendencies. The first is an identification with Africa that is, as cultural critic Paul Gilroy notes, both partial and selective ("Family Affair," 307). For example, Nathan and Julia Hare's advocacy of polygamous families idealizes cowife cooperation and male support, but "ignores cross-generational conflict and intrafamily rivalry" (White, 75). In a similar spirit of obliteration, nationalists who embrace the autonomous, monogamous, conjugal heterosexual family as the domestic ideal suppress their indebtedness to European and Euro-American nationalist notions of proper family life. Their vision of kinship differs radically from the consanguinity and polygamy practiced by African-America's ethnic ancestors (Sudarkasa).

The second tendency is the aforementioned essentialism—the notion that there is one true African diaspora consciousness and cultural system, one black ontology that crosses state boundaries and ethnic groups. Molefi Asante's *Afrocentricity* prominently argues this point, and is also unrelenting in its homophobia. In her essay "Postmodern Blackness" bell hooks speaks to the genealogy of essentialist longings in African America:

The unwillingness to critique essentialism on the part of many African Americans is rooted in the fear that it will cause folks to lose sight of the specific history and experience of African-

Americans and the unique sensibilities and culture that arise from that experience. . . . There is a radical difference between a repudiation of the idea that there is a black "essence" and recognition of the way black identity has been specifically constituted in the experience of exile and struggle. (*Yearning*, 29)

This same tendency obliterates both the historical specificities of African-American culture and cultural diversity within Africa.

A third current runs steadily through many nationalist polemics: the notion that black queerness is fundamentally an epiphenomenal consequence of white supremacy (Madhubuti, 73–74; Welsing, 86). The invocation of white racism constructs a mythical and asocial queerness. The gays and lesbians who stalk their pages are not members of black churches, clubs, schools, and neighborhoods (they are, of course, products of dysfunctional homes). It is here that Lubiano's analysis lends itself to a deeper analogy: just an abstraction of "blackness" as victim rallied community sympathy for Clarence Thomas, so an abstraction of queerness enables the cultural nationalist line.

Consider the extent to which many straight African Americans partake of "don't ask, don't tell," offering acceptance of queers in return for the silence, shame, and terror of the closet. Lesbians and gays who consent to this form of heterosexism are not so easily viewed as beyond the boundaries of "blackness." However, when recast as marked carriers of white oppression, these same folk can elicit black condemnation.

In locating the genesis of black homosexual outside black communities, both cultural nationalists and those not so specifically identified restore the possibility of a normal, healthy black sexuality. Restoration of health requires recovery from the corrosive influences of white supremacy that have weakened heterosexual bonds (and therefore male supremacy) in African-American communities. The alleged consequences of weakened heterosexual bonds are numerous and pernicious, but the allegations of black male emasculation and familial breakdown resonate most powerfully within this context.

The stigmatization of black families and sexualities has been and remains a crucial component in the constitution of black consciousness.

Unlike their white counterparts, African Americans live without the benefit of an assumed familial and sexual wellness. Individual white families can and do manifest numerous and myriad behaviors, but dominant narratives rarely read such events as revelation of an intrinsic and pervasive group cultural chaos. The cultural presumption of black sexual deviance nurtures African-American predispositions to keep at arm's length those individuals and behaviors that may reconfirm aberration. It sustains selective and convenient appropriations of Africa, essentialism, and the white causality model. Thus, racialized discourse of families and sexuality profoundly mediate the meanings of queerness for many African Americans. The stakes are not merely homosexuality, but blackness itself.

Black lesbian scholar E. Frances White also speaks to the nexus of sexuality and race. In a recent essay White reflects upon her attendance of a Sister Souljah concert at Hampshire College (Harper, Cerullo, and White). Souljah is the sole female member of the rap group Public Enemy and became the object of national press attention during the 1992 presidential campaign. President-to-be Bill Clinton chastized her imagining and calling for a week where armed blacks used their guns on whites instead of on one another.

White describes Souljah's performance as one that scripted racialized roles for the audience. Asians were cast as all-powerful enemies of black people; Latinos "could have a role as long as they identified unconditionally with African Americans" (White, 35). At the center stood African Americans, and Sister Souljah was there to instruct them in the means to achieving authentic blackness. It was this process that began to unsettle some students. In proscribing the parameters of blackness, Souljah began to step on more than a few toes. Her injunction against interracial relationships disturbed the students who were either involved in such relationships or children of such unions. But it was her homophobia that really rocked the collective boat.

White proposes that Souljah's heterosexism revealed to students the source of her discursive power: ". . . the power of this performance depended upon attacks on group after group, until virtually everybody had some part of their identity marginalized" (35). Souljah was uncompromising in her position that a strong black community requires strong heterosexual bonds. Listen to White's explanation of the centrality of Souljah's heterosexism:

> One of the reasons that it was so central was that it built on a long tradition of discourse on race that we see in African American nationalist discourse. Afrocentric discourse, and even racist white discourse. It is a way of seeing "The Problem" in the Black community as one of failed family bonds—failed heterosexual bonds, in particular. You can read anyone from Ron Karenga to Patrick Moynihan, from Haki Madhubuti to Bill Moyers, you will find that the problem with the Black community is that we have weak heterosexual bonds. Thus the building blocks for a strong community don't include welfare dependent families, single parent female-headed households, and especially they don't include gay, lesbian, and bisexual family members. (35–36)

White closes by noting that the postconcert debates demonstrated the disruptive powers of sexuality. Many students rejected the notion that "queer" is a white thing.

BEING SEEN IN BLACK AND WHITE

Sistah Souljah clearly had no time for black queers. We are cast out of the fold of blackness, a part of the racial-national problem, not its solution. According to E. Fran White's report, Souljah also banished blacks with white partners from the kingdom. This moment in her performance serves as a pointed reminder that interracial relationships remain a flash point in many black communities. Straight African Americans have long struggled over the racial credentials of blacks with white partners. Black-white relationships frequently have served as the site for the contestation of the meaning of blackness.

The vast majority of public conversations about interracial relationships take heterosexuals as their subjects. Among African Americans, questions of racial loyalty and race-gender ideology figure prominently in the discussion, and the prototypical relationship of concern is that between a black man and a white woman. The questions that often inform the conversations are familiar: To what extent is his choice confirmation of racist and sexist notions of beauty, femininity, and womanhood? Is her choice of him and his choice of her rooted in the titillation provided by the forbidden, more pleasurable and exotic sexual "other"? Is she, for him, a symbolic manifestation of his longing for a status often denied in a racist and patriarchal social order? Is he black identified?[10]

Black and white gays and lesbians are generally nonsubjects in straight folk's cultural meditations on eros, love, and intimacy across racial lines. In those few moments where the topic has come up in my presence, the interrogators are more likely straight women than men, and the questions posed reflect the complexities of racial politics and identification across and within sexual orientations. Several of the men who have questioned my choice of a partner were political allies on the left who concluded that a white partner signifies a slavish and uncritical rejoicing in all things culturally "white." For these leftist cultural and political nationalists, it was my partner's race, not my work, that was the final determinant of political legitimacy. The verdict: not black enough.

Nationalist paternalism remains outrageous and oppressive, although familiar. I am reminded of similar admonitions regarding my feminism at earlier points in my life. Critical conversations about and struggles against sexism, I was and am still told, are evidence of white blight and anathema to black self-determination. I continue to note the extent to which some leftist cultural nationalists are at home in their willingness to proscribe the contours of sexually correct blackness.

However, I had no such reference point for the questions posed and the pain expressed by straight black women. The first time a straight sister asked why I was with a white woman, I assumed that this was the standard racial authenticity test. Yet this same woman affirmed my regard for black lives. The second time a group of black women raised "the question," I was working with them in a black studies context, and my commitment to progressive, antiracist, and feminist politics was evident. In each case, my questioners were more troubled by my partner's race than by my sexual orientation. Why am I not with a black woman?

This time, clarification came via a recollection of that which I had initially overlooked: these straight women were, in effect, identifying with and speaking on behalf of the black lesbians who were not my partners. As such, they were empathetically, and across lines of sexual orientation, articulating the pain of rejection. Since they are not lesbians, we could not, of course, be lovers. Nonetheless, this concrete reality did not impede these straight women from reading my relationship with Elizabeth as rejection of black women—a rejection of myself, a rejection of them.

These racialized and gendered readings of black and white women together occurred when my queerness was a known, a given. When my sexual orientation is unknown and heterosexuality is assumed, an entirely different reading surfaces. In these contexts Elizabeth and I have learned how a black and white lesbian couple can elicit very explicit readings of public interracial togetherness. Our invisibility as lesbians unveils the assumption that interracial relationships must inevitably and predictably be a reenactment of white supremacy.

My experience in the park recalls this country's historically gendered legacy of African-American servitude. It is only within the past thirty years that black women have collectively moved out of domestic work and into the clerical and service occupations of the service economy. Many African Americans born after World War II have parents or grandparents who worked in white homes as housekeepers and providers of child care. Their child-care needs and solutions did not warrant public debate and concern. The much-needed and long-overdue public debates about working women's unmet need for reliable and affordable child care is all too recent, and coincides with the increase in married white women's labor-force participation.

When political and policy elites openly address these issues, the race and class divisions among women loom large. In 1992 we collectively learned that President Clinton's executive cabinet appointees hired undocumented women workers of color because they could not find U.S. citizens to care for their children. Thus, they continued the long-standing tradition of employing their housekeepers and nannies in unprotected labor markets. In 1994 and 1995, the denizens of welfare reform insist that recipients of AFDC enter the labor market, but refuse to address their long-term needs for child care, health care, education, and a living wage. It can only be a matter of time before the policy wizards suggest that states send welfare mothers into professional homes—another fortuitous example of the market economy's miraculous ability to reproduce racialized class relations.

Given this historical context, it is not that surprising that middle-class white women of suburban Maryland assumed that I worked for Elizabeth. My casual empiricism suggests that although few of them employ African-American women in their homes, a fair number employ African nationals, Latinas, and Afro-Caribbean women. The globalized economy has generated new cadres of child-care workers but has preserved North-South political economic hierarchies. It is in this context that our neighbors defined Elizabeth's and my identities and relationship. The possibility that we might be partnered lesbians remains unthinkable. What was imagined is a racialized class provisioning of child care.

Thus, in the presence of our children, I often am read as their paid care provider. In their absence the interpretive lens nonetheless retains its power. I recall for example, our experience at the University of Richmond in the fall of 1992. A few campus progressives organized an oppositional speak-out the night before the presidential debate to be held at their campus. They invited me, I accepted, and Elizabeth joined me. At the hotel desk, I said, "Reservation for Dr. Rhonda Williams, please." The clerk, a young African-American woman, completed her paperwork, then handed the registration form to Elizabeth, saying, "Here you go, Dr. Williams." Elizabeth handed the paper to me, and said to the clerk, while gesturing in my direction, "*She* is Dr. Williams."

We were stunned by this conversation and subsequently discussed at length the racial mediations that structured the exchange. Once again, in the absence of an overt expression or articulation of intimacy, the clerk assumed our "straightness." What we found truly remarkable was this young black women's presumption that I was not asking for my own reservation—I could not be "Dr. Williams." Rather, in that moment the clerk imagined that I worked for Elizabeth in some capacity, and was speaking *for* her in that capacity. In this young black woman's experience, blacks and whites appear together at her desk as employee and employer. In the collision of class and race identification, our being social peers was just as inconceivable as our being social queers.

BEING POLITICAL

The Hampshire students who rejected Souljah's efforts to essentialize race had their counterparts at the University of Maryland. Several African-American students—all male—addressed the black student population on the dangers of a narrowly confined blackness. David Terry opined that "homosexuality is not a burdening problem in the black community. . . . If there is a problem within the black community, it is on the part of 'we' the heterosexual members" (Terry, 2). Timothy Dixon lamented the "small-mindedness" and "stupidity" of his peers (Dixon, 2). Two young men came to my office to share with me their personal support and to let me know that they were taking up the queer cause in the dormitories.

I noted the absence of young women visitors, the dearth of young women who challenge heterosexism in the black papers. I am reminded of Makeda Silvera's ruminations on some black women's fear of losing the heterosexual privilege, the only privilege many know (Silvera, 1992). I wonder to what extent masculine privilege empowered the young men who publically affirmed my sexual orientation. Would they have felt equally at liberty to speak out if the queer in question was a gay brother?

As one semester passes into the next, I regularly encounter students responding to the news of my queerness. First-year students hear it in the large lecture course, and/or receive a briefing from their older peers. Those who frequent the Afro-American studies office witness a small community of black folks struggling to embrace (sometimes with more ease than others) the diversity of our collective. The departmental space provides many students an example of how they might live and work in principled solidarity with their queer brothers and sisters. They see professors, staff, and students affirming our "pomo-homo" family.[11]

Like their elders, some students have greater difficulty with Elizabeth's whiteness than with my queerness. For these students, my having a white partner contradicts my antiracist teaching, research, and politics. Whether straight or gay, they feel betrayed. Many have never known or loved a principled antiracist white person; many do not believe such persons exist. I am reminded of the ongoing necessity for cultural and political works that might expand their racial imaginations.

NOTES

I thank Elizabeth Seydi, Katie King, M. V. Lee Badgett, Wahneema Lubiano, and the editorial collective of the Center for Advanced Feminist Studies at the University of Minnesota for insightful comments.

1. This paragraph employs a diversity of self-referential terms: lesbian, dyke, queerness. My use of these terms has shifted over the years, and not in some ideologically recognizable pattern. My current penchant for "queer" reflects my delight in the term's definitional fuzziness, its overdetermination. I draw inspiration from Phillip Brian Harper's assertion that "queer includes within it a necessarily expansive impulse" (Harper, Cerullo, and White, 30), and Oscar Montero's proposition that "Queer theory skirts identity, sometimes literally, and brings other identities, ethnic, racial, and national, into play" (Montero, 17).

2. In their 1981 dialogue, Barbara Smith and Beverly Smith previewed some of the issues raised here. Barbara Smith suggests that racist sexual stereotypes shape homophobia in black communities. Beverly Smith conjectures that racism's dichotomies give black folks the option of coding lesbianism white. This essay revisits these issues and seeks to extend and amplify their earlier observations (Smith and Smith, 124).

3. Simmons (1991) concisely and critically reviews cultural nationalist positions on black homosexuality.

4. The literature on racial representations, racial meanings, and the racializations of western political economies and cultures continues to grow. For important examples, see Omi and Winant, Gooding-Williams, Butler, Goldberg, Christian, hooks, and Jewell.

5. The academic year 1994–95 marks the thirtieth anniversary of the publication of Daniel P. Moynihan's *The Negro Family: The Case for National Action*. Now known as the Moynihan Report, this monograph popularized the notion that slavery had created a Negro-American subculture that is matriarchal and therefore pathological. According to Moynihan and his disciples, it is this familial dysfunction that impedes black social development, and not contemporary forms of economic and cultural racism. Sociologist William J. Wilson's 1987 treatise *The Truly Disadvantaged* affirmed the prevalence of pathology among the black urban poor, but argued that dein-

dustrialization, not slavery, is the source of female-headed households (i.e., the loss of manufacturing jobs for high school–educated men devastated the employment possibilities for those same men, resulting in a decline in marriage rates). Challenges to Moynihan and Wilson abound. Reed (1990) provides a solid contemporary example.

6. Wilson (1987) focused much underclass debate in the late 1980s and early 1990s. For a compelling discussion of "the underclass" as a racialized and gendered ideological discourse, see Reed (1990).

7. Dumm (1993) discusses the intensification of state monitoring and control of urban black America.

8. I thank Elizabeth Seydi for articulating this contradiction so clearly in our conversations about sexuality and race and thereby sending me in the directions developed in this essay.

9. In this context "kin" are a group of people who consider themselves family or relatives. The rules for defining kin vary widely across cultures, time, and place but often imply notions of responsibility and obligation.

10. Writers speaking from radically divergent perspectives will nonetheless converge on these questions. Feminist bell hooks and leftist philosopher Cornel West reflect upon these themes in *Breaking Bread* (Boston: South End, 1991, 114–17). Their conversation explores how our white supremacist culture's affirmation of whiteness mediates male (and female) notions of beauty and femininity. Nathan and Julia Hare similarly explore at length black men's collective valorization of white/light skin and women (*Crisis in Black Sexual Politics* [San Francisco: Black Think Tank, 1989], 69–77).

11. Gay and black, Brian Freeman, Bernard Branner, and Eric Gupton cowrote *Fierce Love*, their collection of stories on sex, life, and love. They premiered their show in January 1991 at Josie's in San Francisco. Freeman's boyfriend dubbed the trio "Pomo Afro Homos" (as in postmodern African-American, and homosexual), a name embraced by many in the queer media (Freeman, 59). Their performance group and others like them bring black queers out of the closet and into the light.

WORKS CITED

Butler, Judith. "Endangered/Endangering: Schematic Racism and White Paranoia." In *Reading Rodney King, Reading Urban Uprising*, edited by Robert Gooding-Williams. New York: Routledge, 1993.

Christian, Barbara. "What Celie Knows That You Should Know." In *The Anatomy of Racism*, edited by David Goldberg. Minneapolis: University of Minnesota Press, 1990.

Clark, Cheryl. "The Failure to Transform: Homophobia in the Black Community." In *Home Girls: A Black Feminist Anthology*, edited by Barbara Smith. Latham, N.Y.: Kitchen Table: Women of Color Press, 1983.

Dixon, Timothy. Article in *The Eclipse*, a student newspaper, University of Maryland, College Park, March 23, 1992.

Dumm, Thomas. "The New Enclosures: Racism in the Normalized Community." In Gooding-Williams, *Reading Rodney King*.

Freeman, Brian. "Pomo Afro Homos Presents *Fierce Love*." *Outlook* 4, no. 2 (Fall 1991).

Gilroy, Paul. *The Black Atlantic: Modernity and Double Consciousness*. Cambridge Mass.: Harvard University Press, 1993.

———. "It's a Family Affair." In *Black Popular Culture*, edited by Gina Dent. Seattle. Bay Press, 1992.

Goldberg, David. "The Social Formation of Racist Discourse." In *The Anatomy of Racism*, edited by David Goldberg. Minneapolis: University of Minnesota Press, 1990.

Gooding-Williams, Robert. "Look! A Negro." In *Reading Rodney King*.

Gresham, Jewell Handy. "The Politics of Family in America." *Nation*, July 24 and 31, 1989.

Harper, Phillip, Margaret Cerullo, and E. Frances White. "Multi/Queer/Culture." *Radical America* 24, no. 4 (September-December 1990; published April 1993).

hooks, bell. *Black Looks: Race and Representation*. Boston: South End, 1992.

———. *Yearning: Race, Gender, and Cultural Politics*. Boston: South End, 1990.

Jewell, K. Sue. *From Mammy to Miss America and Beyond*. New York: Routledge, 1993.

Lorde, Audre. "I am Your Sister: Black Women Organizing Across Sexualities." In *A Burst of Light*. Ithaca, N.Y.: Firebrand Books, 1988.

Lubiano, Wahneema. "Black Ladies, Welfare Queens, and State Minstrels: Ideological War by Narrative Means." In *Race-ing Justice, En-gendering Power*, edited by Toni Morrison. New York: Pantheon, 1992.

Madhubuti, Haki. *Black Men: Obsolete, Single, Dangerous? Afrikan American Families in Transition: Essays in Discovery, Solution, and Hope*. Chicago: Third World Press, 1990.

Montero, Oscar. "Before the Parade Passes By: Latino Queers and National Identity." *Radical America* 24, no. 4 (September-December 1990; published April 1993).

Omi, Michael, and Howard Winant. *Racial Formation in the United States from the 1960's to the 1980's*. London: Routledge, 1986.

Phélan, Shane. "(Be)Coming Out: Lesbian Identity and Politics." *Signs* 18, no. 4 (1993).

Reed, Adolph. "The Underclass as Myth and Symbol." *Radical America* 24, no. 1 (January 1990).

Silvera, Makeda. "Man Royals and Sodomites: Some Thoughts on the Invisibility of Afro-Caribbean Lesbians." *Feminist Studies* 18, no. 2 (Fall 1992).

Simmons, Ron. "Some Thoughts on the Challenges Facing Black Gay Intellectuals." In *Brother to Brother*, edited by Essex Hemphill. Boston, Alyson Publications, 1991.

Smith, Barbara and Beverly Smith. "Across the Table: A Sister-to-Sister Dialogue." In *This Bridge Called My Back: Writings by Radical Women of Color*, edited by Cherrie Moraga and Gloria Anzaldua. Latham, N.Y.: Kitchen Table: Women of Color Press, 1981.

Sudarkasa, Niara. "African and Afro-American Family Structure: A Comparison." *The Black Scholar*, November-December 1980.

Terry, David. Article in *The Eclipse*, a student newspaper, University of Maryland, College Park, March 23, 1992.

Welsing, Frances Cress. "The Politics Behind Black Male Passivity, Effeminisation, Bisexuality, and Homosexuality." In *The Isis Papers*, Chicago: Third World Press, 1991 (essay originally printed in 1974).

White, E. Frances. "Africa on My Mind: Gender, Counter Discourse, and African American Nationalism." *Journal of Women's History* 2, no. 1 (Spring 1990).

Wilson, William J. *The Truly Disadvantaged*. Chicago: University of Chicago Press, 1987.

RETHINKING VERNACULAR CULTURE

Black Religion and Race Records in the 1920s and 1930s

■

Evelyn Brooks Higginbotham

I F BLACK RELIGIOUS CULTURE in its varied beliefs and practices has fostered bright and shining stars such as Martin Luther King, Jr., Malcolm X, Marian Anderson, Aretha Franklin, Jesse Jackson, and Cornel West, then as this list of names suggests, black religious culture has played a significant role in the contestation of ideologies in African-American communities. This contestation occurs between the middle class and working class, and it also occurs within the working class itself. Unfortunately, the trend in recent scholarship has not given the religious culture of the working class the attention it deserves. Some of the most imaginative and analytically sophisticated studies tend to privilege the secular life of black working-class communities. Such studies often draw upon the "race records" of the 1920s and 1930s, linking blues records with socioeconomic processes of migration and urbanization. They focus on the lyrics of the blues and the lives of blues singers as emblematic of sexual freedom, iconoclastic values, and an overall culture of resistance to the hegemony of middle-class ideology.[1] Implicitly, if not explicitly, the blues is deemed the "authentic" signifier of African-American culture.[2] Blues culture, working-class culture, and "blackness" become virtually synonymous. The religious culture of the working poor, when visible at all, appears as an anomaly or false consciousness. The blues and church are thus counterposed as cultural icons of class division. Perhaps this representation of working-class religion stems from the belief that African-American Christianity is white-derived, middle-class in orientation, and thus less authentically black. Or conversely, perhaps religion among the poor is not taken seriously because it is perceived as otherworldly, lower-class escapism, having no ideological implications and playing no strategic role in struggles over moral and cultural authority.

The race records of the 1920s and 1930s are useful for analysis, since they included not only the blues but also the explicitly religious articulations of the black working class.[3] Companies such as Okeh, Victor, Vocalion, and Paramount recorded vernacular discourses of religion in the form of sermons and gospel music, called gospel blues, as eagerly as they recorded the raunchiest blues lyrics.[4] The religious records tapped into the cultural repertoire of storefront Baptist churches and the rising numbers of Holiness and Pentecostal churches in urban ghettos. Langston Hughes recalled his impressions of the Holiness churches in Chicago around the time of World War I: "I was entranced by their stepped-up rhythms, tambourines, hand clapping, and uninhibited dynamics, rivaled only by Ma Rainey singing the blues at the old Monogram Theater."[5] Just as Hughes had juxtaposed the songs of the church with the blues, this odd coupling of the sacred and profane appeared regularly in newspaper advertisements for race records. Paramount Records informed the readers of the *Chicago Defender* that they could "get these Red-Hot Blues and Inspiring Spirituals" through mail order. Okeh included in a single advertisement blues singer Lonnie Johnson and gospel singer Jessie May Hill. Featuring Johnson's "Mean Old Bed Bug Blues," the advertisement read: "Bedbugs big as a jackass bite you and stand and grin. Then drink a bottle of bed bug poison and come and bite you again. The Hottest Blues You Ever Heard." Yet the same advertisement listed "Sister Jessie May Hill and Sisters of the Congregation singing 'Earth Is No Resting Place.'"[6]

If, as some scholars suggest, advertising's juxtaposition of religious and blues records served as an affront to the pious, the coupling nonetheless offers an analytical rubric for disentangling the working class from its exclusive identification with blues culture. Clearly, the church was just as indigenous to the working poor as was the blues. On one level the popularity of the sermons and gospel songs speaks to an emotional folk orality that contested the ethics and aesthetics of the black middle class. Not through the counterculture of the blues, but rather through vernacular discourses of religion, the black poor waged a struggle over cultural authority that ultimately subverted the hegemonic values and aesthetic standards of the traditional Protestantism of the black middle class. On another level the religious race records speak to the existence of multiple and conflicting subcultures within the black working class, indicating differences of consciousness, values, and lifestyle even among the most poor. The religious culture of the poor, as evidenced in the Pentecostal and Holiness churches, for example, embraced a strict moral code that denounced the fast and free lifestyle of blues culture.[7] In the dialect, imagery, and rhythms of the black poor, the religious race records repudiate sexual freedom, gambling, drinking, womanizing, and general defiance of the law. Nina Simone reminisced about her working-class family: "Mama and them were so religious that they wouldn't allow you to play boogie-woogie in the house, but would allow you to use the same boogie-woogie *beat* to play a gospel tune."[8]

The religious race records of the 1920s gave a new public dimension to black religion and especially to the working-class churches. The records validated the creative energies of the rural folk, turned urban proletariat, as an alternate, competing voice within African-American communities. At the most prosaic levels, the ascendant voice of southern folk culture challenged the middle-class ideology of racial uplift as pronounced by educated religious leaders of the late nineteenth century. The latter group had defined racial progress not merely in the context of black-white relations but also in the context of a class-based contestation over group beliefs and practices. Educated religious leaders emphasized written texts and rational discourses in the struggle for the advancement of their people.[9] These religious leaders articulated sentiments similar to W. E. B. Du Bois's viewpoint that the black colleagues brought African Americans "in contact with modern civilization."[10] Commitment to collegiate education figured prominently in their belief in an intellectual and professional vanguard—the Talented Tenth as Du Bois characterized the black elite at the turn of the century.

As time and schooling distanced African Americans further and further from their slave past, many became self-conscious, conflicted, even critical of the culture of their forebears. From gentle persuasion to ridicule and punishment, white and black missionary teachers sought the demise of the older forms of singing and worship. In 1870, Elizabeth Kilham, a white northern teacher among the freedman, acknowledged the impact of education on the younger generation:

> The distinctive features of negro hymnology, are gradually disappearing, and with another generation will probably be obliterated entirely. The cause for this, lies in the education of the younger people. . . . Already they have learned to ridicule the extravagant preaching, the meaningless hymns, and the noisy singing of their elders. Not perhaps as yet, to any great extent in the country; changes come always more slowly there, but in the cities, the young people have, in many cases, taken the matter into their own hands, formed choirs, adopted the hymns and tunes in use in the white churches. . . .[11]

It is interesting that Kilham, while praising the shift to white hymns, conceded the slowness with which blacks in the countryside assimilated. Bishop Daniel Alexander Payne of the African Methodist Episcopal Church recalled his frustrating experience in a rural church in South Carolina.

> After the sermon they formed a ring, and with coats off sung, clapped their hands and stamped their feet in a most ridiculous and heathenish way. I requested the pastor to go and stop their dancing. At his request they stopped their dancing and clapping of hands, but remained singing and rocking their bodies to and fro. This they did for about fifteen minutes. I then went, and taking their leader by the arm requested him to desist and to sit down and sing in a *rational* manner. I told him also that it was a heathenish way to worship and disgraceful to themselves, the race, and the Christian name.[12] (my emphasis)

Payne's plea for a "rational manner" of singing formed part of the larger assimilationist project of ridding the black community of sensuality, intemperance, "superstition," and the emotional style of worship practiced in the hush harbors of the slave era. His emphasis on a calm, intellectually oriented religious expression signaled the growing class and cultural differences that would surface prominently as rural southern migrants poured into the northern cities. For Bishop Payne, loud and emotive behavior constituted more than an individual's impropriety or doctrinal error. It marked the retrogression of the entire racial group. In the midst of heightened racial discrimination and social Darwinist thought, educated leaders decried the moaning and bodily movements of black worship.[13] Educated African Americans such as James Trotter posited that vocal and instrumental music in the form of the "noble organ . . . sacred chant, the prayer or thanksgiving, uttered in melodious song by the choir or by all the congregation" served as an antidote to "the cares and wild passions" of the world. For Trotter music functioned as a civilizing force, a "source of refinement and pleasure . . . to the possessor himself, and by which he may add to the tranquillity, the joys, of his own and the home life of his neighbors and friends."[14]

Literacy and published texts came to be linked increasingly to the expression of religious culture. The Reverend Sutton Griggs, a college-educated Baptist minister and novelist, typified the black middle class in its preference for print discourse, thus implicitly devaluing the interpretative authority of illiterate leaders. He proclaimed, "To succeed as a race, we must move up out of the age of the voice. . . ."[15] Educated leaders perceived the medium of print as a source of communication and power. They made continual appeals for the publication of texts that would present the African-American side of history and instill pride in their people. They commonly used the term "distinctive literature," referring to any text that was written and/or published by African Americans.[16] Yet the phenomenal rise in literacy among African Americans in the decades after the Civil War occurred with unsettling consequences for traditions of black worship. Calling attention to the clash between literate and oral traditions in the postbellum South, Elsa Barkley Brown describes the conflict surrounding the introduction of printed songbooks in the First African Baptist Church in Richmond. The adoption of hymnals superseded the older practice of "lining out hymns," a practice increasingly labeled "unrefined" and a vestige of slave culture by educated blacks and whites. Lining out had not required literacy, but only an able song leader to introduce each verse of song, which in turn was followed by the congregation's repetition of the verse. The introduction of hymnals, however, disadvantaged the illiterate, since it reconfigured the collective voice to include the literate only. For the illiterate, asserts Elsa Barkley Brown, "it was the equivalent of being deprived of a voice, all the more significant in an oral culture."[17] Efforts to supplant the oral culture by a literate one were depicted by the black poet Daniel Webster Davis in the 1890s. In "De Linin' ub de Hymns," Davis employs dialect in order to voice the critique of uneducated African Americans against the cultural transformations taking place:

Dar's a mighty row in Zion, an' de debbil's gettin' high,
....
'Twuz 'bout a bery leetle thing—de linin' ub a hymn.
De Young folks 'tain't stylish to lin' um out no mo';
Dat dey's got edikashun, an' dey wants us all to know
Dey likes to hab dar singin'-books a-holin' fore dar eyes,
An' sing de hymns right straight along 'to manshuns in de skies.'
....
An' ef de ol' folks will kumplain 'cause dey is ol' an' blind,
An' slabry's chain don' kep' dem back frum larnin' how to
    read—
Dat dey mus' take a corner seat, an' let de young folks lead.
....
De ol'-time groans an' shouts an' moans am passin' out ub
    sight—
Edikashun changed all dat, an' we belebe it right,
We should serb God wid 'telligence; fur dis one thing I plead:
Jes' lebe a leetle place in church fur dem ez kin not read.[18]

An entire genre of race literature arose in the late nineteenth century for the purpose of "uplifting" the black masses culturally, politically, and economically. The rise of literacy had been foundational to the evolution of a black reading public, and it was this very readership that constituted the race market so crucial to the success of church-based entrepreneurship. Many local religious presses as well as the large denominational ones (the A.M.E. Book Concern, the A.M.E. Sunday School Union Press, the A.M.E. Zion Book Concern, the A.M.E. Zion Publication House, the National Baptist Publishing Board, and the Sunday School Publishing Board of the National Baptist Convention, U.S.A., Inc.) figured significantly in the production of hymnals, church literature, newspapers, and to a lesser extent works of fiction. For example, the earliest novels of Frances Ellen Watkins Harper appeared in syndicated form in the *Christian Recorder* of the A.M.E. Church.[19] Literature produced by African Americans strove to negate the pejorative racial images prevalent in film, media, art and scholarly and popular books. Photographs in black-owned periodicals often depicted middle-class men and women in the act of reading. Captions to such photographs made reference to the cultivation of the "higher arts" and sought to convey images of refinement and civility, material comfort and respectability. The conflation of musical taste and literature culture is apparent in the 1904 issue of the *Voice of the Negro*, which featured a photographic series of "representative" black men and women. A caption to a photograph of a young black woman read: "An admirer of Fine Art, a performer on the violin and the piano, a sweet singer, a writer—mostly given to essays, a lover of good books, and a home making girl."[20]

It is no small irony, then, that the newly urbanized southern folk ushered in the "age of the voice" at the height of the renaissance of the black literati.[21] During the 1920s and 1930s the black working class effected the shift to an emotional folk orality that challenged the cultural authority of the black middle class. The migrants built storefront churches, established sects and cults, and "infiltrated" and transformed many of the "old-line" Baptist and Methodist churches with the gospel blues, a twentieth-century musical innovation with roots in the slave past. Historian Lawrence Levine conveys this blend of old and new in the religious culture of the migrants:

While many churches within the black community sought respectability by turning their backs on the past, banning the shout, discouraging enthusiastic religion, and adopting more sedate hymns and refined concertized versions of the spirituals, the Holiness churches constituted a revitalization movement with their emphasis upon healing, gifts of prophecy, speaking in tongues, spirit possession, and religious dance. Musically, they reached back to the traditions of the slave past and out to the rhythms of the secular black musical world around them. They brought into the church not only the sounds of ragtime, blues and jazz but also the instruments.[22]

The public emergence of a folk orality can be attributed to both the massive migration of southern blacks to northern cities and to a triumphant American commercialism, which during the 1920s turned its gaze upon black consumers. Through advertising, department stores, catalog shopping, and installment buying, the new commercial culture made its impact on the Great Migration. The recently arrived migrants soon became a consuming public, hungry for their own musical styles and for an array of products with a racial appeal.[23] They swelled the ranks of the race market and reconfigured black supply and demand well beyond the small entrepreneur and communities of readership at the turn of the century. Historian Jackson Lears describes the commercial culture of America in the 1920s as quite different from the past: "the older culture was suited to a production-oriented society of small entrepreneurs; the new culture epitomized a consumption-oriented society dominated by bureaucratic corporations."[24]

Race-consciousness, creative expression, and the black church itself became implicated in America's growing corporate capitalism. Nowhere is this more evident than in the nexus between working-class religion and the record industry. The record industry tapped into the cultural repertoire of the black working-class churches, drawing upon and promoting the very folk traditions that the middle class had sought to eradicate. While the commodification of black religious culture and the attendant reality of white-controlled profits speak to the problematic aspects of the race records industry,[25] it cannot be denied that this commodification was made possible by the matrix of exchange inherent in the black working-class church. The church was and is at once the producer of musicians and music forms as well as a consumer market with changing tastes. Technological advancement and the consequent rise of the record and broadcast industries, along with mass advertising in the national black press, e.g., the *Chicago Defender*, all worked together to effect the commodification of the religious experience. This process of religious commodification calls to mind philosopher Kwame Anthony Appiah's analysis of modernity in regard to Max Weber's characterization of charismatic versus rational authority.

> What we can see . . . is not the triumph of Enlightenment capital-R Reason—which would have entailed exactly the end of charisma and the universalization of the secular—not even the penetration of a narrower instrumental reason into all spheres of life, but what Weber mistook for that: namely, the incorporation of all areas of the world and all areas of even formerly "private" life into the money economy. Modernity has turned every element of the real into a sign, and the sign reads "for sale"; this is true even in domains like religion. . . .[26]

If African-American religion succumbed to the commercialism and consumerism of the 1920s, it did so while harnessing new venues for working-class cultural production. A new public voice, indeed a charismatic authority, rivaled the authority of the educated black leadership. The nineteenth century had witnessed the ascendancy of the middle class as the literate public voice of the race. The twentieth century witnessed the ascendancy of the black working class as the oral narrator of modernity.[27] Growing working-class consumerism, coupled with black middle-class disdain for the cultural styles of the poor, had initiated this important shift to working-class orality within the black public sphere. Even the Reverend Sutton Griggs, who had earlier admonished his people to "move up out of the age of the voice," recorded sermons on the Victor label during the 1920s.[28] However, the rise of race records should not imply a false dichotomy between reading and oral/aural constituencies. More often than not, the two constituencies were one and the same, since record consumers looked primarily to black newspapers for the advertisement of new record releases and for coverage on the personal lives and public appearances of recording stars.

Blues scholar Paul Oliver notes that religious records enjoyed a popularity equal to that of the blues, and possibly greater.[29] Produced in three-minute and six-minute sound bites, these records attempt to re-create the black worship experience, presenting highly emotional preaching, moaning, ecstatic audience response, vocal and instrumental accompaniment. Oliver recounts their unrestrained quality: "The preacher develops his subject, often speaking in a direct address at first and moving to a singing tone as he warms to his theme. . . . Urged on by the murmurs, cries, shouts of approval and encouragement from the congregation, he might struggle for the right words, 'straining' with constricted throat . . . 'moaning,' 'mourning,' 'whooping.'"[30]

Building on patterns from the folk tradition and thus rejecting a rational, dispassionate style, the recorded sermons and religious songs were especially appealing to the waves of rural migrants who poured into northern cities, uprooted and in search of cultural continuity.[31] Record companies catered to the migrants' preference for a "down-home," i.e., more rural, southern style by adopting such phrases as "old-fashioned," "real Southern style" and "old-time" in their record titles and advertisements. Paramount proudly announced its "latest new electric method" of record production in its advertisement for *Old Time Baptism* by the Reverend R. M. Massey. Okeh Records invoked similar images of an immediate and authentic black religious experience in its advertisement of two sermons by the Reverend F. W. McGee and his congregation: "They make you feel as if you're right in the church. You hear it all just as it actually happens. The preacher's burning words . . . spontaneous shouts from the congregation . . . and the low-pitched hum of musical instruments."[32] Musical accompaniment in recorded sermons often included the moaning sounds of women in the background, a boogie-woogie piano or the sounds of cornet, guitar, and drums. The sermons met with instant success. The Reverend J. C. Burnett's sermon, the *Downfall of Nebuchadnezzar*, sold eighty thousand records within months of its release in November 1926. Interestingly, the sermon begins in the tradition of the slaves with the lining out of the hymn *I Heard the Voice of Jesus Say*.[33] The sale of Burnett's record quadrupled the normal sale of a Bessie Smith record. By the end of the 1930s, the number of black preachers, male and female, on record had soared from six to seventy, while more than 750 sermons had been recorded.[34]

Also popular during the 1920s and early 1930s were the religious records of male and female singers, especially those identified with the storefront Baptist, Holiness, and Pentecostal churches. The strictly musical records outlived the sermons in their appeal to consumers.[35] Arizona Dranes, the blind vocalist, who sang for Okeh Records, played in a piano style reminiscent of ragtime and boogie-woogie as she rendered the songs of black Pentecostalism to record consumers across the nation. The records of Sanctified singers (Paul Oliver's term for female singers in the Pentecostal and Holiness churches) such as Jessie May Hill, Leora Ross, Bessie Johnson, Melinda Taylor, and Rosetta Tharpe with her gospel hybridization of jazz and swing, were widely distributed in black communities.[36] Sanctified singers did not limit themselves to the piano, but employed secular accompaniment—guitars, jug bands, and tambourines. Oliver notes that blues singers even cut religious records, after record promoters convinced them of the lucrative nature of the religious market. Classic blues queens, such as Bessie Smith, Sara Martin, Clara Smith, and Leola Manning claimed at least one sacred song in their repertoire of otherwise secular recordings.[37]

The standard hymn, with its implicit connotations of order and respectability, yielded ineluctably to improvisation and earthy rhythms. The capitulation of middle-class notions of assimilation and respectability to the new "gospel blues" occurred most glaringly in the black Baptist church.[38] This shifting emphasis is epitomized by the musical styles of Marian Anderson and Mahalia Jackson, both of whose musical talents were discovered and nurtured in the church. During the first two decades of the twentieth century, the talents of the future opera star Marian Anderson grew to maturity under the influence of the musical traditions of Philadelphia's Union Baptist Church. By age thirteen she was promoted to the adult choir, having sung in the junior choir since she was six. Her sense of music and its cultural meaning was informed by traditional hymnody and orchestral performances. Black hymnody in this setting is reminiscent of Houston Baker's discussion of the "mastery of form." Baker identifies such mastery as a strategy efficaciously adopted in the name of group advancement, but clearly based upon the acknowledgment of an appeal to white America's hegemonic cultural styles and values, i.e., the nation's *standards*.[39] The church's annual concerts frequently engaged tenor Roland Hayes who "sang old Italian airs, German Lieder, and French songs exquisitely." Anderson recalls in her autobiography that "even people with little understanding of music knew it was beautiful singing, and they were proud Mr. Hayes was one of their own and world famous."[40]

Mahalia Jackson's talents were cultivated in the musical traditions of the southern black church. She began her singing career in New Orleans, the birthplace of jazz. She performed in an up-tempo rhythm expressive of what Michael W. Harris terms "indigenous black religious song in a down-home manner."[41] Her singing group, while popular in the South, met with initial disfavor after she migrated to Chicago in 1927 at the age of sixteen. In his study of the rise of gospel blues, Harris notes that Jackson was once thrown out of a church—the minister shouting, "Get that twisting and jazz out of the church."[42] Similar views are expressed in the poem "When Mahalia Sings" by Quandra Prettyman. Although the poem tells of Prettyman's eventual respect for the emotional religiosity of the working poor, the excerpt below emphasizes her initial mockery of the "holiness rhythms" of the storefront churches:

> We used to gather at the high window
> of the holiness church and, on tip-toe
> look in and laugh at the dresses, too small
> on the ladies, and how wretched they all
> looked—an old garage for a church, for pews,
> old wooden chairs. It seemed a lame excuse
> for a church. Not solemn or grand,
> with no real robed choir, but a loose jazz band,
> or so it sounded to our mocking ears.
> So we responded to their hymns with jeers.[43]

Mahalia Jackson's gospel blues appealed greatly to the swelling numbers of poor, Deep South migrants to Chicago. Jackson gave new voice to an old spirituality as she regularly performed at storefront churches. By 1932 she was receiving invitations from the established, old-line churches and would soon sing at the annual meetings of the National Baptist Convention.[44] The gospel blues had subverted the central, if not hegemonic position of standard hymnody even in these churches. Far less concerned about the gaze of white America in the projection of an African-American image, the gospel blues evoked the call and response of blacks themselves.

Nor did church leaders continue to link inextricably racial progress with their congregants' mastery of Western expressivity and styles of decorum. At issue here is more than the contestation between middle-class and working-class cultures; it is rather the interpenetration of the two. While both Marian Anderson and Mahalia Jackson enjoyed enormous fame throughout their lives, the musical repertoire of urban black Baptist churches came increasingly to identify (although not without contestation) the old-line voice with European hymns, while associating the modern with the more spontaneous, emotive style of down-home religious culture.[45] The transition of black church discourses symbolized the responsive soundings of a people in transition from an old to a new order. The commodification of black religious culture roared along with the 1920s as a marker of the decade's preoccupation with the black vernacular.[46]

Yet the contestation of cultures occurred not merely between the working class and the middle class. Division and dispute occurred within the working class itself. While the musical form of gospel blues incorporated the rhythmic patterns and sounds of secular blues, ragtime, and jazz, the lyrical content of gospel blues were embedded in institutions and belief structures that repudiated secular blues themes. Enjoying a prominence that was not confined to a particular congregation or region, men such as the Reverends E. D. Campbell, A. W. Nix, J. M. Gates and women such as the Reverends Leora Ross and Mary Nelson brought messages of doom and salvation to African Americans throughout the nation. Through recorded sermons and songs they drew upon biblical passages in their denunciation of crime, liquor, dancing, women's fashions, gambling, and fast living in general.[47] In *Better Get Ready for Judgement* the Reverend

Mary Nelson sings in a strong a capella voice, condemning the hypocrites, drunkards, liars, and adulterers.[48] The recordings constituted vernacular discourses of religion, calling attention to the conditions of ghetto life in the everyday language of the poor and uneducated.

The railroad train figures prominently in the religious race records, just as it does in the blues. In discussing the blues, literary scholars Houston Baker and Hazel Carby point to the train's varied meanings of freedom and loneliness for male and female migrants.[49] However, in the religious race records, the train symbolizes a vehicle of judgment—an image altogether different from its metaphorical usage in the secular blues. For example, the Reverend J. M. Gates's sermon, *Death's Black Train Is Coming*, portrays the train as an instrument of retribution for fast living. The most popular use of the train motif was Reverend A. W. Nix's *Black Diamond Express to Hell*.[50] The Vocalion advertisement announced: "Here she comes! The 'Black Diamond Express to Hell' with Sin, the Engineer, holding the throttle wide open; Pleasure is the Headlight, and the Devil is the Conductor. You can feel the roaring of the Express and the moanin' of the Drunkards, Liars, Gamblers and other folk who have got aboard. They are hell-bound and they don't want to go. The train makes eleven stops but nobody can get off." The route of the train included stops at "Liars's Ave., Dance Hall Depot, and Stealing Town."[51]

Themes of justice to the wicked and proud abound in the recorded sermons. Against the background of moaning voices and cries of amen, Reverend Burnett began his blockbuster hit, the *Downfall of Nebuchadnezzar*, by prophesying the inevitable ruin of people who hold themselves in high estimation and manipulate the weak. Burnett's message serves as a promise to the oppressed: God will bring down the liars, backsliders, and rich men.[52] A similar theme can be found in Reverend J. M. Gates's record, *Samson and the Woman*. Despite the title, the sermon focuses not on gender but on class and race relations. Gates, like Burnett, targets those people who think that their positions of strength, privilege, and power over others will last forever. Those on top will be leveled in time, he proclaims repeatedly in the sermon.[53] Gates was one of the most popular of the recorded preachers, holding contracts with five different record companies during the 1920s. Titles of his recorded sermons reveal concern about rising crime, e.g., *The First Born Was a Murderer, Did You Spend Christmas in Jail?, Death Might Be Your Santa Claus, No Room in the Jailhouse,* and *Dying Gambler.* Whether sung or preached, the religious race records condemned the growing disorder, alienation, and criminal elements in the urban setting, but they did so in the common, everyday language of the black working class.[54] The vernacular discourses of religion constituted a moral idiom for distinguishing the personal and collective identity of the "righteous" from other working-class identities (e.g., blues people). The messages in the recorded sermons and songs articulated shared meanings and constraints for evaluating and interpreting social reality. They sought to establish boundaries around the lives of the black poor in the effort to shield them from dangers that were perceived as emanating from both outside and inside their own communities.

At issue here are not only conflicting value systems but internally generated norms. This latter point is often overlooked by scholars who too readily attribute efforts to restore "moral order" to the intentionality, ideology, and disciplinary mechanisms of the middle class. The middle class certainly played a role in disciplining the poor and in policing black women's bodies, as Hazel Carby perceptively discusses, but so, too, did Pentecostal churches.[55] Nor were notions of "moral panic" situated solely within a 1920s bourgeois ideology. The quest for moral order is replete in the sermons, gospel songs, and religious institutions of the working class. The storefront Baptist, Pentecostal, and Holiness churches along with a variety of urban sects and cults, e.g., Father Divine's Peace Mission movement and Daddy Grace's United House of Prayer, were doubtless more effective than middle-class reformers in policing the black woman's body and demanding conformity to strict guidelines of gender roles and sexual conduct.[56] Within these religious traditions, an impassioned embrace of outward emotion and bodily movement went hand-in-hand with the rejection of sexual contact outside of marriage, secular dancing, and worldly indulgence.

In conclusion, I offer these comments on religion and race records in order to ponder competing values and moral discourses within the black working class. Juxtaposing the sacred and profane forces a rethinking of the oft-rendered image of a working class that is the monolithic and coherent bearer of an "authentic" black consciousness. Black working-class culture, as the generative site of the blues and the zoot suit, produced as well Pentecostalism and the Nation of Islam.[57] Religious culture, like the blues, found expression in the black vernacular.

NOTES

1. See, for example, Houston A. Baker Jr., *Blues, Ideology, and Afro-American Literature: A Vernacular Theory* (Chicago: University of Chicago Press, 1984); Hazel V. Carby, "Policing the Black Woman's Body in an Urban Context," *Critical Inquiry* 18 (Summer 1992): 738–55; Carby, "'It Jus Be's Dat Way Sometime': The Sexual Politics of Women's Blues," in *Unequal Sisters: A Multi-cultural Reader in U.S. Women's History*, ed. Vicki L. Ruiz and Ellen Carol DuBois, 2nd ed. (New York: Routledge, 1994), 330–41.

2. See Ann duCille's important critique that this emphasis has caused the blues to be thought of as a "metonym for authentic blackness." Ann duCille, "Blues Notes on Black Sexuality: Sex and the Texts of Jessie Fauset and Nella Larsen," *Journal of the History of Sexuality* 3 (January 1993): 418–44, esp. 419–20. Published since the presentation of this paper at the Race Matters Conference in April 1994 is Farah Griffin's rich interdisciplinary study of the migration narrative. See Farah Jasmine Griffin, *"Who Set You Flowin'?": The African-American Migration Narrative* (New York: Oxford University Press, 1995), 61–63. Griffin draws some of her analysis of working-class religion from an earlier version of this paper, in particular Evelyn Brooks Higginbotham, "'Out of the Age of the Voice': The Black Church and Discourses of Modernity" (paper delivered at the Conference on the Black Public Sphere in the Era of Reagan and Bush, University of Chicago, October 14, 1993.

3. I am focusing on religious records in contradistinction to the interesting work of scholars of religion who locate religious inflections (theology and theodicy) in blues and rap. For example, Jon Michael Spencer finds in the blues and Michael Dyson finds in rap and in the songs of Michael Jackson moral reflections on evil, hypocrisy, suffering, justice, and biblical lore. See Jon Michael Spencer, *Blues and Evil* (Knoxville: University of Tennessee Press, 1993), xxviii, 35, 43–53. Michael Eric Dyson, *Reflecting Black: African-American Cultural Criticism* (Minneapolis: University of Minnesota Press, 1993), 35–60.

4. I am indebted to the following scholars for their pioneering work on race records in both the blues and religious traditions: Paul Oliver, *Songsters and Saints: Vocal Traditions on Race Records* (Cambridge: Cambridge University

Press, 1984); Robert M. W. Dixon and John Godrich, *Recording the Blues* (New York: Stein & Day, 1970); Jeff Todd Titon, *Early Downhome Blues: A Musical and Cultural Analysis* (Urbana: University of Illinois Press, 1977); Tony Heilbut, *The Gospel Sound: Good News and Bad Times* (New York: Simon & Schuster, 1971).

5. Hughes is quoted in Lawrence Levine, *Black Culture and Black Consciousness: Afro-American Folk Thought from Slavery to Freedom* (New York: Oxford University Press, 1978), 180.

6. The advertisement appeared in the *Chicago Defender*, October 8, 1927, 8.

7. See the following: Cheryl Townsend Gilkes, "'Together and in Harness': Women's Traditions in the Sanctified Church," *Signs: Journal of Women in Culture and Society* 10 (Summer 1985): 679; Arthur Huff Fauset, *Black Gods of the Metropolis: Negro Religious Cults of the Urban North* (Philadelphia: University of Pennsylvania Press, 1944); Melvin D. Williams, *Community in a Black Pentecostal Church: An Anthropological Study* (University of Pittsburgh Press, 1974); Arthur E. Paris, *Black Pentecostalism: Southern Religion in an Urban World* (Amherst: University of Massachusetts Press, 1982).

8. Levine, *Black Culture*, 200

9. Evelyn Brooks Higginbotham, *Righteous Discontent: The Women's Movement in the Black Baptist Church, 1880–1920* (Cambridge, Mass.: Harvard University Press, 1993), 42–46.

10. W. E. Burghardt Du Bois, "The Talented Tenth," in Booker T. Washington et al., *The Negro Problem: A Series of Articles by Representative Negroes of Today* (New York: James Pott, 1903), 54–55.

11. Elizabeth Kilham, "Sketches in Color," is quoted in Dena J. Epstein, *Sinful Times and Spirituals: Black Folk Music to the Civil War* (Urbana: University of Illinois Press, 1977), 277.

12. Daniel Alexander Payne, *Recollections of Seventy Years* (New York: Arno Press and the New York Times, 1969), 253–54.

13. Levine, *Black Culture*, 162–66; also see analysis of the "politics of respectability" in Higginbotham, *Righteous Discontent*, 187–99.

14. James M. Trotter, *Music and Some Highly Musical People* (Chicago: Afro-American Press, 1969; reprint of 1880 ed.), 58–59, 285.

15. Sutton Griggs is quoted and discussed in Wilson Jeremiah Moses, *The Golden Age of Black Nationalism, 1850–1925* (New York: Oxford University Press, 1978), 170–93.

16. Virginia W. Broughton, "Need of Distinctive Literature," *National Baptist Union* 13 (December 1902).

17. Elsa Barkley Brown, "Negotiating and Transforming the Public Sphere: African American Political Life in the Transition from Slavery to Freedom," *Public Culture* 7 (November 1994): 135–36; Levine, *Black Culture*, 24.

18. Daniel Webster Davis, 'Weh Down Souf and Other Poems (Cleveland: Helman-Taylor Co., 1897), 54–56, as quoted in Brown, "Negotiating and Transforming the Public Sphere," 136.

19. Frances Smith Foster, ed., Minnie's Sacrifice; Sowing and Reaping; Trial and Triumph: Three Rediscovered Novels by Frances E. W. Harper (Boston: Beacon Press, 1994), xxiv–xxvi.

20. For a discussion of the role of photographic imagery in racial reconstruction, see Henry Louis Gates, Jr., "The Trope of a New Negro and the Reconstruction of the Image of the Black," Representations 24 (Fall 1988): 141.

21. For discussion of the literati during the Harlem Renaissance, see David Levering Lewis, When Harlem Was in Vogue (New York: Oxford University Press, 1989; originally published by Knopf, 1981), 119–55.

22. Levine, Black Culture, 179–80.

23. For a discussion of black consumerism during the 1920s and 1930s, see Liz Cohen, Making a New Deal: Industrial Workers in Chicago, 1919–1939 (New York: Cambridge University Press, 1990), 147–58.

24. Richard Wightman Fox and T. J. Jackson Lears, eds., The Culture of Consumption: Critical Essays in American History, 1880–1980 (New York: Pantheon, 1983), 3, also ix–xiii.

25. For a discussion of the inability of a black-owned record company, the Black Swan Company, to compete successfully against the large white corporations, such as Victor and Paramount, see Dixon and Godrich, Recording the Blues, 13, 21–32, 44.

26. Kwame Anthony Appiah, In My Father's House: Africa in the Philosophy of Culture (New York: Oxford University Press, 1992), 145.

27. Here I am reminded of Houston Baker's brilliant discussion of the "blending . . . of class and mass—poetic mastery discovered as a function of deformative [subversive] folk sound—constitutes the essence of black discursive modernism." Baker, Modernism and the Harlem Renaissance, 93; the oral narrative in literature is described by Henry Louis Gates, Jr., as the "speakerly text." See Gates, The Signifying Monkey: A Theory of African-American Literary Criticism (New York: Oxford University Press, 1988), xxv–xxvi, 181.

28. Sutton Griggs, A Hero Closes a War, Victor 21706-B (1928), and A Surprise Answer to Prayer, Victor 21706-A (1928); Oliver, Songsters and Saints, 146–47.

29. Paul Oliver discusses the popular appeal of the recorded sermons of black Baptist, Holiness, and Pentecostal preachers in Oliver, Songsters and Saints, 140–228; Dixon and Godrich, Recording the Blues, 38, 56–57.

30. Oliver, Songsters and Saints, 155.

31. Record companies began to scour southern cities and hamlets in the mid-1920s in search of down-home religious and secular talent. Jeff Titon argues,

however, that part of the return to the old-time was part of a "folk" vogue that swept American culture in the post–World War I period as a counter-voice to the increasing sophistication and slickness of urbanity and the Jazz Age of the 1920s. Titon argues that race records must be seen as a part of this larger vogue, which also included "hillbilly" music, Broadway plays about mountain life in North Carolina and Kentucky during the 1923–24 season, and a general romanticization of a simpler, agrarian society. Titon, *Early Downhome Blues*, 215–16, 243–45.

32. *Chicago Defender*, October 1, 1927, and May 12, 1928.

33. See the analysis of recorded sermons in Michael Harris's biography of Thomas A. Dorsey: Michael W. Harris, *Rise of Gospel Blues: The Music of Thomas Andrew Dorsey in the Urban Church* (New York: Oxford University Press, 1992), 156–63.

34. Oliver, *Songsters and Saints*, 140–45, 155, 159.

35. Recorded sermons seem to have enjoyed the greatest popularity between 1926 and 1931. The onset of the Great Depression caused a precipitous de-cline in the release of sermonic records. Gospel music records continue to be popular to this day. Moreover, gospel queens outlasted the classic blues singers of the 1920s in popularity. Dixon and Godrich, *Recording the Blues*, 85; Oliver, *Songsters and Saints*, 188–98, 203–5; Heilbut, *The Gospel Sound*, 9–35.

36. Oliver, *Songsters and Saints*, 183–87. See advertisements for Rev. Leora Ross's *Dry Bones in the Valley* and *A Gambler Broke in a Strange Land*, Okeh 8486, and Jessie May Hill's *The Crucifixion of Christ* and *God Rode in the Windstorm*, Okeh 8490, in the *Chicago Defender*, August 27, 1927, and September 24, 1927; also Jerma Jackson, "Testifying at the Cross: Thomas An-drew Dorsey, Sister Rosetta Tharpe, and the Politics of African-American Sacred and Secular Music" (Ph.D. diss., Rutgers University, 1995), 157–80, 263–71.

37. Oliver, *Songsters and Saints*, 203–5.

38. Harris, *Rise of Gospel Blues*, 182–208.

39. Houston A. Baker, Jr., *Modernism and the Harlem Renaissance* (Chicago: University of Chicago Press, 1987), 93.

40. Anderson notes that her church made possible her initial training at the studio of Giuseppe Boghetti by helping to pay the costs for instruction. Mar-ian Anderson, *My Lord, What a Morning* (New York: Viking Press, 1956), 7, 23–38, 49.

41. Michael Harris notes that Mahalia Jackson received voice training from gospel-blues songwriter Thomas Dorsey, then music director at Pilgrim Bap-tist Church in Chicago but formerly a blues lyricist and piano accompanist to Ma Rainey, Bessie Smith, and other blues queens. Harris, *Rise of Gospel Blues*, 259–60.

42. Quoted in ibid., 258; Mahalia Jackson noted in her autobiography: "In those days the big colored churches didn't want me and they didn't let me in. I had to make it my business to pack the little basement-hall congregations and store-front churches and get their respect that way. When they began to see the crowds I drew, the big churches began to sit up and take notice." Mahalia Jackson, *Moving' On Up* (New York: Hawthorn Books, 1966).

43. I am indebted to Quandra Prettyman for permission to reprint this poem, which is found in its entirety in Arnold Adoff, comp., *The Poetry of Black America: Anthology of the Twentieth Century* (New York: Harper & Row, 1973).

44. Harris, *Rise of Gospel Blues*, 258–71.

45. Ibid., 269–70.

46. The new urban context of the 1920s unleashed strivings for "authentic" racial expression in music (blues and jazz), in literature (Harlem Renaissance writers such as Zora Neale Hurston and Langston Hughes), and in political movements such as Marcus Garvey's Universal Negro Improvement Association. Black church culture must be situated in this historical context.

47. Oliver, *Songsters and Saints*, 145, 155, 159.

48. Ibid., 146; Rev. Mary Nelson, *Better Get Ready for Judgement*, Vocalion 1109-B.

49. Baker argues that the train represents the migrants' perceptions of freedom and mobility. However, Carby argues that the train imagery holds distinctively gendered connotations, since male blues singers more frequently associate the train with freedom and mobility than women. For blues women, train images often convey meanings of desertion and loneliness. See Baker, *Blues, Ideology, and Afro-American Literature*, 11–12; Carby, "'It Jus Be's Dat Way Sometime,'" 335.

50. In the religious race records, the train represents the vehicle of punishment to the wicked and salvation to the righteous. See Rev. J. M. Gates, *Death's Black Train Is Coming*, Victor 20211 (1926); Rev. A. W. Nix, *Black Diamond Express to Hell*, which was issued in six parts. Parts 1 and 2 appeared on Vocalion 1098 in May 1927, parts 3 and 4 on Vocalian 1421, released in November 1929, and parts 5 and 6 on Vocalion 1486 in June 1930. Nix also recorded *White Flyer to Heaven*, Vocalion 1170 (1927). Dixon and Godrich, *Recording the Blues*, 57; Paul Oliver, Max Harrison, and William Bolcom, *The New Grove Gospel, Blues, and Jazz with Spirituals and Ragtime* (New York: Norton, 1986), 194–95.

51. Dixon and Godrich, *Recording the Blues*, 39, 57.

52. Rev. J. C. Burnett, *The Downfall of Nebuchadnezzar*, Columbia 14166 (1926).

53. Gates, *Samson and the Woman*, Victor 21125 (1927).

54. Gates, *The First Born Was a Murderer*, Victor 21125 (1927); *Death Might Be Your Santa Claus*, Okeh 8413 (1926); *Did You Spend Christmas in Jail?*, Okeh 8753-A; *No Room in the Jailhouse*, Okeh 8753-B (1929); and *Dying Gambler*, Okeh 8387 (1926); Oliver, Harrison, and Bolcom, *The New Grove Gospel*, 194–95.

55. Carby, "Policing the Black Woman's Body," 739–55.

56. Hans A. Baer and Merrill Singer, *African-American Religion in the Twentieth Century: Varieties of Protest and Accommodation* (Knoxville: University of Tennessee Press, 1992), 147–78, 215–21; Jill Watts, *God, Harlem U.S.A.: The Father Divine Story* (Berkeley: University of California Press, 1992), 161–62.

57. "I knew that our strict moral code and discipline was what repelled them most," stated Malcolm X in reference to the fact that many blacks came to hear him but far fewer joined the Muslims. He continued: "No Muslim who followed Elijah Muhammad could dance, gamble, date, attend movies, or sports, or take long vacations from work." Malcolm X with the assistance of Alex Haley, *The Autobiography of Malcolm X* (New York: Ballantine, 1973), 221; for a brilliant analysis of the zoot suit culture that attracted the young Malcolm, see Robin D. G. Kelley, "The Riddle of the Zoot: Malcolm Little and Black Cultural Politics During World War II," in *Malcolm X: In Our Own Image*, ed. Joe Wood (New York: St. Martin's Press, 1992), 155–82.

WHAT IS BLACK CULTURE?

David Lionel Smith

■

Could this compulsion to put invisibility down in black and white
be thus an urge to make music of invisibility?

—Ralph Ellison

I

A T THE END OF Amiri Baraka's play *Dutchman*, the protagonist Clay delivers a rambling monologue, expressing his indignation at insults from his antagonist, Lula. He complains: "If I'm a middle-class fake white man . . . let me be. . . . It's none of your business. You don't know anything except what's there for you to see. An act. Lies. Device. Not the pure heart, the pumping black heart."[1] Subsequently, he compares himself to Charlie Parker and Bessie Smith, declaring that "if Bessie Smith had killed some white people she wouldn't have needed that music. She could have talked very straight and plain about the world" (*Dutchman*, 35). A moment later the white woman Lula, perhaps inspired by his call for "a simple knife thrust," stabs him to death.

This notorious scene, like many works of the Black Arts movement, which *Dutchman* anticipates, conflates the anxiety over racial identity with attempts at cultural criticism. Despite his bland facade, Clay argues, his unseen self is truly black; and true blackness is angry. Black art, however, is "artifice," "lies," a sublimation of the honest racial anger that would otherwise express itself as physical violence. Obviously, to associate blackness with violence is politically dubious, and it leads to an antiaesthetic that defines black art as the expression of violent passion. We know that such thinking led the Black Arts critics to dismiss nearly all of the African-American literature written prior to 1965. This attitude is neatly articulated in Larry Neal's influential essay "And Shine Swam On": "Listen to James Brown scream. Ask yourself, then: Have you ever heard a Negro poet sing like that? Of course not . . . Our music has always been far ahead of our literature."[2] Unfortunately, in subordinating poetry to singing, Neal fails to consider that poetry may have its own unique cultural work to do. Besides, James Brown does more musically than just scream.

Whether such an aesthetic of violent passion harnessed the best creative energies of its adherents is a question that we might best answer by asking ourselves how many Black Arts works we continue to read for our own pleasure rather than for purposes of teaching and historical study. Though Black Arts theory may have reflected honestly the anger and rebelliousness of its era, it too often followed the blueprint established by Baraka's Clay, combining shrill assertions about black identity with reductive and self-serving exercises in cultural criticism. By the mid-1970s, Black Arts critics such as Baraka and Neal began to moderate their views, developing broader and less condescending approaches to the study of culture. In any case, I would argue that the impasse reached by Black Arts theorists was largely due to inherent entailments of racial thinking, not to failures of their own intelligence. America has always defined the Negro as a child of nature, not a man or woman of culture. Thus, given the common sense of our culture, "black art" is a contradiction in terms.

Is "black culture" also a contradiction in terms? Hasn't America taught us to associate blackness with savagery, ignorance, crime, and inferiority—the very antitheses of "culture"? Blackness has signified spontaneity, not self-consciousness, the lack of culture, not cultural difference; and correspondingly, black people have been regarded by America as social problems, not social partners. This being the case, perhaps my subtitle ought to be, with an apologetic nod to W. E. B. Du Bois: "How Does It Feel to Be an Oxymoron?" As most black intellectuals have always recognized, this dilemma is the precondition of black consciousness in America. In this essay I want to consider some entailments of thinking about blackness and culture.

II

Before we can define "black culture," we need first to define or to identify "black people." Otherwise, "black culture" becomes a floating signifier, detached from any particular social grounding. Unfortunately, no one has ever succeeded in producing an adequate definition of this social category. Black people can have white skin, blue eyes, and naturally straight hair; they can be half, three-quarters, seven-eighths or more white; they can even deny or not know that they are black. Claim what they will or look as they may, they are still by law and custom black. Race is a slippery concept in our society. In effect, race is a set of social prescriptions invented by slaveholders and their descendants to exploit and constrain persons classified as black. These white supremacists maximized the socially inferior category by relegating to it everyone who possessed even the remotest of African ancestry. Though such counterintuitive accounts of blackness make a mockery of scientific reasoning and even of common understandings of mixing (as in painting, cooking, or animal husbandry), the social utility of racial hierarchy is immediately obvious, and thus we have accepted foolishness in the service of utility. No one can define blackness, but we Americans embrace it as a matter of common sense.

For the sake of argument, let us accept race as an a priori. Does blackness entail specific forms of culture? If so, how do we know what those forms are? When Wynton Marsalis plays a Haydn concerto or Leontyne Price sings a Verdi opera, is that black culture? Similarly, when Dr. John plays the blues or Travis Tritt sings soul, is that black culture? In all these cases, our answer is probably no. Yet black people relish a game invented by James Naismith, a white man. Don't we commonly accept basketball as part of black culture? Do we exclude John Coltrane from black culture because he plays a French saxophone or spurn B. B. King's blues if his Lucille is a Gibson guitar? Is participation in black culture a biological privilege, or can anybody join? Conversely, is black culture obligatory for black people, and does blackness preclude them from mastering nonblack cultural modes? Such questions are impertinent, because in the absence of fundamental definitions, they cannot be answered. Besides, they defy our racial common sense. We feel that we know who and what is truly black. So what if we cannot explain what constitutes that blackness?

I want to argue that our reliance on "common sense" racial notions subverts our ability to produce accurate theoretical or even descriptive accounts of our social and cultural circumstances. This is not to imply, however, that we can simply dismiss racial categories. Spurious or not, they continue to inform our consciousness. The challenge is to understand what race is, how it functions, and ultimately to theorize how we might endeavor within a culture bound by race to subvert the subordinating strictures that race was designed to perpetuate.

III

In his essay "Critical Notes on an Attempt at a Popular Presentation of Marxism by Bukharin," Gramsci defines common sense as

> the world conception absorbed uncritically by various social and cultural circles in which the moral individuality of the average man is developed. Common sense is not a single conception, identical in time and space: it is the 'folk-lore' of philosophy and like folk-lore it appears in innumerable forms: its fundamental and most characteristic trait is that of being (even in single brains) disintegrated, incoherent, inconsecutive, in keeping with the social and cultural position of the multitudes whose philosophy it is.[3]

Viewed sentimentally, common sense appears to be a natural endowment of the folk—a bedrock of wisdom that only fools would challenge. For Gramsci it is a primary impediment to the liberation of the masses, because it is an undifferentiated mix of habit, superstition, fact, hearsay, dissent, prejudice, etc.: the ideology of common experience. Common sense is not critically self-conscious, and its function is to facilitate conformity and adaptation to familiar circumstances. It thrives on familiarity and fears change, and therefore common sense is profoundly conservative. Thus, paradoxically, those who wish to change the status quo must combat common sense and thereby risk acquiring the semblance of fools.

Race is a commonsense notion. It falls apart under rational scrutiny, yet it is exceedingly difficult for us to attack. The blackness that marks us off for permanent subordination and various forms of abuse is also what gives us a sense of identity, community, and history. It is our "we." Thus, to assault racial identity makes us appear foolishly in rebellion against common sense; and even worse, it seems to be a self-loathing assault against ourselves and our community. The self-vindicating character of common sense gives notions like race a powerful durability. Common sense, the conservative, self-perpetuating ideology of common folk, poses a special problem for progressive intellectuals, who are by definition committed to social change.

Gramsci's argument regarding the relationship between intellectuals and the folk has often been misrepresented. His term "organic intellectuals" has frequently been taken to mean intellectuals from the grass roots or intellectuals who really are attuned with and embedded in their culture. Such a misreading appeals to the nostalgic impulses of critics who feel troubled by their distance from the actual day-to-day lives of the folk with whom they identify themselves. Black intellectuals ensconced in white institutions are especially susceptible to this dilemma. It is tempting for such critics to believe that sharing the tastes of their communities for certain music, films, sports figures, etc., and declaring those enthusiasms makes them "organic intellectuals." Whether they invoke Gramsci or not, many contemporary cultural critics hold such a view. This sentimentalized notion of identifying with the folk is, needless to say, the exact opposite of what Gramsci advocated.

The opening of Gramsci's essay "The Formation of Intellectuals" provides his most familiar statement regarding "organic intellectuals":

Every social class, coming into existence on the original basis of an essential function in the world of economic production, creates with itself, organically, one or more groups of intellectuals who give it homogeneity and consciousness of its function not only in the economic field but in the social and political field as well. (*The Modern Prince*, 118)

This suggests a close correlation between intellectuals and the class they represent. We should note, however, that Gramsci's examples in the paragraphs that follow are dominant classes such as capitalists and aristocrats, who constitute the hegemonic elite of society. The organic intellectuals of these classes, as Gramsci argues here and in other works, such as *The Modern Prince*, are rarely useful models for intellectuals representing subordinate classes to emulate. Indeed, the organic intellectuals of the dominant classes are comfortably ensconced in hegemonic institutions such as the academy and the church. Gramsci's sympathy, then, is with the organic intellectuals of the oppressed class, not with all organic intellectuals.

For Gramsci the fundamental problem is how to bring into existence a self-conscious proletariat. The organic intellectuals he envisions to awaken the proletariat to its historical destiny must, of course, be organized into a vanguard: the Communist Party. In order to succeed, they must undo the work of indoctrination and acculturation that the hegemonic intellectuals—professors, lawyers, bankers, clerics, etc.—have so successfully perpetuated. Furthermore, they must unmake indigenous peasant and proletarian culture in order to remake it. The various essays and musings collected in Gramsci's *Prison Notebooks* are primarily concerned with theorizing what this work might entail within the specific social context of Fascist Italy. African Americans are not necessarily analogous to the proletariat, but the challenge for intellectuals is analogous, and Gramsci provides us a splendid model of seriously revolutionary cultural criticism. For intellectuals who represent the interests of an oppressed group, and not their oppressors, it is not enough to be merely "organic." One must challenge the acculturation—the common sense—that holds one's group in oppression. One must challenge, not endorse, hegemonic consensus. In short, the "organic intellectuals" of an oppressed group must be the most thorough, unsparing, and demanding critics of that culture.

African-American intellectuals have generally adopted the opposite strategy, embracing the affirmation of racial identity as an obligatory gesture of solidarity. This gesture has been conventionalized in various forms. For example, popular black musical forms—spirituals, blues, soul, rap, etc.—are routinely treated as synecdoches of black culture, and by celebrating these forms, black intellectuals from Douglass to ourselves have identified themselves with "the people." This gesture is doubtless heartfelt, but in scholarly contexts, it often displaces serious critical engagement with the actual complexities and multicultural origins of black music and offers instead cultural criticism as an act of self-vindication. This poses a fundamental question for us to consider: Is the purpose of our writing on black culture to affirm or to alter blackness as we know it? If we seek the latter, how is such transformation to be achieved?

Dutchman provides a useful vehicle for considering this question. Baraka's Clay exemplifies the cultural critic as self-vindicator. There is a fundamental conflict between the requirements of an adequate cultural criticism and the personal, psychological compulsions of Clay to articulate black culture in terms of his own self-expressive needs. To say this is not to invoke some antiquated distinction between objective and subjective expression. Clay's account is inadequate by other, simpler criteria. For example, he substitutes ideological declaration for descriptive accuracy. How can he infer that Bessie Smith's unstated premise is "Kiss my unruly black ass"? Though his claim sounds plausible, he offers no textual evidence to support it. Thus, if we accept his view of Bessie Smith, it can only be because we find him, not his argument, persuasive. As presented, his argument is intuitive rather than analytical, and insofar as we take seriously the notion that critical discourse should be analytical, we must correspondingly hesitate to endorse under this heading assertions such as Clay's. Obviously, Clay's speech is a dramatic moment in a play, not an essay in cultural criticism. On the other hand, there is no dramatic necessity that his tirade be expressed as a sweeping claim about black cultural history, complete with biographical illustrations. In effect, Baraka uses the dramatic moment as a platform on which cultural criticism struts about in the guise of spontaneous emotion.

Clay's statement about Bessie Smith and Charlie Parker links lowdown and high-brow artists and thereby purports to designate some general truth about black culture. Both artists, according to Clay, are essentially defined by the equation of blackness and anger. But in fact, Clay is making a statement about himself—very literally so in the play—and by framing it as a statement about black culture in general, he pursues the rhetorical objective of legitimating his own views and personality by representing himself as typically "black," just like Smith and Parker. In effect, Clay's monologue is a very fine instance of personal essay, which uses its engagement with the external world as a mode of self-expression. Personal essay, in this instance, is compelling because it renders the world in terms of Clay's experiences and insights; but it is problematic because it also imposes Clay's limitations upon the world that it renders.

Those limitations are quite apparent in Clay's representation of Smith's and Parker's art. According to Clay, their only artistic inspiration is anger at white people, which they sublimate as music in lieu of committing honest acts of violence. This is perhaps a clever adaptation of Freud's aesthetic theories, but at the same time, it dismisses the role of imagination, intelligence, discipline, and hard work in the making of blues and jazz, not to mention the spectrum of other normal emotions, such as love, sadness, and amusement. The narrowness of Clay's own obsessions leads to a critical argument that is stiflingly reductive.

At the same time, his strident claims about black culture divert attention away from his own specific neuroses. As his comments throughout the play suggest, Clay is painfully insecure about his merits as a poet, his middle-class, New Jersey background, and even his name. When Lula condemns "those hopeless colored names creeping out of New Jersey," such as Lloyd, Norman, Leonard, Warren, and Everett, Clay responds: "Gag . . ." (*Dutchman*, 15). Everett is, in fact, the author's own name: Everett LeRoi Jones. Even in his long soliloquy, Clay pauses to voice his anxieties about being marginal and irrelevant to other black people, lamenting: "My people. They don't need me to claim them. . . . They don't need all those words" (*Dutchman*, 37–38). Rather than elaborate this worry in more detail, however, Clay turns instead to a hollow threat that middle-class, assimilationist Negroes like himself may one day rise up to murder white people. Thus, by invoking reductive stereotypes of black anger as cultural essence, the insecure poet recasts himself as the avenging hero. To such pomposity, Lula's deflating knife thrust may be the aptest response.

IV

In *The American Evasion of Philosophy*, Cornel West argues that "once one gives up on the search for foundations and the quest for certainty, human

inquiry into truth and knowledge shifts to the social and communal circumstances under which persons can communicate and cooperate in the
process of acquiring knowledge."[4] In this pragmatist spirit I propose that
we ought to abandon attempts to understand race and blackness in terms
of foundations and definitional certainty. Instead, we should take our actual experience of race and blackness as our starting point. I mean both
our historical experience and our autobiographies, but since blackness is a
social rather than a personal concept, the former must be considered primary. We must understand what it means to be socially constituted as
black, but beyond this, insofar as we are committed to inquiry as praxis,
we must also seek to understand the point of leverage that blackness gives
us to make ourselves a force for change. Indeed, to acknowledge openly
the arbitrariness of racial categories will be an important, though not sufficient, step toward the demystification of America's exploitative racial
culture.

Du Bois described brilliantly the dilemma of the black professional
class as a particular form of double consciousness, a "contradiction of double aims" felt by those "striving to be a co-worker in the kingdom of culture."[5] This dilemma for Du Bois was not just psychology but rather a
direct reflection of contradictory facts. Black intellectuals are implicated
in white culture by their educations and in black culture by social, political, and emotional ties, thereby representing both and neither. Because
the impulses of black and white America conflict, the plight of the black
professional is to ascertain how to avoid being "torn asunder." Du Bois's sociological insight is even more pertinent now than it was in 1903; and as
I have indicated, it is reflected in the nature of much African-American
cultural criticism.

Du Bois was right to describe such double consciousness as debilitating. Still, we have an opportunity, even an obligation, to recognize that
our peculiar position gives us a unique standpoint, an enabling standpoint, as critics of modern and postmodern culture. Georg Lukács made
an analogous point regarding the historical perspective of the proletariat:

> . . . the same growth of insight into the nature of society, which
> reflects the protracted death struggle of the bourgeoisie, entails a

steady growth in the strength of the proletariat. For the proletariat the truth is a weapon that brings victory; and the more ruthless, the greater the victory. This makes more comprehensible the desperate fury with which bourgeois science assails historical materialism; for as soon as the bourgeoisie is forced to take up its stand on this terrain, it is lost. And, at the same time, this explains why the proletariat and *only* the proletariat can discern in the correct understanding of *the nature of society* a power-factor of the first, and perhaps decisive importance.[6]

Needless to say, the class relations articulated by Marxist analysis describe a very precise historical development. The situation of African Americans is not equivalent to that of the proletariat. My point is not to posit such an equivalence but rather to suggest that understanding Lukács's class analysis may help us to think in a more sophisticated way about the standpoint of blackness.

For Lukács, the proletariat has a special destiny, contradicting its actual position as an oppressed and exploited class, to triumph over the bourgeoisie and to usher in a new epoch of social life. The proletariat is a majority, and unlike the bourgeoisie, a minority class that must rule through coercion and deception, its best interest is served by a will to truth. Only by comprehending the truth of its social position can the proletariat end bourgeois oppression; and the greater its oppression, the greater its need to comprehend the truth of its historical situation. One cannot claim for African Americans the historical role of the proletariat, but the experience of slavery, exploitation, and racist oppression constitutes blackness as a unique standpoint of historical consciousness. Consequently, certain aspects of American history and culture cannot be adequately understood unless the critically self-conscious African-American perspective is adequately taken into account. The challenge is to become critically self-conscious regarding the entailments of our own social position.

Cornel West addressed this problem explicitly when he called for black intellectuals to "articulate a new 'regime of truth' linked to, yet not confined by, indigenous institutional practices, permeated by the kinetic orality and emotional physicality, the rhythmic syncopation, the protean improvisation and the religious, rhetorical and antiphonal repetition of African-American life." American racial discourse assigns to black intellectuals a generic mandate to address the Negro Problem. As West's work so splendidly exemplifies, we can claim a larger role for ourselves by envisioning "the emergence of new cultural forms which prefigure (and point toward) a post-Western civilization."[7]

But even as we expand our purview, we ought also to reexamine our work as critics of black culture, talking into account the issues raised by Gramsci's critique of common sense. To what degree do our practices as critics reinforce the established, repressive, commonsensical notions of race, blackness, and culture? We must have the courage to risk alienating ourselves by challenging common sense, by being true critics and not mere celebrants of black culture, and by subverting the premises that define blackness. Perhaps in losing ourselves, we will find ourselves. As Walter Benjamin reminds us, "in every era the attempt must be made anew to wrest tradition away from a conformism that is about to overpower it. . . . Only that historian will have the gift of fanning the spark of hope in the past who is firmly convinced that *even the dead* will not be safe if the enemy triumphs. And this enemy has not yet ceased to be victorious."[8] Benjamin refers here to the constant struggle to control how the past is understood and what facts and persons are included or excluded in the official accounts. In our own context, so long as the slave master's racial prescriptions dictate our categories and areas of inquiry, the enemy remains triumphant.

V

In his seventh thesis on the philosophy of history, Benjamin describes the spectacles staged by victors:

Whoever has emerged victorious participates to this day in the triumphal procession in which the present rulers step over those who are lying prostrate. According to traditional practice, the spoils are carried along in the procession. They are called cultural treasures, and a historical materialist views them with cautious detachment. . . . They owe their existence not only to the efforts of the great minds and talents who have created them, but also to the anonymous toil of their contemporaries. There is no document of civilization which is not at the same time a document of barbarism. . . . A historical materialist therefore dissociates himself from it as far as possible. He regards it as his task to brush history against the grain. (*Illuminations,* 256–57)

Though Benjamin obviously refers here to Nazi spectacles, he also refers more broadly to those struggles that define cultural and historical discourse. Nazis are not the only ones who repress dissenting voices and exclude subordinate groups from their official accounts. Every group that endeavors to assert its own cultural hegemony writes histories that engage in its own version of this process. It is easy enough to embrace Benjamin's sympathy with victims; but we must also note the thoroughness of his skepticism, which looks coldly upon every victor and every document. To rub history against the grain is to raise the ragged ends and expose imperfections. This conception of the critic as a detached but committed observer produces a quite different kind of cultural criticism from the affirmative, in-group partisanship that has been the preferred mode among African-American intellectuals. Perhaps we need more skepticism.

In this context the work of Cornel West is especially pertinent. Throughout his career West has been a truly critical cultural critic. While he can be almost reverential in his appreciations of figures such as James Baldwin and Marvin Gaye, West has always offered balanced assessments, and his judgments can be astringently unsentimental. His "The Dilemma of the Black Intellectual," arguably the most influential of his essays, exhibits his remarkable combination of broad erudition, judiciousness, and scalpel-like analysis. It offers a historical overview of black intellectuals, an analysis of the social factors that have facilitated or impeded black intellectual production, an assessment of various intellectual traditions and models, and a set of recommendations for developing a new cadre of black intellectuals.

Eschewing the self-advertisement, the self-vindication, and the opportunistic embracing of black culture that have characterized so much of African-American cultural criticism, West offers instead a harsh critique of the failure of black intellectuals as a class, asserting that the quality of black intellectual production is actually worse in the postintegration era than it was previously. His criticisms, however, are not in the spirit of trashing other black people but rather of advocating specific higher standards of performance. Thus, he concludes his essay with a call for the "Black intellectual as critical organic catalyst," and offers a brief blueprint for the social networks and institutional structures needed to develop such scholar-activists. West's self-conscious nod toward Gramsci reflects his fundamental scholarly commitment that one must both master and transcend the work of earlier theorists. This essay, then, is Cornel West's effort to assess the value of Marxism, Foucault, Gramsci, and others in the process of appraising and reconceiving the work of black intellectuals. This is a cultural criticism that endeavors not just to interpret the world but to change it.

This point has been lost on some of Cornel West's critics. Some have complained, for example, that his emphasis on African-American "nihilism" in *Race Matters* blames the victims and offers validation to the arguments of conservatives. Some conservatives may, indeed, have seized upon this point and, with blatant intellectual dishonesty, used it to buttress their own "black pathology" assertions. West's conception, however, has only the most superficial connection to such arguments. Nihilism, for him, is a cultural manifestation of conditions created by capitalism: "a jungle ruled by a cutthroat market morality devoid of any faith in deliverance or hope for freedom." Consequently, in West's view the behavior so commonly described as "black pathology" is rather "the tragic response of a people bereft of resources in confronting the workings of U.S. capitalist society."[9] Unlike the work of conservatives who demonize black people in order to justify reactionary social policies, West's critique of nihilism endeavors to provide a thorough understanding of the black situation—both objective and subjective—as a necessary first step in a process of social redemption and transformation. Such cultural criticism is, in the best sense, an act of social commitment.

VI

Cultural criticism, like any other form of inquiry, raises questions and offers analyses; but more fundamentally, it constitutes its own object of study. When we examine instances of cultural criticism, we necessarily attend to explicit assertions, but we also should scrutinize the vision of culture implicit in the framing of those assertions. Thus, we assess Clay's declarations regarding Bessie Smith and Charlie Parker, but we should also examine the depiction of Clay, Lula, and the entire symbolic universe constituted within the play *Dutchman*. Clay's declarations as a cultural critic may strike us as self-serving, naive, and wrong-headed; but the value of the play should not be reduced to our judgment regarding one character's pontifications. Clay is not just an interpreter of black culture; he is, like the play itself, a manifestation of black culture. He represents a particular social type within a specific historical moment—the young, middle-class, black male aesthete—replete with the quirks and preoccupations of that class. Thus, we can see Clay's ideas in association with a social type, an individual, and a rhetorical situation. Baraka may or may not have endorsed the views expressed by Clay. Regardless, he has created a cultural artifact that we may analyze at any of several levels. The choice is ours whether to join in Clay's parade or to brush him against his grain.

Because of the complex layering that is inherent to literary works, literary artists are among our most valuable cultural critics. We take for granted the value of literature as a mode of expression. Perhaps we would be wise to think more seriously about literature as a mode of knowledge. To illustrate this point, let us consider a passage from Toni Morrison's novel *The Bluest Eye*. After recounting the personal history of Cholly Breedlove, a pathetic drunkard and incestuous child molester, the author comments:

> The pieces of Cholly's life could become coherent only in the head of a musician. Only those who talk through the gold of curved metal, or in the touch of black-and-white rectangles and taut skins and strings echoing from wooden corridors, could give true form to his life. Only they would know how to connect the

heart of a red watermelon to the asafetida bag to the muscadine to the flashlight on his behind to the fists of money to the lemonade in a Mason jar to a man called Blue and come up with what all of that meant in joy, in pain, in anger, in love, and give it its final and pervading ache of freedom. Only a musician would sense, know, without even knowing that he knew, that Cholly was free.[10]

A character such as Cholly poses a daunting challenge: how does one depict a monster without rendering him subhuman? Morrison rises brilliantly to this challenge, constructing an account of Cholly's personal history that makes his sensibility and behavior altogether comprehensible. What Morrison composes is not an argument or explanation; it is more like a musical score, assembled from the fragments of Cholly's life. Aptly, she frames her conclusion to this passage as a tribute to musicians.

The wise, poignant beauty of this tribute to musicians demonstrates that a great literary artist can indeed make known unspeakable things and need not defer to sociologists, critics, or even musicians. Morrison allows us to hear the music of Cholly's invisibility. Furthermore, her narrative encourages us to view Cholly sympathetically but critically, and to understand him without identifying with him or excusing his behavior. In addition to its lyricism, this novel embodies the detachment that Benjamin advocates. Like Ellison's *Invisible Man*, *The Bluest Eye*, published in 1970 during the Black Arts era, is a profound inquiry into black culture and how individuals are shaped by their social experiences. Both novels present narrators who are at once critical and self-critical. Some of the most cogent African-American cultural criticism, I would argue, is to be found in the works of literary artists—especially Ellison and Morrison. The function of cultural criticism is to analyze culture, but more fundamentally, to define what we understand culture to be.

What, then, is black culture? No one can answer this question definitively, because "black culture" is not a fixed, single thing "out there" in the empirical world. It is, rather, a complex and ambiguous set of processes and interactions, facts and fantasies, assertions and inquiries, passionately held and passionately contested. The cultural identity that we designate "blackness" is intangible, yet its effects are powerfully immediate. This explains the cogency of Ellison's suggestive metaphor: the music of invisibility. In our effort to hear, play, and understand that music, we enact and discover who and what we are.

NOTES

1. LeRoi Jones, *Dutchman and The Slave* (New York: Morrow, 1964), 34.
2. Larry Neal, *Visions of a Liberated Future* (New York: Thunder's Mouth Press, 1989), 20–21. LeRoi Jones makes a similar point in his essay "The Myth of a Negro Literature," collected in his *Home*.
3. Antonio Gramsci, *The Modern Prince and Other Writings* (New York: International Publishers, 1957), 90.
4. Cornel West, *The American Evasion of Philosophy* (Madison: University of Wisconsin Press, 1989), 213.
5. W. E. B. Du Bois, *The Souls of Black Folk*, in *Writings*, ed. Arnold Rampersad (New York: Library of America), 365.
6. George Lukács, "Reification and the Consciousness of the Proletariat," in *History and Class Consciousness* (Cambridge, Mass.: MIT Press, 1971), 68 (emphasis in original). See also p. 149 and passim.
7. Cornel West, *Keeping Faith* (New York: Routledge, 1993), 82.
8. Walter Benjamin, *Illuminations* (New York: Schocken, 1969), 255. I have retranslated this passage in order to convey Benjamin's sense of historical contingency. See Benjamin, *Illuminationen* (Frankfurt: Suhrkamp, 1969), 271–72.
9. Cornel West, *Race Matters* (Boston: Beacon, 1993), 16.
10. Toni Morrison, *The Bluest Eye* (New York: Holt, Rinehart & Winston, 1970), 125.

WORKS CITED

Baraka, Amiri. *See* LeRoi Jones.
Benjamin, Walter, *Illuminations*. New York: Schocken, 1969.
  German: *Illuminationen*. Frankfurt, Suhrkamp, 1969.
Du Bois, W. E. B. *The Souls of Black Folk*. In *Writings*, edited by Arnold Rampersad. New York: Library of America, 1986.
Ellison, Ralph. *Invisible Man*. Revision. New York: Vintage Books, 1992.
Gramsci, Antonio. *The Modern Prince and Other Writings*. New York: International Publishers, 1957.

Jones, LeRoi. *Dutchman and The Slave*. New York: Morrow, 1964.
————. *Home*. New York: Morrow, 1966.
Lukács, Georg. *History and Class Consciousness*. Cambridge: MIT Press, 1971.
Morrison, Toni. *The Bluest Eye*. New York: Holt, Rinehart & Winston, 1970.
Neal, Larry. *Visions of a Liberated Future*. New York: Thunder's Mouth Press, 1989.
West, Cornel. *The American Evasion of Philosophy*. Madison: University of Wisconsin Press, 1989.
————. *Keeping Faith*. New York: Routledge, 1993.
————. *Race Matters*. Boston: Beacon, 1993.

PLAYING FOR KEEPS

Pleasure and Profit on the Postindustrial Playground

■

Robin D. G. Kelley

I don't like to dream about gettin paid, so I
Dig into the books of the rhymes that I made. . . .

—Eric B. and Rakim, "Paid in Full"

If you can run ball for 6–7 hours, you have already established
your ability to work.

—James Spady, "Running Ball"

Graffiti writing for the unemployed black ghetto kid may have
developed because there is little else to do but street wisdom tells
you to turn it to your advantage. The rap insists on self-realisation
but on your own terms, to be unafraid of established channels,
but to use them on your own terms, i.e., rip them off.

—Atlanta and Alexander, "Wild Style: Graffiti Painting"

NIKE, REEBOK, L.A. GEAR, and other athletic shoe conglomerates have profited enormously from postindustrial decline. TV commercials and print ads romanticize the crumbling urban spaces in which African-American youth must play, and in so doing they have created a vast market for overpriced sneakers. These televisual representations of "street ball" are quite remarkable; marked by chain-link fences, concrete playgrounds, bent and rusted netless hoops, graffiti-scrawled walls, and empty buildings, they have created a world where young black males do nothing *but* play.

And yet, representations of the ghetto as a space of play and pleasure amid violence and deterioration are more than simply products of the corporate imagination. Inner-city public parks and school facilities *are* falling apart or disappearing at an alarming rate. The writings of "aerosol artists" *have* altered concrete walls, abandoned buildings, and public transportation; some have created masterpieces amid urban rubble, most have highlighted the rubble by "tagging" public structures with signs and signatures. Play areas—like much of the inner city—have become increasingly fortified, caged in by steel fences, wrought-iron gates, padlocks, and razor-sharp ribbon wire. The most striking element in this postindustrial urban spectacle are the people who occupy these urban spaces. Parks and school-yards are full of brown bodies of various hues whose lack of employment has left them with plenty of time to "play." In other words, while obscuring poverty, unemployment, racism, and rising police repression, commercial representations of the contemporary "concrete jungles" powerfully underscore the link between urban decline, joblessness, and the erosion of recreational spaces in the inner city. At the same time, they highlight the historic development of "leisure" time for the urban working class and, therefore, offer commodities to help fill that time. The difference between the creation and commodification of urban leisure at the turn of the century and now, however, is that opportunities for wage labor have virtually disappeared and the bodies of the displaced workers are overwhelmingly black and brown.

The purpose of this essay is to offer some suggestive observations about the relationship between the rise of permanent unemployment, the transformation of public space, and the changing meanings and practices of "play" for African-American urban youth. The approach I take challenges the way work and leisure have been dichotomized in studies of the U.S. working class. In much of this literature, play is seen as an escape from work, something that takes place on the weekends or evenings in

distinctive spaces set aside for leisure. Indeed, these leisure spaces constitute the flip side of work, for, as cultural critic Paul Gilroy puts it, the body
"is here celebrated as an instrument of pleasure rather than an instrument
of labor."[1] What I am suggesting, however, is that the pursuit of leisure,
pleasure, and creative expression is *labor*, and that some African-American
urban youth have tried to turn that labor into cold hard cash. Thus, "play"
has increasingly become, for some, more than an expression of stylistic innovation, gender identities, and/or racial and class anger increasingly it
is viewed as a way to survive economic crisis or a means to upward mobility. Having stated the essential outlines of my argument, however, let me
add a few clarifications and caveats. First, I am in no way suggesting that
this kind of self-commodification of "play" is emancipatory, revolutionary,
or even resistive. Rather, it comprises a range of strategies within capitalism—some quite entrepreneurial, in fact—intended to enable working-
class urban youth to avoid dead-end, low-wage labor while devoting their
energies to creative and pleasurable pursuits. These strategies do not un-
dermine capitalism; profits generated by the most successful ventures simply buttress capital and illustrate, once again, its amazing resilience and
elasticity, even when the commodities themselves offer ideological challenges to its basic premise. Furthermore, these strategies do not necessarily improve the position of the entire black community, nor are they
intended to. On the contrary, in some instances they might have negative
consequences for African Americans—i.e., through the circulation of
representations that ultimately undergird racist ideologies or "success"
narratives that take racism off the hook by demonstrating that "hard
work" in the realm of sports or entertainment is all one needs to escape
the ghetto. Second, I am not suggesting that all or even most youth
engaged in these forms of play are trying to turn their efforts and skills
into a commodity. Nor am I suggesting that the self-commodification
of "play-labor" is unique to black community—though the structural
position of working-class African Americans in political and cultural
economy of the U.S. terrain lends itself to these kind of opportunities.
In a nation with few employment opportunities for African Americans
and a white consumer market eager to be entertained by the "other,"
blacks have historically occupied a central place in the popular-culture

industry. Thus, while the postindustrial city has created a different set of opportunities for and limitations on black youths' efforts to turn play into a means of escape wage labor, what I discuss below has a much older trajectory.

■

Economic restructuring leading to permanent unemployment, the shrinking of city services, the rising number of abandoned buildings, the militarization of inner-city streets, the decline of parks, youth programs, and public schools, all have altered the terrain of play and creative expression for black youth. The loss of manufacturing jobs was accompanied by expansion of low-wage "service" jobs—those of retail clerks, janitors, maids, computer programmers and data processors, security guards, waitresses, cooks, etc.—which tend to be part-time and to offer limited health or retirement benefits. By Reagan's second term, over one-third of black families earned incomes below the poverty line. For black teenagers, the unemployment rate increased from 38.9 percent to 43.6 percent under Reagan. And in midwestern cities—once the industrial heartland—black teenage unemployment rates ranged from 50 to 70 percent in 1985.[2] Federal and state job programs for inner-city youth were also wiped out at an alarming rate. In California, both the Neighborhood Youth Corps and the Comprehensive Employment and Training Act (CETA) were dismantled, and the Jobs Corps and Los Angeles Summer Job Program have been cut back substantially.[3]

Massive joblessness contributed to the expansion of the underground economy, and young people, not surprisingly, are among its biggest employees. The invention and marketing of new, cheaper drugs (PCP, crack, synthetic drugs, etc.) combined with a growing fear of crime and violence, the transformation of policing through the use of new technologies, and the erosion of youth programs and recreational facilities, have had a profound impact on public life. When the crack economy made its presence felt in poor black communities in Los Angeles, for instance, street violence intensified as various gangs and groups of peddlers battled for control over markets. Because of its unusually high crime rate, L.A. gained the dubious distinction of having the largest urban prison population in the country. Yet, in spite of the violence and financial vulnerability that went along with peddling crack, for many black youngsters it was the most viable economic option.[4]

While the rise in crime and the ascendance of the crack economy, however, might have put money into some people's pockets, for the majority it meant greater police repression. Black working-class communities in L.A. were turned into war zones during the mid-to-late 1980s. Police helicopters, complex electronic surveillance, even small tanks armed with battering rams became part of this increasingly militarized urban landscape. Housing projects, such as Imperial Courts, were renovated along the lines of minimum-security prisons and equipped with fortified fencing and an LAPD substation. Imperial Court residents were suddenly required to carry identity cards and visitors were routinely searched. As popular media coverage of the inner city linked drugs and violence to black youth, young African Americans in Los Angeles and elsewhere were subject to increasing police harassment and, in some cases, were feared by older residents.[5]

In trying to make sense of the intensification of violence and crime in the inner city during the past two decades, we must resist the tendency to romanticize the past, to recall a golden age of urban public life free of violence and conflict. At the turn of the century, for example, bloody turf wars were common among European immigrant youth. Recalling his youth on the Lower East Side of Manhattan, Communist writer and activist Mike Gold wrote:

> The East Side, for children, was a world plunged in eternal war. It was suicide to walk into the next block. Each block was a separate nation, and when a strange boy appeared, the patriots swarmed. . . . The beating was as cruel and bloody as that of grown-ups; no mercy was shown. I have had three holes in my head, and many black eyes and puffed lips from our street wars. We did it to others, they did it to us. It was patriotism, though what difference there was between one East Side block and another is now hard to see.[6]

In addition to Jewish and Italian gang violence, historian Cary Goodman points out that some of the most vicious fights that erupted in the Lower

East Side during this era took place between socialists and anarchists. Likewise, in Philadelphia during the 1950s, gangs fought with zip guns and switchblades, which resulted in even more deaths and serious injuries than did the turn-of-the-century street wars.[7]

The difference between then and now is not the levels of violence or crime (indeed, few criminologists are willing to admit that the crime rate in predominantly white turn-of-the-century cities was often higher then than it is now). Rather, it is a combination of the growing importance of street gangs in the urban political economy and the dramatic improvement in technology that is different. Taking advantage of the gaping hole left by the disappearance of a viable local economy, some gangs have become businesses, distributors of illegal and *legal* goods and services, and they generally define their markets by territory. The very technological revolutions that enable them to connect up with international cartels, expand their venues, or maintain contact with one another (through reasonably priced pagers, laptop computers, and handheld fax machines) has also increased the stakes by facilitating greater investment diversity and territorial reach.[8]

More important, the proliferation of inexpensive and powerful semiautomatic weapons is what distinguishes the 1990s from the 1950s, or for that matter, from the 1890s. The National Rifle Association, the nation's largest lobby against gun control, played a major role in ensuring the availability of firearms. Backed by huge weapons manufacturers and armed with one of the wealthiest political action committees in the country (its annual budget is close to $30 million and in the 1992 elections it contributed $1.7 million to House and Senate candidates), the NRA has fought tenaciously against bans on the kinds of automatic assault weapons that are appearing more frequently in inner-city communities. Under Reagan, whose presidential campaign received strong backing from the NRA, the regulatory power of the Bureau of Alcohol, Tobacco, and Firearms (ATF) was weakened considerably. By the mid-1980s, obtaining a license to sell guns became so easy that potential dealers needed only to pay a mere $30 fee and undergo an unusually casual background check. According to one report, "the ATF's background checks were once so lax that the agency even issued licenses to dogs." Ironically, the *fear* of crime partly explains the success of the NRA lobby and their closest allies, gun manufacturers and distributors. During the past decade, the gun industry has banked on the fear of crime to sell their products, focusing attention less on the hunting market and more on citizens' desire to protect themselves and their property. After a sales slump in the early 1980s, gun sellers not only expanded their marketing strategy to women and teens but brought back cheap semiautomatic pistols, which are frequently used in street crimes. In the end, however, middle-class families concerned about crime—not the criminals—are the primary consumers of handguns. In 1992 alone, estimated sales of firearms totaled more than $774 million.[9]

The fear of crime has also spawned new developments in late-twentieth-century urban architecture. The design of the built environment has had a profound impact on how public space is defended and protected, which in turn shapes the way people interact with one another. The work of Camilo José Vergara and Mike Davis powerfully illustrate the degree to which cities are built and conceived as fortifications against the presumed criminality and chaos of the streets. Vergara writes: "Buildings grow claws and spikes, their entrances acquire metal plates, their roofs get fenced in. . . . Even in areas where statistics show a decrease in major crime, fortification continues to escalate, and as it does, ghettos lose their coherence. Neighborhoods are replaced by a random assortment of isolated bunkers, structures that increasingly resemble jails or power stations, their interiors effectively separated from the outside. . . . In brick and cinder block and sharpened metal, inequality takes material form."[10]

Recession and Reagan-era budget cuts, combined with the militarization of urban life, has devastated inner-city public recreational facilities and altered the landscape of play significantly. Beginning in the 1970s, a wave of public recreational-service employees were either furloughed, discharged, or allowed to retire without replacement; the service and maintenance of parks and playgrounds was cut back substantially; many facilities were eliminated or simply deteriorated by attrition; and the hours of operation were drastically reduced. During the mid-1970s, for instance, Cleveland's recreation department had to close down almost $50 million worth of facilities. In New York City, municipal appropriations for parks dropped by more than $40 million between 1974 and 1980—a 60 percent cut in real dollars. Staff cutbacks were even more drastic: between the late 1960s and 1979, the number of park employees dropped from almost 6,100 to 2,600. To make matters worse, a growing number of public school yards in inner-city communities have become inaccessible during after-school hours.[11]

More recently, we have witnessed a growing number of semipublic-private play spaces like "people's parks" that require a key (e.g., the playground in Greenwich Village that services residents of New York University–owned apartments) and highly sophisticated indoor play areas that charge admission. The growth of these privatized spaces has reinforced a class-segregated play world and created yet another opportunity for investors to profit from the general fear of crime and violence. Thus, in the shadows of Central Park, Frederick Law Olmsted's great urban vision of class integration and public sociability, high-tech indoor playgrounds such as Wondercamp, Discovery Zone, and Playspace, charge admission to eager middle- and upper-class children whose parents want a safe play environment. Protection from the outside is emphasized; at Playspace, for example, young workers are expected to size up potential customers before "buzzing" them in. While these play areas are occasionally patronized by poor and working-class black children, the fact that most of these indoor playgrounds are built in well-to-do neighborhoods and charge an admission fee ranging between $5 and $9 prohibits poor families from making frequent visits.[12]

Privatization has also adversely affected public parks. Parks directors in several big cities, notably New York, have turned to "public-private partnerships" and begun to charge "user fees" in order to make ends meet. New York City's Department of Parks and Recreation has already transferred zoos, skating rinks, and parking lots to private operators, and there has been discussion of contracting out recreational and maintenance services to private companies. Moreover, during the 1980s the city and state used tax abatements as a way of encouraging private developers to build parks and plazas, which usually manifest themselves as highly surveilled "arcades, interior atriums, and festival marketplaces attached to office and condominium towers." The move toward private ownership of public space is powerfully captured in a plaque located on a plaza in midtown Manhattan: "PUBLIC SPACE, Owned and Maintained by AT&T."[13]

Of course, I do not want to exaggerate the impact of the disappearance of public play areas on urban youth. In New York, for example, the sidewalks and streets have long been a more desirable place to play, not just for children but for adults as well. In the immigrant working-class neighborhoods of the Lower East Side during the early twentieth century, parents preferred to be within hearing distance of their children, and the streets were often crowded with kids. Scenes of dozens of Jewish and Italian kids surrounding an open fire hydrant on a hot summer day in the 1920s are not much different from similar scenes of Harlem in the early 1970s. Young and old kids have constantly carved out space on the sidewalk for jacks, craps, double Dutch, hopscotch, and handball, and the streets more broadly have been used as stickball diamonds that incorporate existing landmarks (cars, fire hydrants, etc.) as bases. Moreover, since 1909, the New York Police Athletic League has run an annual program whereby they block off traffic through selected streets during the summer in order to create more safe places to play.[14]

But as the streets become increasingly dangerous, or are perceived to be so, more and more young children are confined indoors, limited to backyards, or (for those who can afford it) shuttled to the city's proliferating "discovery zones." For inner-city families, the threat of drive-bys have turned porches and front doors, which once spilled out onto sidewalks and streets as extensions of play areas, into fortified entrances with iron "screen" doors that lock from the inside. Sadly, the increasingly common practice of placing iron gates over windows and doors is partly responsible for a rise in fire-related deaths in urban black communities.

The simultaneous decline in employment opportunities, public leisure spaces for young people, and overcrowded, poorly funded public schools and youth programs simply expanded an urban landscape in which black teenagers—the throwaways of a new, mobile capitalism—became an even larger, more permanent (and in the minds of many, more menacing) presence in parks and street corners. The growing numbers of young brown bodies engaged in "play" rather than work (from street-corner bantering, to "malling," to basketball) has contributed to popular constructions of the "underclass" as a threat and has shaped urban police practices. The invention of terms such as "wilding," as literary scholar and cultural critic Houston Baker points out, reveal a discourse of black male youth out of control, rampaging teenagers free of the disciplinary strictures of school, work, or prison.[15]

I want to argue instead that many of these young bodies are not merely idle bystanders. They are not uniformly devoid of ambition or a work ethic either. Increasingly, young people have tried to turn play into an alternative to unfulfilling wage labor. Basketball, for black males at least, not only embodies dreams of success and possible escape from the ghetto, but in a growing number of communities pickup games are played for money much like cards or pool. While it is true that some boys and young men see basketball as a quick (though *never* easy) means to success and riches, it is ludicrous to believe that everyone on the court shares the same aspirations.[16] In the context of a game with competition, it becomes clear very quickly who can play and who cannot. Most participants are not deluding themselves into believing that it is an escape from the ghetto; rather, they derive some kind of pleasure from it. But for that small minority who hold on to the dream and are encouraged, the work ethic begins quite early and they usually work harder than most turn-of-the-century child wage workers. As cultural critic James Spady observes in the epigraph above, running ball all day long is evidence of a work ethic. Besides, black working-class men and their families see themselves as having fewer career options than whites, so sports has been more of an imagined possibility than becoming a highly educated professional—"it was *the* career option rather than *a* career option," writes Michael Messner.[17] Nowhere is this better illustrated than in the highly acclaimed documentary film *Hoop Dreams*. Charting the tragic lives of Arthur Agee and William Gates, two young talents from the South Side of Chicago who were recruited by a white suburban Catholic high school to play ball, the filmmakers capture the degree to which many black working-class families have invested their hopes and aspirations in the game of basketball.[18]

Not surprisingly, the vast majority are disappointed. Of the half-million high school basketball players in the U.S., only 14,000 (2.8 percent) play college ball, and only 25 of those (.005 percent) make it to the NBA. More generally, only 6 or 7 percent of high school athletes ever play college sports; roughly 8 percent of draft-eligible college football and basketball players are drafted by the pros, and only 2 percent ever sign a contract. The chances of attaining professional status in sports are approximately 4 in 100,00 for white men, 2 in 100,000 for black men, and 3 in 1,000,000 for U.S.-born Latinos.[19]

Practically all scholars agree that young women and girls have had even fewer opportunities to engage in either work or play. They have less access to public spaces, are often responsible for attending to household duties, and are policed by family members, authorities, and boys themselves from the "dangers" of the streets. Aside from the gender division of labor that frees many boys and men from child-care responsibilities, house cleaning, etc., the fear of violence and teen pregnancy has led parents to cloister girls even more. Thus, when they do spend much of their "play" time in the public spaces of the city, parent-imposed curfews and other pressures limit their time outside the household.

Controlling women's access to public space is just part of the story. Because sports, street gambling, hanging out in parks and street corners, and other forms of play are central to the construction of masculinity, boys, young men, and authority figures erect strict gender boundaries to keep women out. In fact, one might argue that play is at least as important, if not more, than work in shaping gender identities. After all, our sense of maleness and femaleness is made in childhood, and the limits, boundaries, and contestations in the world of play constitute key moments in the creation and shaping of gender identity.[20] And given the transformation of the labor market in the age of multinational capital, the gendering and gender-policing of play has enormous implications. With the extension of a service-based economy (often gendered as feminized or servile labor) and the rise of permanent unemployment, work no longer seems to be a primary factor in the construction of masculinity—if it ever was.

The policing of these boundaries have a material element as well; they ultimately help reproduce gender inequalities by denying or limiting women access to the most potentially profitable forms of creative leisure. Of course, girls and young women do participate in mixed-gender play, and some even earn the right to participate in the men's world of play. For instance, women do play basketball, occasionally with the fellas, but they have fewer opportunities for pickup games, to participate in organized "street" leagues, or to dream that honing one's skills could land a college scholarship or trip to the pros. Yet, despite the policing of gender boundaries, which tends to become more rigid when children reach preadolescence, girls find forms of homosocial play and pleasure that they defend and protect. And like boys' games and mixed-gender play in declining urban centers, modern social reformers have occasionally tried to turn these forms into "supervised play" as a way to build self-esteem, discipline, and the work ethic (though these virtues were allegedly instilled in young girls through "domestic science" programs). The most fascinating example is the Double Dutch League of New York, originally founded in 1973 by the Police Athletic League (PAL) and later sponsored by McDonald's restaurant. Girls were organized into teams that competed in the plaza at the Lincoln Center for the Performing Arts for scholarship money and other prizes. Some of the crews, like the Jazzy Jumpers and the Ebonnettes, became fairly big in New York and nationally.[21]

Double dutch is a very old jump-rope game in which participants skip over two ropes spinning in opposite directions. Although it is not exclusive to African-American youth, it has been a cultural mainstay among black urban girls for decades. Double dutch is not a competitive sport; rather, it is a highly stylized performance accompanied by (frequently profane) songs and rhymes and can involve three or more girls. Two girls turn the rope (though boys occasionally participated as "turners," especially if they were under big sister's supervision) while one or sometimes two participants "jump in."[22] The good jumpers perform improvised acrobatic feats or complicated body movements as a way of stylizing and individualizing the performance. What is particularly interesting about the Double Dutch League is the degree to which its male founders, like its president David Walker, saw the game in terms of the peculiar needs and interests of girls. Walker explained that he had been thinking about activities for girls, especially after failing to attract many girls to his bicycling program. Walker explained, "When I heard the expression double dutch, about a thousand bulbs lit in my mind. I started realizing it was an activity that girls really related to. . . . Mothers did it when they were kids. . . . See the relationship—mother—clothesline—daughter. . . ." Moreover, he believed it was an important activity for controlling inner-city girls and teaching them the benefits of competition. Once PAL and other groups began institutionalizing double dutch, the jumpers who participated in these formal contests found the improvisational character of the game sharply circumscribed. Within the PAL-sponsored contests and demonstrations, moves became highly formalized and choreographed, despite the fact that League organizers encouraged innovation. Contestants were judged on speed and accuracy—criteria that simply were less important on the streets. The organizers even tried to sever its inner-city linkages by referring to double dutch as "street ballet" and by practically eliminating the verbal component so essential to the activity. Few girls participated in these tournaments, in part because there was little incentive. The financial promise of basketball (which could still be played without supervision) was missing in double dutch.[23]

Even more than sports and various school-yard games, forms of "play" that fall outside the pale of recreation—visual art, dance, music, etc.—offered black urban youth more immediate opportunities for entrepreneurship and greater freedom from unfulfilling wage labor. Performance and visual arts, in particular, powerfully dramatize how young people have turned the labor of play into a commodity, not only to escape wage work but to invest their time and energy in creative expression, or what ethnographer and cultural theorist Paul Willis calls "symbolic creativity." As Willis argues, constructing an identity, communicating with others, and achieving pleasure constitute the labor of creating art in everyday life. Hence, it is in the realm of "symbolic creativity" that the boundaries between work and play are perhaps most blurred, especially as these forms become commodified.[24]

The struggle to carve out a kind of liminal space between work and play, labor and performance, is hardly new. Today in the streets of New Orleans children as young as five years old maintain a tradition of street performance, playing "second line" jazz in makeshift marching bands throughout the French Quarter. And the subway stops and downtown sidewalks of New York, Washington, D.C., Atlanta, Oakland, and elsewhere are filled with young black musicians of mixed talent trying to make a living through their craft. Perhaps the most famous young black "street musician" is Larry Wright, a talented percussionist who milked a plastic bucket and a pair of drumsticks for every timbre and tonality imaginable. He began performing on street corners in New York City as an adolescent, earning change from passersby who found his complex polyrhythms appealing. His mother encouraged Larry to pursue his art, which ultimately earned him acceptance into New York's highly competitive High School for the Performing Arts. When he was still only fifteen, two filmmakers "discovered" him and made a half-hour video about his life and music that put his name in circulation—and the rest, as they say, is history. After an appearance in the film *Green Card*, a Levi's commercial shot by Spike Lee, and a Mariah Carey video, his example spawned a number of imitators throughout the country. I've seen kids in front of the Pavilion (an eatery and shopping center on Pennsylvania Avenue in Washington, D.C.) with white buckets and sticks trying to reproduce his sound.[25]

White street performance is as old as cities themselves, new technologies and the peculiar circumstances of postindustrial decline have given rise to new cultural forms that are even more directly a product of grassroots entrepreneurship and urban youths' struggle over public space. These forms demanded specific skills, technical knowledge, and often complicated support systems that provided employment and investment opportunities for nonperformers. The most obvious example is hip-hop culture, a broad cultural movement that emerged in the South Bronx during the 1970s. But even before the hip-hop scene blew up in New York City as an alternative vocation for black and Latino kids, the slums of Washington, D.C., became a source of both musical inspiration and entrepreneurial imagination. Out of D.C.'s black ghettos emerged a highly percussive music called go-go, which indirectly influenced the direction of East Coast hip-hop. Originating in the late 1960s, when go-go guru Charles Brown formed a dynamic band called the Soul Stirrers, go-go had always been a distinctive Washington, D.C., style. The bands tended to be large—sometimes a dozen pieces—and were characterized by heavy funk bass, horns, rhythm guitar, and various percussion instruments—from snares, congas, and cowbells to found objects. Like hip-hop and other black Atlantic musical traditions, go-go music places a premium on sustaining the rhythm and getting the dancers involved in the performance through call and response. Just as hip-hop DJs keep the dancers on the floor by playing a seamless array of break beats, go-go bands play continuously, linking different songs by using a relentless back beat and bass guitar to string the music together into an intense performance that could last an hour or more.[26]

Go-go groups like Trouble Funk, EU (Experience Unlimited), Redds and the Boys, Go-Go Allstarz, Mass Extension, and the appropriately named Junkyard Band were products of high school and junior high inner-city music programs. Some band members met at high school marching band competitions or were involved in summer youth projects intended to get kids off the streets. As black D.C. artist and activist Malik Edwards remembers, "It was just kids trying to play their music, bands trying to out-jam each other. EU came out of the Valley Green Courtesy Patrol summer project, which got them some instruments through the community center and a place to practice." Performing on cheap, often battered instruments, young go-go musicians created a distinctive "pot-and-pan" sound. "The sound was created out of inefficient instruments, just anything they could do to make an instrument," recalls go-go promoter Maxx Kidd. Yet, these artists still made the most popular music in the District, sometimes performing to capacity dance crowds in school gyms, parks, recreation centers, empty warehouses, rented hotel ballrooms, and a vast array of go-gos (clubs) in the neighborhood.

With few exceptions, no one really got rich off go-go. Throughout the 1970s neither radio stations nor the record industry took an interest in this new urban music. Despite the initial lack of commercial interest, go-go gave up-and-coming musicians a space to learn their craft, perform for audiences, make a little money on the side, and an opportunity for creative expression. Ironically, it is precisely because the early go-go scene remained free of major corporate investment that it spawned a fairly lucrative underground economy for inner-city youth who sold bootleg tapes, made posters, organized dances, made and repaired musical instruments, and indirectly benefited from the fact that black working-class consumers spent their money on local entertainment.[27] Unfortunately, just as go-go began building an international following and the record industry took a greater interest in the mid-1980s, its popularity in D.C. began to decline. Moreover, it never achieved the kind of following hip-hop enjoyed; after hit songs by EU, Trouble Funk, and Charles Brown, the big studios lost interest in go-go soon thereafter. There is still a vibrant go-go scene in Washington, but it is only a fraction of what it was a decade ago.

Hip-hop, on the other hand, was more than music; it embraced an array of cultural forms that included graffiti art and break dancing as well as rap music. Because each of these forms generated different kinds of opportunities and imposed different sorts of limitations, we must examine them separately. We might begin with the oldest—and perhaps least lucrative—component of hip-hop culture: graffiti. Of course, various forms of wall writing go back centuries, from political slogans and gang markings to romantic declarations. But the aerosol art movement is substantially different. Calling themselves writers, graffiti artists, aerosol artists, and subterranean guerrilla artists, many of the young pioneers of this art form treated their work as a skilled craft and believed they were engaged in worthwhile labor. During the 1970s, some graffiti artists sold their services to local merchants and community organizations, and a handful enjoyed fleeting success in the SoHo art scene.

Subway trains provided the most popular canvases. They not only enabled the artist to literally circulate his or her work through the city, but many young people thought of themselves as waging war against the New York City Transit Authority. They felt the transit police were repressive, the fares were too high, and trains assigned to poor communities like Harlem and the South Bronx were inferior. Writers often "bombed" the interiors of trains with "tags"—quickly executed and highly stylized signatures, often made with fat markers rather than spray cans. Outside the trains they created "masterpieces," elaborate works carefully conceived and designed ahead of time. Good writers not only had to be skilled artists, but because they were breaking the law by defacing property, they had to work quickly and quietly. They often executed their work in complete darkness, sometimes beginning around 2 or 3 A.M. The threat of arrest was constant, as was the potential of being seriously injured by a moving train or the electrified "third rail." Most artists protected themselves by working in "crews" rather than as lone individuals. From the outset women writers like Lady Pink, Charmin, and Lady Heart were part of these crews and most worked alongside male artists, though female writers had to battle male sexism and protect themselves from possible sexual assault while executing their work.[28]

By the early 1970s, graffiti writing became a widely debated and discussed phenomenon, becoming the subject of several dramatic and documentary films. Although this partly explains the mainstream art world's fleeting interest in aerosol art, the fact is, graffiti writers themselves took the first initiative. Through organizations such as United Graffiti Artists (UGA) and the Nation of Graffiti Artists (NOGA), some of the leading artists attempted to market their work collectively and establish ties to art dealers and downtown galleries. Launched in 1972, UGA's initial mission was to redirect graffiti into socially acceptable avenues and to get black and Puerto Rican kids off the street. Very quickly, however, it became a primary vehicle for exposing a fairly exclusive group of aerosol artists to galleries and dealers. A year after its founding, the UGA exhibited graffiti on canvases at the Razor Gallery in SoHo (downtown Manhattan). The paintings were priced between $200 and $3,000, and several of the pieces sold.[29] NOGA artists also enjoyed a few fleeting successes in the mid-1970s. Unlike UGA, which had a small membership of selected artists, NOGA was founded as a community youth artists' collective open to just about everyone. With the assistance of former dancer and entrepreneur Jack Pelsinger and graphic artist and gallery manager Livi French, two veterans of the New York arts scene, NOGA arranged several exhibits in public venues throughout the city. They could not command as much as the UGA artists for their work; NOGA writers rarely sold canvases for more than $300 and 25 percent of their proceeds went back to the organization to pay for supplies. Because they were not regarded as legitimate artists, institutions that hired them to paint large-scale murals frequently saw no need to pay them. Author Craig Castleman relates one such incident in which Prospect Hospital in the Bronx commissioned NOGA artists to produce a mural:

> When the mural was complete, Jacob Freedman, director and owner of the hospital, thanked the artists and had the mural

rolled and taken into the hospital. He then started back to his office. At that point, Jack [Pelsinger] related, "I asked him for the
money. 'What money?' he said. 'The money for the artists!' He
acted like he didn't understand. It was like he was saying 'What!
Pay kids for painting a mural for my hospital!' Well, I kept after
him and finally he coughed up a hundred dollars. A hundred dollars for a mural that had taken all day to complete."[30]

While UGA members demanded higher prices, in some ways they did not
fare much better in terms of earning respect as legitimate artists. Those
who tried to branch out beyond graffiti were often discouraged, and
gallery and museum directors who invited them to show their work
tended to treat them in an incredibly disrespectful manner. After arrang-
ing a show at the Chicago Museum of Science and Industry in 1974, museum staff not only refused to help them hang their own show but put the
artists up at the YMCA rather than at a nearby hotel.[31]

In any event, the American and European art world's fascination with
aerosol artists did not last long, and it was largely limited to male writers
since "high art" critics viewed graffiti as the embodiment of an aggressive
masculine street culture. (Many of the artists also promoted this image;
the UGA, for example, systematically denied women membership.) The
only graffiti writers who made it big were the Haitian-born Jean-Michel
Basquiat and a white artist named Keith Haring, both of whom have since
died. To most veteran writers, Basquiat and Haring were peripheral to the
graffiti scene since neither had done a train piece.[32] Nevertheless, the
overnight success of these major artists, especially Basquiat, gave hope to
some writers that the visual arts might offer a lucrative alternative to low-
wage labor and an opportunity to live off of their own creativity. And for
some writers, hard work and talent paid off. St. Maurice, a veteran writer
from Staten Island whose parents were artists, pursued his art professionally and eventually opened a frame shop. All twelve original members of
UGA went on to either college or art school, and most of them became
professional artists.[33]

Writers most committed to the genre, however, wanted to get paid
but were unwilling to "sell out." Despite a strong desire to make money

from their work and to become full-time artists, few writers wholeheartedly embraced the downtown art scene. As Lady Pink explained it:

> Painting on canvas or a gallery's walls removes the element of risk, of getting one's name around, of interaction with one's peers and one's potential younger rivals. The pieces in galleries cease to be graffiti because they have been removed from the cultural context that gives graffiti the reason for being, a voice of the ghetto.[34]

And as the risks increased, the number of masterpieces in the public sphere slowly dwindled, and with it went the excitement of the downtown art world. By the late 1970s, the city launched a fairly successful (and very expensive) war against subway graffiti. In 1977 the MTA began spending $400,000 per year cleaning the trains with petroleum hydroxide and huge buffing machines. They also protected the train yards with attack dogs and $24 million worth of new fencing topped with ribbon wire, a razor-sharp form of barbed wire that ensnares and shreds the body attempting to cross it. Ironically, while the MTA largely succeeded in keeping the trains graffiti-free, aerosol art literally exploded throughout other city spaces and has spread throughout the world during the 1980s and 1990s. Tagging can be found in virtually every urban landscape, and masterpieces continue to pop up on the sides of housing projects, school yards, abandoned buildings and plants, under bridges, and inside tunnels that service commuter trains.[35]

Why does aerosol art lose its value soon as it is removed from its sites of origin—the urban jungle? On the surface the answer seems obvious: it is regarded by artists and critics as more authentic when it is produced illegally and can simultaneously deface property while conveying a message. Yet, when we compare "graffiti" with basketball, it is interesting to note that the latter does not lose its street credentials once individuals take their skills into more bourgeois, institutionalized contexts. Indeed, stories of black college players who were "discovered" on the playgrounds of some horrific metropolitan ghetto have become stock narratives among sportscasters and columnists. By contrast, once a piece of aerosol art enters the hallowed space of a museum or gallery, it is instantly dismissed as inauthentic or constructed for viewers as an extreme example of "outsider art." The different responses to sports and graffiti, I believe, are linked to the very nature of sports as a spectacle of performing bodies. The physicality of certain sports (like basketball), the eroticizing and racializing of the bodies participating in these spectacles, and the tendency to invest those bodies with the hopes, dreams, and aspirations of a mythic, heroic working class, keep most popular, commercialized team sports at a safe distance from the world of high culture. Visual arts are a different story; it is precisely the similarities in form and technique (not to mention aesthetics) that pushes graffiti uncomfortably close to the official realm of modern art. And as residents of newly gentrified communities know, policing becomes more intense when the threat is in close proximity. Moreover, when the creative product is the body itself rather than a painting, a sculpture, a book, or even a musical score, it is rendered as less cerebral or cognitive and thus, inadvertently, devalued. It is not ironic, for example, that the media paid as much attention to Jean-Michel Basquiat's physical appearance as to his paintings.[36]

As aerosol art was pushed further underground, rap music emerged from the underground with a vengeance. Young West Indian, African-American, and Puerto Rican DJs and MCs in the South Bronx plugged their sound systems into public outlets and organized dance parties in school yards and parks, partly as a means to make money. A whole underground economy emerged, which ranged from printing and selling T-shirts advertising crews, to building speakers, reconfiguring turntables, buying and selling records and bootleg tapes, to even selling food and drink at these outdoor events.[37] The real money, however, was in promoting, DJ-ing, and rapping. In fact, production and performance of hip-hop music not only required musical knowledge but skills in electronics and audio technology. It's not an accident, for instance, that most pioneering hip-hop DJs and graffiti artists had attended trade and vocational schools. Others got their start DJ-ing for house parties, a practice particularly common in Los Angeles. L.A. hip-hop DJ G-Bone recalls, "I got out of high school, working at Fox Hills [mall] [I] must have been making minimum wage, about three dollars then, we came up with the DJ idea . . . we started buyin' records from Music Plus with our whole paycheques. . . . All we had was two speakers, Acculab speakers and a home amp with tubes and a Radio Shack mixer that didn't have crossfaders. They made it with buttons."[38] Calling themselves Ultrawave Productions, they started out making $60 a gig before muscling out another neighborhood DJ company (Baldwin Hills Productions) for clients. Then their fee shot up to $150. Young rappers and DJs also made money by selling homemade tapes on the streets or through local record shops willing to carry them. Toddy Tee's hit song "Batteram" started out as a street tape, and Oakland rapper Too Short sold homemade tapes for several years before getting a record contract.

Serious DJs invested the money they made doing dances and house parties in better equipment. Dr. Dre, formerly of the now defunct rap group Niggas with Attitude, used the money he made DJ-ing in high school to set up a four-track recording studio above his mother's garage in Compton. "That's how I learned how to use the board and everything. From the four track I advanced to the eight track and then fucking around in a little demo studio we had, using the money we had from DJing we bought a few things for a little twelve track studio." After selling street tapes for a while, he finally put his music on vinyl—before he got a record contract. Dre remembers, "We was just sellin' 'em out the trunk, trying to make money, we sold close to ten thousand records right out the car before we got signed."[39]

Break dancing, like rap music, apparently emerged in the South Bronx during the 1970s. The word "break" refers to "break beats"—fragments of a song that dancers enjoyed most and that the DJ would isolate and play over and over by using two turntables. The breakers were sometimes called "B-boys" or "B-girls" for short. Thanks to popular films such as *Flashdance*, most people have some familiarity with break dancing—the head and back spins, the jerky body movements of the "Electric Boogie" and the "Egyptian."[40] Performed by men and women, sometimes in "crews" that did choreographed and "freestyle" moves before audiences and often in competition with other crews, breaking involved incredible body contortions and acrobatic feats. What many outsiders fail to appreciate, however, is the amount of practice and body conditioning required to execute moves like spinning on one's hand or head. Besides rigorous physical preparation, break dancers constantly risked injury, particularly since they generally performed on the streets and sidewalks. Some placed a flattened cardboard on the hard concrete, but it was not enough to protect them from serious injuries ranging from stress fractures and scrotal contusions to brain hemorrhaging. Training and discipline were of the utmost importance if dancers wanted to avoid injury. One particularly dangerous move was the "suicide," where the dancer does a front flip and lands on his or her back. As Dee-rock of the Furious Rockers put it, "It can be dangerous. . . . If you don't learn right, you'll kill yourself."[41]

Perhaps more than most dance crazes, breaking ultimately became a contest over public space. It was a style performed in malls, hallways, and especially city streets. Historian and cultural critic Tricia Rose explains:

> Streets were preferred practice spaces for a couple of reasons. Indoor community spaces in economically oppressed areas are rare, and those that are available are not usually big enough to accommodate large groups performing acrobatic dances. In addition, some indoor spaces had other drawbacks. One of the breakers with whom I spoke pointed out that the Police Athletic League [of New York], which did have gymnasium-size space, was avoided because it was used as a means of community surveillance for the police. Whenever local police were looking for a suspect, kids hanging out in the PAL were questioned.

But despite the fantasy scenes of dancers taking to the streets in films like *Fame* and *Flashdance*, breakers did not go unmolested. There were several cases in which break dancers were arrested for disturbing the peace or "attracting undesirable crowds" in public spaces such as shopping malls.[42]

One of the main reasons break dancers performed in public was simply to make money. Like athletes, graffiti artists, and rap musicians, break dancers were not only willing to work within the marketplace, but they actively promoted the commodification of the form as an alternative to dead-end wage labor. The Furious Rockers, a predominantly Puerto Rican group from Brooklyn, were typical of most crews—at first. They began performing at Coney Island amusement park for nickels and dimes, carrying only a boom box and a flattened cardboard box, and within months graduated to local gigs in New York public schools. Then they got a real break: choreographer Rosanne Hoare "discovered" them and arranged appearances on NBC's *Today* show and in Gene Kelly's film *That's Dancing!*[43]

While most break dancers continued to hustle coins and dollar bills for their street-corner performances, the overnight success of the style itself and its rapid appropriation by advertising firms, professional dance schools, and the entertainment industry raised the stakes considerably. It suggested to young practitioners that break dancing was worth pursuing professionally. Some, like the Rock Steady Crew, appeared in several movies that focus on hip-hop culture, including *Beat Street*, *Breakin'*, and *Wild Style*. Burger King, Panasonic, Pepsi, and Coca-Cola have all used break dancers in their commercials. All of these "breaks" left a deep imprint on young up-and-coming breakers that their craft might lead them out of the ghetto and into a worthwhile career and financial security.[44] But as one of the pioneers of break dancing, the Rock Steady Crew's Crazy Legs, put it, "We got ripped off by so many people." As inner-city black and Puerto Rican youth who lacked professional status within the entertainment industry, they were frequently hired by downtown clubs to perform for their elite clientele and paid virtually nothing. Indeed, the very fact that the Furious Rockers even had an agent was unusual. The film industry did not do much better, either paying break dancers less than union scale or hiring professional dancers to learn the moves so as to bypass the problem of hiring nonunion labor. Bedsides, like most dance trends, breaking declined almost as rapidly as it came into style.[45]

Perhaps because break dancing was both a skill that could be learned by professional dancers and a component of hip-hop that was ultimately subordinated to rap music—serving more or less as a colorful backdrop to the MC and DJ—breakers had far fewer opportunities to market their skills. Besides, breaking was introduced to the wider consumer audience without the overwhelming emphasis on the ghetto origins of the performers that one finds in rap and graffiti. Television shows like *Star Search* promoted suburban white preteens performing the most clichéd routines that combined breaking and gymnastics. We might add, too, that hip-hop culture, in particular, and dance and visual arts, in general, simply lack the institutional reward structures one finds in college and professional sports. The chances of landing a college scholarship or getting commercial endorsements (unless one is marketing malt liquor to underaged drinkers) on the basis of one's skill as an MC, a break dancer, or aerosol artist are slim indeed. Rap music is the only potential money-maker, and the most successful artists usually earn a fraction of what star athletes make. Given the wider range of financial opportunities available in sports, is it any wonder that athletics (including basketball) continue to be the most multiracial realm of "play-labor" and the most intensely defended as a "color-blind" site of cultural practice?

None of these realms of play-labor, however, claim to be "gender-blind." Participants in, and advocates for, sports, hip-hop, and go-go erect gender boundaries to maintain male hegemony in the areas of production, promotion, and performance. Of course, music and the arts offered women more opportunities for entry than the highly masculinized and sex-segregated world of sports. Women not only persevered to become respected graffiti artists in spite of the pressures against them, they had been part of the rap scene since its inception. At the same time, gender boundaries within hip-hop were vigilantly policed at all levels of production. Young men often discouraged or ridiculed women MCs; such women were often denied access to technology, were ignored, or were pressured by gender conventions to stay out of a cultural form identified as rough, profane, and male. Indeed, one might argue that rap music's misogyny is partly a function of efforts of male hip-hop artists to keep it a masculine space. On the other hand, because the record industry markets rap as a profane, masculine "street" music, selling the bodies of the performers is as important as producing the music. Perhaps this may explain why, during the formative years of rap music, it was easier for women to get on the mic at a local place like the Hevalo Club in the Bronx than to secure a record contract. Hip-hop, like other contemporary popular music, has become a highly visual genre that depends on video representations to authenticate the performer's ghetto roots and rough exterior. In a world of larger-than-life B-boys surrounded by a chaotic urban backdrop, there are few spaces for women outside the realm of hypermasculinity. Sometimes women rappers might challenge hypermasculine constructions of hip-hop, but rarely do they step outside of those constructions. While there is something strangely empowering about women being able to occupy that profane, phallocentric space through which to express their own voices, it none-theless sets limits on women's participation and ensures male dominance in the hip-hop industry.[46]

On the other hand, women have been essential to the hip-hop and go-go scene as consumers and participants. The pioneering DJs made their money by throwing parties, either in small underground clubs or at outdoor events. In order to ensure women's presence at these heterosocial affairs, gender differences shaped admissions policies substantially. Be-cause women do not have the same access to cash wages, or unfettered moment through public space, they were often subsidized at these gather-ings (almost every night was ladies' night; many house parties in Califor-nia charged men and admitted women free). This should not be surprising since men depend on the presence of women for their own pleasure in the context of heterosexual exchange.

Indeed, it is in the world of sexuality that young men, more than young women, become consumers in the urban marketplace. In this com-plicated arena of public play, sex is one of the few realms of pleasure in which young women could make money. By exploring how young women have tried to turn the commodification of their own bodies and sexuality into "pleasure and profit" for themselves, however, I am not arguing that heterosexual relations are merely extensions of the marketplace. I am not suggesting that black working-class urban youth have no genuine loving relationships, even when economic transactions are involved. Rather, I am merely suggesting that because black women have less access than black men to public space, employment opportunities, entrepreneurial opportunities, and the most lucrative cultural opportunities, it has a pro-found impact on their daily social relations. For poor young black women, sex is one of the few "hustles" they have since virtually every other avenue is closed to them.

Sex, whether it is sexual intercourse or public expressions of sexuality, is a very complicated issue to think about in terms of the kinds of entre-preneurial activities I've outlined thus far. It is equally complicated when we consider the fact that sex is almost never performed or experienced in a context of pure pleasure. It carries with it the potential for deep emotional ties, scars, and/or obligations (i.e., fidelity, devotion, possession, agreed-upon codes of public behavior, etc.) between partners. Sex, therefore, is not simply another game or performance. Although all forms of play operate within discrete relations of power (indeed, the very notion of "leveling the playing field" acknowledge deep power relations in sports itself), the ideological and emotional currents that shape sexual encounters push the issue of power to the foreground. Sex, after all, is neither competition nor an expression of aesthetic value, though in practice it might contain elements of both. For example, heterosexual courtship for men is often highly competitive, analogous to hunters competing for game, which they display as a way of demonstrating their prowess. The physical attractiveness of the "prey" also enhances the hunter's claims of prowess. Although consensual sexual intercourse itself may contain elements of competition and value an aesthetic of form, ideally it is people enjoying and partaking in the erotic, sensual pleasures of the body—someone else's and/or their own. Realistically, I think it is safe to say, sex involves control and manipulation, not just physically and emotionally but discursively.

When we examine the commodification of sex in relation to our argument about how displaced urban youth turn forms of "play" into paid labor, discursive constructions of sex as a source of power become extremely important. These discourses powerfully reproduce a gender hierarchy in which professionalization ultimately increases the value of men's sexuality while devaluing women's sexuality. The "pimp," whose very survival depends on the commodification of sex and the private ownership of women's bodies, is considered a heroic figure rich in sexual prowess. On the other hand, when women presumably use sex as a lever to obtain nice things or even decent treatment, they are labeled "hos," "gold diggers," and "skeezers." It is a discourse that absolves men of responsibility, erasing their own participation in the sexual transaction. While women are constructed as possessing extraordinary sexual powers, when they do employ their sexuality as an exchange value, their prowess and worth are sharply downgraded. The contrast with other forms of play-labor we've discussed is striking. Unlike sports and most aspects of hip-hop culture (with the possible exception of aerosol art), when women's sexual exercises remain just "play" and are not widely circulated, they are more highly valued. If she turns "professional" and earns money and becomes more highly circulated, she loses "value."[47]

The most unambiguous example of the professionalization of sex is obviously prostitution. The word "prostitution," however, carries enormous moral connotations and focuses attention solely on the woman rather than the men who are equally involved in the transaction, both as consumers and employers. Few female prostitutes describe their work as creative or fulfilling in the same way that graffiti artists, athletes, or musicians do. And, in most cases, it is not autonomous work but an exploitative wage relationship—piece work is perhaps a better description. Because streets are dominated and controlled by men, prostitutes often require protection; even if they are not assaulted, the fear of assault is constantly circulated. Most important, women turn to prostitution for the money.[48]

On the other hand, when discussing prostitution in a heterosexual context, we run the risk of stripping women of any agency or removing from the transaction the issue of female desire. For instance, while prostitution offered women a means of income, we must consider the extent to which anonymous sex was a source of pleasure. Furthermore, in light of the ways in which black women's sexual expression or participation in popular amusements (especially in heterosocial public places) has been constrained historically, black women's involvement in the pleasure industry might be seen as both typical and transgressive. Typical in that black women's bodies have historically been exploited as sites of male pleasure and embodiments of lasciviousness; transgressive in that women were able to break the straitjacket of what historian Evelyn Brooks Higginbotham calls the "politics of respectability" in exchange for the possibility of female pleasure. It is also potentially empowering since it turns labor not associated with wage work—sexual play and intercourse—into income.[49]

One young Harlem woman, simply identified as "Margo," who turned to prostitution as early as fifteen, took pleasure in the fact that she could earn an average of $200 per customer for doing something she enjoyed— having sex. As the product of an abusive home and grinding poverty, Margo sold her body as a means of survival. At the same time, by describing prostitution as her "pastime" rather than her job, she indirectly illustrated the pleasure she sometimes derived from the transaction:

> If a guy approached me and said I was beautiful and asked how much would it cost him to have me, I would tell him whatever came to my mind. If he looked well dressed and clean I would say $200, $300, $400. It depended on my mood. If I was real horny, I would react quicker but that didn't mean the price went down. I would just choose someone who I thought was good looking. Someone who I thought would be pleasant to fuck.[50]

Sex, in Margo's view, was undoubtedly labor, but it was unlike the wage relationships that dominate the labor market. Besides, she found a way to bypass a pimp and work for herself, which meant that she kept all of her earnings. "It was sort of like getting your cake and eating it too," she pointed out. "You wake up, eat, sleep, you don't punch no clocks, you don't conform to no rules and regulations or courtesy to co-workers, customers, bosses, clients, patients, staff, etc. Best of all, you don't pay taxes either."[51]

Margo's world is hardly ideal, and it certainly does not challenge the structures of capitalism. On the contrary, her decisions are driven somewhat by capitalist principles: namely, reducing labor expenditures and maximizing profit. However, she is resisting what would otherwise be her fate in an increasingly service-oriented, low-wage economy with shrinking opportunities for working-class ghetto residents. She exercises some control over the labor time, retains the full fee for her services, and often enjoys the work she performs. For her, sex is both work she can earn money from and play she can enjoy.

All of these examples, in their own unique way, reveal the dialectical links between "work" and "play" within the context of capitalism. Although the concept of "play" in the modern era is inextricably tied to the creation of leisure time as a form of consumption and recuperation for wage workers in a capitalist political economy, play is a form of agency that is generally regarded as pleasurable activities that take place in "free" time. Play undeniably requires labor, but it is usually thought to be creative and fulfilling to those involved; it is autonomous from the world of work. In a postindustrial economy with fewer opportunities for wage work that might be financially or even psychologically fulfilling, art and performance—forms of labor not always seen as labor—become increasingly visible as options to joblessness and low-wage service work. Of course, the opportunities that music, sports, visual arts, and sex offer as alternative roads to upward mobility are actually quite limited. Nevertheless, these arenas have provided young people with a wider range of options for survival, space for creative expression, and at least a modicum of control over their own labor. In other words, neither an entrepreneurial spirit nor a work ethic is lacking in many of these inner-city youths. Indeed, the terms themselves presume a binarism that simply doesn't do justice to the meaning of labor, for they obscure the degree to which young people attempt to turn a realm of consumption (leisure time, play time) into a site of production. Their efforts are clearly within the spirit of laissez-faire, but the definition of "profit" is not limited to monetary gain; equally important are the visceral pleasures of the form, the aesthetic quality of the product, the victory, the praise.

Of course, turning the labor of play into a commodity is hardly new. What is new, however, are the particular cultural forms that have emerged in this era and the structural context of the postindustrial urban political economy. As I've argued above, the decline of recreational facilities and accessible play spaces for inner-city youths has coincided with the transformation of a criminal justice system in which reform is clearly no longer on the agenda. Today, policing the inner city is geared toward the corralling and managing of a young, displaced, and by most estimates permanently unemployed black working-class population. Ironically, while city and state expenditures on parks and recreation dwindle and the corporate sector invests in more class-segregated, forbidding "public" play spaces, a growing number of voices have called for a return to supervised play in order to get kids "off the streets" and instill them with discipline and a strong work ethic. The movement sounds strikingly similar to Progressive-era efforts to replace what appeared to be disorganized street life with middle-class norms and behavior.[52] Not surprisingly, the introduction of an old idea to solve relatively new problems is keeping with the new conservative agenda of the current Republican-dominated Congress under the leadership of Newt Gingrich. (Ironically, whereas the Republicans' "Contract with America"—a highly publicized commitment to sharply limit government and pass a broad plank of extremely conservative legislation—placed emphasis on "family values," crime, and personal safety, they have deeply cut expenditures on recreation and urban development. Instead of supervised play, Gingrich and his followers have favored forms of incarceration, from longer prison sentences to orphanages for children whose parents are deemed incompetent. Suddenly, supervised play seems like the liberal answer to "juvenile delinquency.")

While the movement for organized play has plenty of virtues, I hope we do not make the same mistakes of a century ago; more social control will do little to unleash and develop the creative capacities of black urban youth. Rather than try to change the person through rigid regimentation and supervised play, what needs to be changed are the streets themselves, the built environment, the economy, and the racist discourse that dominates popular perceptions of black youth. The presence of large numbers of African-American and Latino youth together in parks, school yards, subway stations, or on street corners does not necessarily mean they are conspiring to rob somebody. Nor does it mean they are leading a life of idleness.

Finally, in the struggles of urban youths for survival and pleasure inside of capitalism, capitalism has become both their greatest friend and greatest foe. It has the capacity to create spaces for their entrepreneurial imaginations and their "symbolic work," to turn something of a profit for some, for them to hone their skills and imagine getting paid. At the same time, it is also responsible for a shrinking labor market, the militarization of urban space, and the circulation of the very representations of race that generate terror in all of us at the sight of young black men and yet compels most of America to want to wear their shoes.

NOTES

The author wishes to thank Diedra Harris-Kelley, Kyra Gaunt, Wahneema Lubiano, Tricia Rose, James Spady, Cornel West, Michael Eric Dyson, Playthell

Benjamin, Arnold Rampersad, Marya McQuirter, fellows at the Institute for the Humanities (University of Michigan), and several attendees of the Race Matters Conference at Princeton University for their criticisms and insights. The research and writing of this essay was supported by a generous grant from the National Endowment for the Humanities.

1. Paul Gilroy, "One Nation Under a Groove: The Culture Politics of 'Race' and Racism in Britain," in *Anatomy of Racism*, ed. David Theo Goldberg (Minneapolis: University of Minnesota Press, 1990), 274.

2. Nearly half of the unemployed in the 1980s were teenagers, and blacks and Latinos had the highest percentage. Terry Williams and William Kornblum, *Growing Up Poor* (Lexington, Mass.: D.C. Heath, 1985), 5–6.

3. Mike Davis, *City of Quartz: Excavating the Future of Los Angeles* (London: Verso, 1990), 304–7; Edward Soja, *Postmodern Geographies: The Reassertion of Space in Critical Social Theory* (London: Verso, 1989), 197, 201.

4. The idea that unemployed black youth turn to crime because it is more rewarding than minimum-wage service-oriented work has been explored by a number of social scientists. See, for example, Richard B. Freeman, "The Relation of Criminal Activity to Black Youth Employment," in *The Economics of Race and Crime*, ed. Margaret C. Simms and Samuel L. Myers, Jr. (New Brunswick, N.J.: Transaction Books, 1988), 99–107; Llad Phillips and Harold Votey, Jr., "Rational Choice Models of Crimes by Youth," ibid., 129–87; Llad Philips, H. L. Votey, Jr., and D. Maxwell, "Crime, Youth, and the Labor Market," *Journal of Political Economy* 80 (1972): 491–504; Philip Moss and Chris Tilly, *Why Black Men Are Doing Worse in the Labor Market: A Review of Supply-Side and Demand-Side Explanations* (working paper) (New York: Social Science Research Council Committee for Research on the Underclass, 1991), 90–93. For a discussion of the role of gangs in the illicit economy, see Martin Sanchez Jankowski, *Islands in the Street: Gangs and American Urban Society* (Berkeley and Los Angeles: University of California Press, 1991), 119–31. Despite the general perception that dealers make an enormous amount of money, at least one study suggests that the average crack peddler only makes about $700 per month. See Peter Reuter, Robert MacCoun, and Patrick Murphy, *Money for Crime: A Study of the Economics of Drug Dealing in Washington, D.C.* (Santa Monica, Calif: Rand Drug Policy Research Center, 1990); Davis, *City of Quartz*, 322.

5. Davis, *City of Quartz*, 244–51. For discussions of the ways in which the mass media depicts black youth gangs, violence, and the crack economy in inner-city neighborhoods, see Jankowski, *Islands in the Street*, 284–302; Jimmie L. Reeves and Richard Campbell, *Cracked Coverage: Television News, the Anti-cocaine Crusade, and the Reagan Legacy* (Durham, N.C.: Duke University Press, 1994); Herman Gray, "Race Relations as News: Content Analysis," *American Behavioral Scientist* 30, no. 4 (March–April, 1987): 381–96; Craig Reinarman and Harry G. Levine, "The Crack Attack: Politics and Media in

America's Latest Drug Scare," in *Images of Issues: Typifying Contemporary Social Problems*, ed. Joel Best (New York: Aldine de Gruyter, 1989), 115–35; Clarence Lusane, *Pipe Dream Blues: Racism and the War on Drugs* (Boston: South End Press, 1991).

6. Michael Gold, *Jews Without Money* (New York: International Publishers Co., 1930), 42.

7. Cary Goodman, *Choosing Sides: Playground and Street Life on the Lower East Side* (New York: Schocken, 1979), 9; Carl Nightingale, *On the Edge: A History of Poor Black Children and Their American Dreams* (New York: Basic Books, 1993), 15.

8. Jankowski, *Islands in the Streets*, 119–31; Terry Williams, *Cocaine Kids: The Inside Story of a Teenage Drug Ring* (Reading, Mass.: Addison-Wesley, 1989); Jonathan Rieder, "Adventure Capitalism," *New Republic* 19 (November 1990): 36–40; Philippe Bourgeois, "In Search of Horatio Alger: Culture and Ideology in the Crack Economy," *Contemporary Drug Problems* 16 (Winter 1989): 619–49.

9. Josh Sugarmann and Kristen Rand, "Cease Fire," *Rolling Stone Magazine* 677 (March 10, 1994): 31–42, quote on p. 38. This is an excerpt from a report issued by the Violence Policy Center titled *Cease Fire: A Comprehensive Strategy to Reduce Firearms Violence* (Washington, D.C.: Violence Policy Center, 1994). See also, Bruce C. Johnson, "Taking Care of Labor: The Police in American Politics," *Theory and Society* 3, no. 1 (1976): 106; Craig Wolff, "Guns Offer New York Teenagers a Commonplace Deadly Allure," *New York Times*, November 5, 1990; "Guns Take Ever-Higher Toll Among Young Blacks," *New York Times*, March 17, 1991; Davis, *City of Quartz*, 240–48.

10. Davis, *City of Quartz*, chap. 4; Camilo José Vergara, "Our Fortified Ghettos," *Nation* (January 31, 1994): 121, 122.

11. Jay S. Shivers and Joseph W. Halper, *The Crisis in Urban Recreational Services* (Rutherford, N.J.: Fairleigh Dickinson University Press, 1981), 77–79; Roy Rosenzweig and Elizabeth Blackmar, *The Park and the People: A History of Central Park* (New York: Henry Holt, 1994), 502. The increasing costs of policing public recreational facilities also contributed to the budget crisis (Shivers and Halper, *The Crisis*, 106, 248–61).

12. Much of this I learned by taking my four-year-old, Elleza, to these high-tech playgrounds. When we visited Playspace in December of 1994, the employees refused to "buzz" me in at first, partly because they could not see Elleza through the window. When I picked her up and literally pointed to her, they allowed us to enter. For an interesting article about these pay-for-play spaces and the impact they are making on children's play in New York City, see Barbara Ensor, "Fun City," *New York Magazine* (October 24, 1994): 54–57. I should add that given the increasing workload of urban professionals, these "pay-for-play" spaces also offer inexpensive baby-sitting for older children.

13. Rosenzweig and Blackmar, *The Park and the People*, 508–9.
14. Cary Goodman, *Choosing Sides: Playground and Street Life on the Lower East Side* (New York: Schocken, 1979); David Nasaw, *Children of the City: At Work and at Play* (Garden City, N.Y.: Anchor, 1985); Amanda Dargan and Steve Zeitlin, *City Play* (New Brunswick, N.J., and London: Rutgers University Press, 1990), 136.
15. Houston Baker, *Black Studies, Rap, and the Academy* (Chicago: University of Chicago Press, 1993), 46–50; Robin D. G. Kelley, "Straight from Underground," *Nation* 254, no. 22 (June 8, 1992): 793–96; Davis, *City of Quartz*, chaps. 4 and 5; Tricia Rose, *Black Noise: Rap Music and Black Culture in Contemporary America* (Hanover and London: Wesleyan University Press, 1994), 106–14.
16. Nelson George, *Elevating the Game: Black Men and Basketball* (New York: HarperCollins, 1992), 200.
17. James Spady and Joseph Eure, *Nation Conscious Rap* (Brooklyn: PC International, 1991), 262; Michael A. Messner, *Power at Play: Sport and the Problem of Masculinity* (Boston: Beacon, 1992), 52; see also Henry Louis Gates, Jr., "Delusions of Grandeur," *Sports Illustrated* (August 9, 1991): 78.
18. Steve James, Fred Marx, and Peter Gilbert, *Hoop Dreams* (Kartemquit Films, 1994).
19. J. Hoberman, "Making It," *Village Voice*, October 18, 1994; Messner, *Power at Play*, 45. Hoberman's essay is a review of *Hoop Dreams*.
20. Heidi Hartmann, "The Family as the Locus of Gender, Class, and Political Struggle: The Example of Housework," *Signs* 6 (Spring 1981): 366–94; Carolyn Steedman, *Landscape for a Good Woman: A Story of Two Lives* (New Brunswick, N.J.: Rutgers University Press, 1986), 13; Elizabeth Faue, "Reproducing the Class Struggle: Perspectives on the Writing of Working-Class History" (paper presented at Social Science History Association Meeting, Minneapolis, October 19, 1990) (paper in author's possession), 8.
21. Dargan and Zeitlin, *City Play*, 157–61; Williams and Kornblum, *Growing Up Poor*, 77; June Goodwin, "Double Dutch, Double Dutch: All You Need Is a Clothesline and Jet-Propelled Feet," *Christian Science Monitor*, October 7, 1980. Also, Kyra Gaunt, an ethnomusicology student at the University of Michigan, is writing an important dissertation on black girls' culture that includes an extensive discussion of double dutch.
22. As a boy "turner" in New York during the late 1960s and early 1970s, I remember vividly some of the accompanying songs and rhymes. My favorite was "Ain't your mamma pretty / She got meatballs on her titties [breasts] / She got scrambled eggs between her legs / Ain't your mamma pretty." The most popular rhyme at that time went something like this: "_____ and _____ sitting in a tree [any name will do] / K-I-S-S-I-N-G / First comes love / Then comes marriage / Here comes

_____ with a baby carriage / How many babies did she have?" At that point the tempo would pick up and the other participants would count the number of times the jumper could skip without messing up. The final count, of course, equals the number of babies she and her boyfriend will have. For other examples, see Roger D. Abrahams, ed., *Jump-Rope Rhymes: A Dictionary* (Austin: University of Texas Press, 1969); Marjorie Harness Goodwin, *He-Said-She-Said: Talk as Social Organization Among Black Children* (Bloomington: Indiana University Press, 1990); Bessie Lomax Hawes and Bessie Jones, ed., *Step It Down: Games, Plays, Songs, and Stories from Afro-American Heritage* (New York: Harper & Row, 1972).

23. Dargan and Zeitlin, *City Play*, 157, 160–61.

24. Paul Willis, *Common Culture: Symbolic Work at Play in the Everyday Cultures of the Young* (Boulder, Colo., and San Francisco: Westview Press, 1990), 1–5, 65.

25. On Larry Wright, see the film by Ari Marcopoulos and Maja Zrnic, *Larry Wright* (distributed by First Run Icarus Films, 1990). I am basing some of my arguments here on my own observations in several U.S. cities. For a sensitive portrait of a young black homeless man in Washington, D.C., trying to make a living playing flute on the streets, see Courtland Milloy, "Bittersweet Notes from the Street," *Washington Post*, October 3, 1985.

26. Unfortunately, there is very little written on go-go, so some of what I describe comes from my own observations and discussions with friends who grew up in Washington, D.C.—most notably, Marya McQuirter, a history graduate student at the University of Michigan. (I am grateful to Marya for correcting a couple of errors in an earlier draft of this essay.) Nevertheless, there are a few useful articles from the *Washington Post* that I consulted for this essay. See esp. Richard Harrington, "Go-Go: A Musical Phenomenon, Bonding a Community," *Washington Post*, May 19, 1985; Michael Marriott, "Funky Sounds 'Bustin' Loose' in the District," *Washington Post*, October 5, 1984; Courtland Milloy, "Go-Go Goes Across Town," *Washington Post*, July 15, 1985.

27. Richard Harrington, "Go-Go."

28. Some very useful works on graffiti include Craig Castleman, *Getting Up: Subway Graffiti in New York* (Cambridge, Mass.: MIT Press, 1982); Atlanta and Alexander, "Wild Style," 156–68; Martha Cooper and Henry Chalfant, *Subway Art* (New York: Holt, Rinehart & Winston, 1984); Steve Hager, *Hip Hop: The Illustrated History of Breakdancing, Rap Music, and Graffiti* (New York: St. Martin, 1984); Ivor L. Miller, "Aerosol Kingdom: The Indigenous Culture of New York Subway Painters" (Ph.D. diss., Yale University, 1990); Rose, *Black Noise*, 41–47. On women aerosol artists, see esp. Nancy Guevara, "Women Writin' Rappin' Breakin'" in *The Year Left 2*, ed. Mike Davis et. al. (Verso Press: London, 1987), 160–75; Rose, *Black Noise*, 43–44.

29. Castleman, *Getting Up*, 117–25; Hugo Martinez, "A Brief Background of Graffiti," in *United Graffiti Artists Catalog* (n.p., 1975).

30. Castleman, *Getting Up*, 131–32.

31. Ibid., 122–25.

32. Ivor Miller, "Guerrilla Artists of New York City," *Race and Class* 35, no. 1 (July–September 1993): 39; David Brendan Strasser, "'It's the End of the World as We Know It (and I Feel Fine)': Keith Haring, Postmodern Hieroglyphics, Panic Hyperreality" (Ph.D. diss., Bowling Green State University, 1992); on the European art scene's fascination with graffiti, see Atlanta and Alexander, "Wild Style," 156–57; Kirk Varnedoe and Adam Gopnik, *High and Low: Modern Art, Popular Culture* (New York: Museum of Modern Art, New York, 1990), 377–82.

33. Castleman, *Getting Up*, 126; author's conversation with St. Maurice, Staten Island, New York, January 1990. I might add that because graffiti was one aspect of the larger hip-hop culture, some writers, notably Freddy Brathwaite and Rammelzee also produced and performed rap music. Brathwaite, known to the world as "Fab Five Freddy" did attend art school but went on to produce music videos, rap songs, and host the ever-popular *Yo! MTV Raps*. Rammelzee rapped for a while (appearing in Charlie Ahearn's 1982 film *Wildstyle*) and eventually became a noted performance artist. See Atlanta and Alexander, "Wild Style," 158–62; Rose, *Black Noise*, 194.

34. Quoted in Ivor Miller, "Guerrilla Artists of New York City," 39.

35. Joe Austin, "A Symbol That We Have Lost Control: Authority, Public Identity, and Graffiti Writing" (unpublished paper in author's possession).

36. On this last point one need only look at the *New York Times Magazine*'s cover article on Basquiat in February 1985. As the physical embodiment of "primitivism"-meets-modernism, he appeared shoeless but with a shirt and tie. For other examples of Basquiat's body and lifestyle as spectacle, see Lorraine O'Grady, "A Day at the Races: On Basquiat and the Black Art World," *Artforum* 31 (April 1993): 10–12; "Jean-Michel Basquiat: Pop Life," *Economist* 325 (November 21, 1992): 104–5; Martine Arnault, "Basquiat, from Brooklyn," *Cimaise* (November–December 1989): 41–44; Andrew Decker, "The Price of Fame," *Art News* 88 (January 1989): 96–101. On the problem of outsider/insider art and the question of boundaries, see the wonderful catalogue edited by Maurice Tuchman and Carol S. Eliel, *Parallel Visions: Modern Artists and Outsider Art* (Princeton, N.J.: Princeton University Press, 1992); Michael D. Hall and Eugene W. Metcalf, Jr., *The Artist Outsider: Creativity and the Boundaries of Culture* (Washington, D.C., and London: Smithsonian Institution Press, 1994).

37. On the early history of rap music, see Hager, *Hip Hop*; Rose, *Black Noise*; Bill Adler, *Rap: Portraits and Lyrics of a Generation of Black Rockers* (New York: St. Martin, 1991); Nelson George et al., eds., *Fresh: Hip Hop Don't*

Stop (New York: Random House, 1985); Spady and Eure, *Nation Conscious Rap*, xi–xxxi; David Toop, *Rap Attack 2: African Rap to Global Hip Hop* (London: Serpent's Tail, 1991); Brian Cross, *It's Not About a Salary: Rap, Race, and Resistance in Los Angeles* (London: Verso, 1993); and for more on the financial side of hip-hop, see Clarence Lusane, "Rap, Race, and Politics," *Race and Class* 35, no. 1 (1993): 42–47; Alan Light, "About a Salary or Reality?" *South Atlantic Quarterly* 90 (Fall 1991): 855–70.

38. Cross, *It's Not About a Salary*, 162–63; 145.

39. Ibid., 196–97. It is particularly interesting to contrast Dr. Dre's story with that of his former partner, Eazy E (aka Eric Wright). Eazy's more publicized version of NWA's origins suggests that drug money was used to capitalize NWA's initial productions—a narrative that reinforces the idea that "authentic" gangsta rappers have criminal backgrounds. See David Mills, "The Gangsta Rapper: Violent Hero or Negative Role Model?" *The Source*, December 1990, 32; Dan Charnas, "A Gangsta's World View," *The Source*, (Summer 1990), 21–22; "Niggers with Attitude," *Melody Maker* 65, no. 44 (November 4, 1989): 33; Frank Owen, "Hanging Tough," *Spin* 6, no. 1 (April 1990): 34.

40. Rose, *Black Noise*; Nancy Guevara, "Women Writin' Rappin' Breakin'"; Dan Cox, "Brooklyn's Furious Rockers: Break Dance Roots in a Breakneck Neighborhood," *Dance Magazine* 58, no. 4 (April 1984): 79–82; Hager, *Hip Hop*; Peter J. Rosenwald, "Breaking Away '80s Style," *Dance Magazine* 58, no. 4 (April 1984), 70.

41. Quoted in Cox, "Brooklyn's Furious Rockers," 81. A lot has been written on injuries caused by break dancing. For a sample, see Ronald Wheeler and Rodney Appell, "Differential Diagnosis of Scrotal Pain After Break Dancing," *Journal of the American Medical Association* 252 (December 28, 1984): 3336; Philip J. Goscienski and Louis Luevanos, "Injury Caused by Break Dancing," *Journal of the American Medical Association* 252 (December 28, 1984): 3367; Robert A. Norman and Michael Grodin, "Injuries from Break Dancing," *American Family Physician* 30 (October 1984): 109–12; Kui-Chung Lee, "Intracerebral Hemorrhage after Break Dancing," *New England Journal of Medicine* 323 (August 30, 1990): 615–16.

42. Rose, *Black Noise*, 48, 50; Sally Banes, "Breaking Is Hard to Do," *Village Voice*, April 22–28, 1981.

43. Dan Cox, "Brooklyn's Furious Rockers," 79.

44. Rosenwald, "Breaking Away '80s Style," 73–74.

45. Rose, *Black Noise*, 50; and on the training of professional dancers in breakdance techniques, see Joyce Mollov, "Getting the Breaks," *Ballet News* 6 (August 1984): 14–19; Margaret Pierpont, "Breaking in the Studio," *Dance Magazine* 58, no. 4 (April 1984): 82.

46. The best discussion of women's involvement as hip-hop artists can be found

in Rose, *Black Noise*, esp. chap. 5. See also Toop, *Rap Attack 2*, 93–95; Guevara, "Women Writin' Rappin' Breakin'," 160–75. Most of the work on women and rap focuses on representations of women or female rappers, and on representations of sexuality rather than their actual participation as artists, producers, etc.

47. I am especially grateful to Wahneema Lubiano for helping me think through the valuing or devaluing of women's sexuality in relationship to the market. For examples of the celebration of the pimp in literature and popular culture, see Iceberg Slim [Robert Beck], *Pimp: The Story of My Life* (Los Angeles: Holloway House, 1969); Christina Milner and Richard Milner, *Black Prayers: The Secret World of Black Pimps* (New York: Little, Brown, 1972). On the pimp in popular film, see Donald Bogle, *Toms, Coons, Mulattoes, Mammies, and Bucks: An Interpretive History of Blacks in American Films*, rev. ed. (New York: Continuum, 1989), 234–42; Daniel Leab, *From Sambo to Superspade: The Black Experience in Motion Pictures* (Boston: Houghton Mifflin, 1975); David E. James, "Chained to Devilpictures: Cinema and Black Liberation in the Sixties," in Davis et al., *The Year Left 2*, 125–38; H. Rap Brown, *Die, Nigger, Die* (New York: Dial Press, 1969); Bobby Seale, *Seize the Time* (New York: Random House, 1970), and *Lonely Rage* (New York: Times Books, 1978), in which Seale himself takes on the characteristics of a pimp; Eldridge Cleaver, *Soul on Ice* (New York: McGraw-Hill, 1968).

48. For a vivid and detailed description of black teenage prostitutes and pimps during the 1970s and 1980s, see Williams and Kornblum, *Growing Up Poor*, 62–63.

49. My thinking here owes a great deal to Tera Hunter's forthcoming book *Contesting the New South: The Politics and Culture of Wage Household Labor in Atlanta, 1861–1920* (unpublished manuscript), chap. 5; Kathy Peiss, *Cheap Amusements: Working Women and Leisure in Turn-of-the-Century New York* (Philadelphia: Temple University Press, 1986); Hazel Carby, "Policing the Black Woman's Body in an Urban Context," *Critical Inquiry* 18 (Summer 1992): 738–55; Victoria Wollcott, "'I'm as Good as Any Woman in Your Town': African-American Women and the Politics of Identity in Inter-war Detroit" (Ph.D. diss., in progress, University of Michigan).

50. Williams and Kornblum, *Growing Up Poor*, 65–66.

51. Ibid., 66, 69.

52. Goodman, *Choosing Sides*, 28.

BLACK NATIONALISM
AND BLACK COMMON SENSE

Policing Ourselves and Others

■

Wahneema Lubiano

THIS ESSAY ADDRESSES black nationalism as black American common sense—as everyday ideology. I'll begin with definitions. Cultural theorist James Kavanagh explains succinctly: "Ideology designates a rich 'system of representations,' worked up in specific material practices, which helps form individuals into social subjects. . . . [it is] not a set of narrowly 'political' ideas but a fundamental framework of assumptions that defines the parameters of the real and the self—what [Louis] Althusser calls the social subject's '*lived* relation to the real.'"[1] Or, as cultural theorist Laurie Langbauer puts it, "perhaps the simplest definition of the ideological is that it is whatever seems natural."[2] When I say "common sense," then, I refer to ideology lived and articulated in everyday understandings of the world and one's place in it.

I argue here that black nationalism is plural, flexible, and contested; that its most hegemonic appearances and manifestations have been masculinist and homophobic; that its circulation has acted both as a bulwark against racism and as disciplinary activity within the group. I see it as extremely complicated, often reactionary, and dangerously effective in the way that it can and has organized specific groups of black people, under specific circumstances, to ally themselves with harmful and dangerous activities. I take the confirmation of Supreme Court Justice Clarence Thomas to be such an instance. He is far more threatening to black people's (and, indeed, to the larger social formation's) political and economic fortunes and to the fight for social and racial justice than any drug dealer. That is not to deny that some form of black nationalism animates what we can think of as black American common sense. It is important, therefore, to think of it as something with which to engage if we want to do politics within the shifting multiplicities of a group that understands itself as "black."

What is black nationalism? It depends. One way to understand it is to consider the way it functions: (1) It functions as a narrative of political history—a way to narrate a past in relation to that past's and the present's politics. (2) It functions as an articulation; it gives language to, and joins together, things that have no necessary belonging in such a way that the joining makes the connection seem inevitable. (3) It functions as an articulation explaining what is good and beautiful, as style. (4) It functions as a utopian narrative—a rallying cry, an expression of desire. (5) It functions as a critical analysis—an ongoing, ever-renewed critique of black existence against white racial domination as well as an evaluation of black existence within the group. Black nationalism is of inestimable ideological—commonsensical—importance given the reality that U.S. blacks, in their "being-as-a-group" control no means of production, no land mass, and until about thirty years ago, were excluded from meaningful participation in formal, public politics.[3] Necessarily, culture has been our terrain of struggle.

For the moment I will define "nationalism" as the activation of a narrative of identity and interests.[4] Whether or not concrete in the form of a state (or the idea of its possibility), this narrative is one that members of a social, political, cultural, ethnic, or "racial" group relate to themselves, and which is predicated on some understanding—however mythologized or mystified—of a shared past, an assessment of present circumstances, and a description of or prescription for a shared future. Nationalism articulates a desire—always unfulfillable—for complete representation of the past and a fantasy for a better future. It is a social identification. My definition is Weberian in that it draws on his notions of a "community of memories" and a community of shared values, but it also draws on various nineteenth-century black intellectuals' descriptions of their group's political imperatives.[5] (I have in mind here Henry Highland Garnet, Maria Stewart, Martin Delany, Frances E. W. Harper, and the early W. E. B.

Du Bois.) Black nationalism is a form of nationalism generally understood, a relation easily forgotten if it is thought of only as a form of racial
separatism.

Black nationalism, in its broadest sense, is a sign, an analytic, describing a range of historically manifested ideas about black American possibilities that include any or all of the following: racial solidarity, cultural
specificity, religious, economic, and political separatism. (This last has
been articulated both as a possibility within and outside of U.S. territorial
boundaries.) Black nationalism has most consistently registered opposition to the historical and continuing racism of the U.S. state and its institutions. It has been deployed to articulate strategies of resistance.
Bernice Reagon argues:

> You come together to see what you can do about shouldering up
> all of your energies so that you and your kind can survive. . . .
> [T]hat space should be a nurturing space where you sift out what
> people are saying about you and decide who you really are. And
> you take the time to try to construct within yourself and within
> your community who you would be if you were running soci-
> ety. . . . It's nurturing, but it is also nationalism. At a certain stage,
> nationalism is crucial to a people if you are ever going to impact
> as a group in your own interest.[6]

Black nationalism is a constantly reinvented and reinventing discourse that generally opposes the Eurocentricism of the U.S. state, but
neither historically nor contemporaneously depends upon a consistent or
complete opposition to Eurocentrism. As conservative thinker Wilson
Moses argues, black nationalism does not *necessarily* entail a complete rejection of the Euro-American cultural tradition.[7] In fact, one consistent
black feminist critique of black nationalist ideology is that it insufficiently
breaks with patriarchical modes of economic, political, cultural (especially familial), and social circulations of power that mimic Euro-American
modes.

When I say "the state," I mean not only the system of formal government and its attendant means of legislation and policy implementation. I

also refer to what political theorist Tim Mitchell has described as the "common ideological and cultural construct [that] occurs not merely as a subjective belief, incorporated in the thinking and action of individuals [but is] represented and reproduced in visible everyday forms."[8] I agree with Mitchell's assertion that the state's "boundary within society appears elusive, porous, and mobile" (77), and that is no less efficient for being difficult to describe in its presence and effects.

There is no way of being outside the state. We not only make the state in the forms that cohere as the judicial system or Congress, but we encounter it in our public imaginings about the nature of our world. These imaginings are spread through our civil institutions, our educational system, our families, our churches—all the sectors of civil society that we do not generally think of as ground on which the state operates. When we envision what constitutes a safe world for children, or when we talk about what a good person is, or when we fantasize about the good life, our imaginings are very much influenced by how the mechanisms of our daily lives are suggested, produced, maintained, or enforced by powerful state forces, or by powerful entities able to influence or direct the state. And regardless of how unfair it is that particular individuals or particular collections of individuals who exist as social entities (such as corporations or banks) have much more influence on the state compared to those of us without wealth or power, we are nonetheless subject to that state's power. In many cases that means we are subject to the powerful individuals, corporate entities, and other manifestations of the political and economic elite via their influence on the state.

The perspective of black nationalism permits the realization that the dominant operations of the U.S. state have been determined by the interests of the economically most powerful (interests that have served the dominant racial group), and that the dominant discouse of U.S. history has been some form or other of white American nationalism.

Possessed of the terms of black nationalism, let us see how the state functions. The state's role in imagining and representing the nation is of paramount importance in managing the social formation, if, despite the state's "elusive and porous" mobility, we understand its various entities to have the power of and access to forums—civic, institutional, formally and informally political—that allow it to produce and circulate representations of what our social formation is and ought to be. The education system, for example, is of primary importance in the circulation of the state's idea of its subject. And while black Americans are *subject to*, as well as negative *subjects of* that circulation, historically, black nationalism has been the articulated consciousness of black Americans' awareness of their place in the state's intentions.

Black nationalism resists both the U.S. state and its social and racialized domination—including what black social theorist Oliver Cox describes as the tendency of the white bourgeois to proletarianize the entire black American group.[9] In other words, in the eyes of the dominant group there are no necessary *easily* discernible class differences among the black American group members. Black nationalism resists racialized domination for all classes of the group. But it has also historically appealed to the white bourgeois state to protect black people from the worst depredations of unbridled white nationalism. Further, even as it functions as resistance to the state on one hand, it reinscribes the state in particular places within its own narratives of resistance. That reinscription most often occurs within black nationalist narratives of the black family. (Black feminist cultural commentators across two centuries have developed critiques of this familial narrative.)

Black nationalism establishes itself as a counter to the narrativizing of race as class within this social order. While black nationalism has not always, under all circumstances, understood the black struggle to focus on redistribution of wealth, its strategies for "liberation" in the U.S. context have been organized by the fact that within the discourse of white supremacy *all* blacks are equally debased, and that *for the most part* class has not mediated many of the effects of racism. In this way, black nationalism is predicated on the notion of racial solidarity across class lines.

■

Black nationalism is significant for the ubiquity of its presence in black American lives—in those lives' conventional wisdom. Black nationalism is the cultural logic of black peoples' historical self-consciousness.[10] The political realities and possibilities of black nationalism as an organizing discourse include: (1) demystification of white racial domination, (2) the transformative effects of new deployments of it—such as the valorization of black nationalist construction of community against, for example, the capitalist-driven logic and aesthetics of the drug trade, and (3) activation as a bridge to international political awareness. Historically, this last aspect—international political awareness—has manifested itself as Pan-Africanism. As a bridge discourse, black nationalism can begin the work of radicalizing people unaware of international labor politics, for example, by providing a jolt of "recognition" of the exploitative politics of global capitalism's effect on Third World labor. None of what I've been describing is *guaranteed* by black nationalism; the proof of its capabilities rest in its deployments. Black nationalism as constitutive of a political class actually produced labor alliances within black American political struggle of a progressive kind in recent history—and Manning Marable's narrative of 1960s and '70s black nationalism delineates this.[11]

Commonsense black nationalism is evidenced in the repeated calls on the part of some black Americans for "an end to black-on-black violence." Rather than dismissing that language as an expression that further pathologizes black violence (which it does also), we can see it (and also be critical of it) as a way that people try to intervene in what happens within the group. Such language implies black historical awareness in order to stave off what is seen as within-the-group suicidal behaviors. Such usage is a way of saying, "Remember what the dominant group has done to us, and stop doing the same thing." Against the market-driven forces of the drug trade, such a rallying cry is meant as a counter.

■

Commonsense black nationalism's work as counternarrative is aestheticized in popular culture. That common sense is implicitly a part of two sentences—one from Greg Tate and one from Gina Dent—that, at first glance, might seem distant from it: "I don't think anyone . . . wants to give up a certain kind of romance we have with being black" and "We love to be in love."[12] That language is a reminder that whatever other understandings we have about black identity, and despite our quite necessary awareness that race is not a given but an explanation fought over across a specific history, black identity is also a sign for remembering our specificity and aestheticizing our resistance to racist trauma.

I'm describing articulations of the convergences and divergences of black nationalism understood as both a problem and a part of the working arsenal of black American common sense with the goal of illuminating the nature of its functioning in the world. Let me now focus on two examples from black popular culture and an extraordinary moment in recent history, the Million Man March.

My project is to examine the relation between black nationalism and the state. I am thinking through ways to understand just how black nationalist narratives are available to the state for projects that are inimical to the interests of black people in terms of their position within the United States. Therefore, I am concerned with both exploring black nationalism's possibilities and criticizing its problems. My present work addresses those questions by attending to manifestations of black nationalist narrative in mass-distributed cultural productions, and in a moment's movement that embodies the concerns that I address here. Why look at popular culture? For what it has to teach us about the nexus of politics and desire; to look at what one or two cultural producers can make of salient ideas in the world; to think about what an audience can find appealing enough to consume; and to chart what political resonances exist or can be read off the intersection of these things.

I talk about black nationalism generally in order to point up its manifestation in black common sense. I want to use the film *Deep Cover* to talk about the ways that black nationalist family romance can play itself out as an address that not only encourages black audiences to consume with pleasure an appeal to "pro-black family" sentiments, but also provides an aesthetic cover for delineating the ways black nationalism could function, horribly, in "new world order" terms. I also want to use Tupac Shakur's[13] rap song "Keep Ya Head Up" to look at ways that black women are circulated in aesthetic representations that seem to center them within a genre that is accused most consistently of marginalizing the actual women by subjecting their representations to lyrical mistreatment. And I want to focus on the Million Man March as a moment that signals internalizations of conservative state ideology through validations of masculinity, "family," personal responsibility, and the exercise of "control."

■

The film *Deep Cover* illuminates how black nationalism can function as a policing apparatus both by aestheticizing the black nationalist patriarchal family romance and by celebrating the enforcement of the "new world order" in its view of the terms. Sociologist Avery Gordon has called the dynamic to which I refer here "diversity management." She writes, "The management of racial and gender identities and conflicts, or what is otherwise known as diversity management, is a core component of the new corporate culture."[14] In the present moment there are no clearly marked delineations among corporate culture, state culture, and civil society or their interaction. Instead, each is shot through with the others. Within the world of the film, the problematic gender objects and ethnic group representatives are managed—are actually managed, for the most part, right out of existence.

Deep Cover was directed by Bill Duke and written by Michael Tolkin (*The Player*) and Henry Bean (*Internal Affairs*). The major stars are Laurence Fishburne and Jeff Goldblum. The plot setup is easily summarized. A small boy, Russell Stevens (Laurence Fishburne), who sees his drug-addict father killed in the course of a convenience-store holdup (and is left with bloodstained money in his hand), grows up to be a cop recruited as a "deep" undercover drug courier by a white DEA (Drug Enforcement Agency) agent named Carver. This agent tells Stevens that his psychological profile almost perfectly matches that of a criminal. Stevens is given a new identity—John Q. Hull, drug dealer wannabe—and is told to go undercover in order to get to three Latino drug dealers who inhabit three levels in the drug-world hierarchy. Felix Barbossa is "the lieutenant"; Gallegos is "the prince"—in charge of West Coast distribution; and Guzman is "the king"—in charge of drug supply from an unnamed South American country. Possibly, Guzman will be the next president of his country. Carver, the DEA agent, tells Hull to stop after infiltrating level two (Gallegos), and consult with him before proceeding to level three. The drug dealer for whom Hull goes to work and with whom he later becomes partners and friends (after a fashion) is a white Jewish lawyer, David Jason (Jeff Goldblum). He has a beautiful black mistress, Betty McCutheon (Victoria Dillard), who owns an African cultural artifact shop. He is married, with a child and a house in a wealthy suburb.

Two subplots are tied into the primary plot by the end of the movie: (1) Clarence Williams III, plays a good, Christian, black nationalist cop known as Taft; Taft, unaware of John Hull's *real* identity as a cop, runs a consistent black nationalist series of antidrug lectures directed at John; and (2) a small Latino boy, who lives with his crack-addicted mother, is present in the transient apartment building where Hull takes up residence and becomes important in Hull's new existence. By the movie's end John has redeemed himself and his mission; he blows the whistle on the federal government's and DEA's political double dealing when the DEA shuts down the undercover operation because Guzman is the United States' client politico in the region.

■

Black nationalist anxiety over racial virility, or its historical lack, plays itself out continually in black cultural production. My interest here is in examining that anxiety as it plays itself out in a Hollywood film that is about a black undercover cop, but is also—in fascinating ways—a hysterical black nationalist revision of a patriarchal family romance. I say hysterical because the film's obsession with patriarchy is also the terrain for its anxiety over a "sufficient and necessary" heterosexuality. That is to say, its cakewalk to straight black masculine "realness" not only remakes a master narrative, but trips all over its own attempts to discipline its homoeroticism. This hysteria is further complicated in the film's representation of the relations among various ethnicities: the black Americans, the Jewish lawyer, and the Latino drug lords. But the way black nationalism most thoroughly coalesces into a conventional master narrative is by means of its centering of the family romance.

While *Deep Cover* is ostensibly about the drug trade and is even critical of white political complicity in that trade, it is framed on both ends by family narratives. The film's beginning, and structurally essential, point is the father-son scene (a late-twentieth-century "blackened" version of the primal scene) with a conventional enough U.S. black movie scenario of a black junkie robbing a convenience store. The film's ending—structurally anticipated—is the constitution of a new, improved, and multicultural family for the little Latino boy whose "bad" mother, a drug addict named Belinda Chacon, dies.

Throughout the film, family is the moral ground evoked again and again in the rehabilitation of John Hull. The family narrative on display, however, is a departure from the historical black nationalist family narrative with respect to the importance of the mother, who, according to black nationalist convention, is omnipresent as the nurturer of black children, the cultural carrier of antiracist black essence, and the teacher of the community. In contrast, there are no "fit" black mothers (or any mothers of color) left alive or visible in this film until Betty McCutheon, David Jason's mistress, is rehabilitated at the end (but left offscreen) to be the "mother," along with John Hull, the newly crafted "father," of the Latino boy.

McCutheon is the marker for black male reclamation of "his" history. Hull woos McCutheon away from Jason. His ability to overpower her original resistance to and suspicion of him is a reclamation *from the Jewish middleman* of black history and autonomy. It is also Hull's way of claiming his right to male ownership. McCutheon is a dark-skinned black woman (historically important in black nationalist aesthetic terms), and the cultural gatekeeper for African artifacts. Because she represents the commodification of African art, her reclamation is doubly important to a black nationalist project. McCutheon doesn't just switch boyfriends and return to the black homeland via Hull, she also makes the first step to becoming a "fit" mother.

Family—dead or alive, dying or being resurrected—is everywhere in this film. Hull's pedigree is established at the beginning of the film by his own father—a junkie, but one gamely (the film insists), however ineptly, trying to be a good father. The good black cop's family also comes into the narrative when he talks about his children and shows their pictures to Hull during an interrogation. That cop articulates, along with Jerry Carver, the corrupt DEA agent, the tie between the drug trade and killing children and babies. Such articulations are the coming together of family narrative and black nationalist common sense: "Don't destroy your own people." This admonition gains resonance in the dramatic high point when the good cop dies in Hull's arms—dies, in effect, for Hull's "sins" against his people. The death of that *good* father brings Hull back into the black family as well as back into the family of the American state's law-and-order family. Taft, the good, black nationalist cop, dies saying, "You and me are one. Don't forget who you are."

John Hull's patriarchal fitness is established through capitalist family romance convention: the stealing of a great fortune. The means by which he is able to consolidate his position as future patriarch arrives via a rather heavy piece of symbolism: a truck full of money—more than $11 million in smallish bills—that hangs in the air suspended from a large shipping crane as a fairly crude embodiment of drama's "god from the machine." His patriarchal status is secured by the means of that money from above, visibly severed from its means of production. No longer "owned" by the U.S. drug trade or the Latino originators, it is transformed into Hull's "own" money. Money is an absolute (and fetishistically overdetermined) value in the film. It is symbolically found money, reward money, for Hull's unveiling of the drug lord, his destruction of the drug partnership with Jason, his killing of Jason, and, most dramatically, his "uncovering" of U.S. political complicity in the international drug trade. Like all good and wealthy patriarchs, his relationship to the source of his new power is ambiguous, as the awkwardly intrusive voice-over makes clear.

Hull's individual triumph also narratively represents black nationalism overpowering the Jew as middleman between blacks and whites. That triumph is a demonstration of his ability to manipulate others within a system where masculinity is predicated on the ability to dominate others. Jason as the almost-white controller of the female gatekeeper of Africanness is pushed aside as the black male becomes the discipliner of the other ethnic "interlopers" on U.S. terrain—the Latinos.

By a third of the way through the movie, we see the familial structures in place that will be dissolved and reformed: family one, small Latino boy and mother; family two, John Hull (later orphaned) and his father; and family three, drug lord as prince and nephew to the drug-overlord uncle. Any reproductive narrative possibilities of a Latino-Latina family combination are disrupted by John Hull's takeover of the Latino boy after his mother dies. Given the contingent nature of ethnic relations and identity politics in the current U.S. political *mise-en-scène*, this colonizing of the Latino-Latina family combinations by a black American is telling. As ethnic groups struggle to be part of the mainstream, they are often forced to make a place for themselves by serving the interests of the state. Given public hostility to immigration from south of our borders *and* to drug production and distribution that originates in South America, black Americans can be encouraged to make themselves more valued by helping to contain the "threats" coming from "outside."

In black nationalist terms, Hull triumphs over Jason: a white male is dead. A bad, white patriarchy is dissolved. But a black male doesn't just win. A black masculinist version of virile history wins. It does so because the triangle formed by Williams/Taft, Goldblum/Jason, and Fishburne/Hull is shattered. Fishburne/Hull is the ambiguous black cop and drug dealer trembling on the brink of the historical void. He is pulled back from his flirtation with the Goldblum/Jason–directed world of corruption and reminded by Williams/Taft of his history. Taft, the Christian, black nationalist rival for Hull is shot by Jason (the finishing touch of the film's establishment of his supervillainy) because he wants to end both Hull's "flirtation" with his earlier cop history and black male bonding. But Taft (and black history) prove stronger than the attraction that Hull admits he feels for Jason's world: the money, the clothes, the interior design.

Ironically, Taft, embodying black brotherhood, black patriarchy, and selfless devotion to the (white) law, wins back (from the lip of the grave) Hull, not only to black history but also to the master—and the "master's"—narrative. Freed by that murder, Hull rejects Jason's corrupt whiteness, the seduction of his drug world, and the "not real" patriarchy. In their place he gains the "real" things: blackness, black solidarity, legality, and, most important for the overall sociological work performed by this film, the white judicial system. The film's logic makes it necessary for Hull to kill Jason and then leaves Hull fit to fulfill his appointed role in the new, black, grand family narrative.

A new black patriarchy is framed not only by a black American hero killing the Jewish outsider, but also at the expense of the dead, finally femininely quiet, Latina. Hull's voice-over tells us that until Belinda was dead Hull never knew how pretty she was. But she is dead and so are all the black mothers in this film, including a black mother with no existence outside of a wallet photograph.

We watch the creation of a black patriarch. Not all patriarchs are created politically or economically equal, of course, and this one plays a complicated game with the American master narrative. By being true to "himself" and his identifications, Hull is a perfect drug dealer *and* a perfect cop. By not giving up his mission he makes the bust, gets the woman, the family, and $11 million that "doesn't know where it came from." By being "true" to one, two, or three of his "real" selves, he is able to embarrass the U.S. government and expose a corrupt DEA. This is patriarchy with a difference. But within-the-group manhood is tied nonetheless to fatherhood (and, in this film, respect for the law). Fatherhood is the "political imaginary" for many members of the group, male and female, across the political spectrum.[15]

Surely it is not difficult to see, once we interrupt the film's narrative and begin to analyze its workings, how such popular entertainment ideologically supports—even enforces—the following highly problematic and destructive developments: (1) the disproportionate black presence in the military; (2) the increasing popularity in the media and among policymakers of the idea that black males should be subjected to military-style boot camps, ironically giving new force to Senator Moynihan's twenty-five-year-old injunction that the military could make "men" out of black males; (3) black Americans' increasing fetishization of "the family" as a response to state and civil-society attacks on "the black family"; and (4) black love affairs with heroic narratives about powerful male presence. The contest over black subject-making is not only a means of graphing the intersection of identity politics and the political economy, it is the ground on which the state provides itself with the means and repressive apparatus to police the international realm and to remake its own economy.

I'll end this section *Jeopardy* quiz-show style with an answer and then the question that I derive from it. Answer: the romanticized black patriarchal family and its disciplinary possibilities. Question: what is one way that the state can mobilize blackness to do its repressive work and its policing of civil society?

■

Let us consider the interplay of: (1) black nationalism as a cultural narrative that explains many black Americans' understanding of themselves—a kind of common sense even for black people who don't think of themselves as nationalist; (2) the U.S. state's interests and investments in family-values discourse; (3) black heterosexual and heterosexist masculinity; and (4) the simultaneous marginalization of black women—marginalization as politically important and autonomous agents—even as they are represented as vessels, literal bearers, of "the black people."

Any narrative that insists that *responsible reproductive* black masculinity is the central signifier and affirmer of black maleness is a policing of black male sexual desire. It is a means by which black nationalist accounts of and prescriptions for the black family—something historically and aesthetically appealing as resistance to racist demonization of black people—becomes available also for appropriation by the U.S. state for erecting a political disciplinary apparatus in moral terms. I do not want to be misunderstood. I am not saying that black males should take no responsibility for the result of their heterosexual relations and their possible consequences. I am pointing out the dangers of considering such sexuality and its results to be that which signifies black maleness, or that which dignifies it.

Black heterosexual masculinity and desire are represented in black nationalist accounts as the foundation of "the black people" via the establishment of strong black families with strong (and responsible) black patriarchs who will be the means by which the black family is saved. In this construction a family is perceived (and represented) as "weakened" by black female deviance (sexual and economic) or as "weakened" by external factors. Such a narrative makes easier its melding with a pro-family narrative from the larger culture.

It is important to distinguish between the complexity of "family" as a way to describe the work of nurturing and socializing the young, regularizing some form of domestic life, supporting individuals drawn together in collectivities by virtue of kinship *or* by voluntary emotional bonds—without any particular privileging of genders and/or sexual inclinations—from the "family" narrowly invoked by the phrase "family values." That term seeks to enforce a definition of "family" as only a household of people headed by two members of opposite sexes living with progeny produced by one of them—usually the female—and whose finances and decision-making power are largely centered on the male person.

In this moment the U.S. state has made family values a means of policing the exercise largely (but not solely) of female desire, as well as a way to establish that state's moral right to influence and even direct the private sphere. The notion of black peoplehood or black nationalism provides a fecund and appealing ground for the state's project to be made attractive to black people. This is accomplished through that disciplinary project's rhetorical resemblance to the black nationalist family project that projects strong ideas of responsible black male fathering and subordinate black female mothering.

As the U.S. state becomes more and more successful as the articulator of family values, betrayal of the family, as Cora Kaplan argues, becomes as subversive as betrayal of the state.[16] If this sounds far-fetched, read and reread the oceans of ink being spilled over the dangers to the social order posed by pregnant teenagers and/or welfare mothers, and the family-values planks of Newt Gingrich's "Contract with America." The state is not always successful, and people resist in a myriad of ways. However, the fact that the state is not always and completely successful does not lessen either the historical trajectory of its successes or its momentum in the present repressive political climate.

■

Let me turn to Tupac Shakur's "Keep Ya Head Up." I turn to it because it caught the attention of millions of black people who consume rap, and because our consumption of art is part of our world-making. Cultural artifacts do not simply hold up a mirror to what we already think we know, they "make" what we know. This rap song was not only immensely popular, but it was often touted as antisexist and supportive of black women because of its defense of young black mothers and welfare mothers. It is also beautiful—the lyrics, his voice, the refrain—the voices singing in harmony "keep ya head up." It includes a nod to an older black R&B group and a sentimental ballad favorite—the Five Stairsteps and "Ooh, Ooh Child"—with its quotation of "things are gonna get easier." And the song fits comfortably within the paradigms of the black nationalist reproductive narrative—peoplehood and children.

The lyrics articulate a combination of black family themes: support for women on welfare and a sense of future possibility for the group through the family. The language evokes a black group past, present, and future, and connects those times to black women and childbearing. Its explicit language of positive dark "roots"—when "black was the thing to be," of "sisters on welfare," "young mothers," of a need to "heal the race . . . [or we'll produce] a race of babies who hate the ladies who make the babies"—and its warning about the insanity of within-the-group violence—"a setup from the outside"—reproduces familiar imperatives. It announces that once we had a healthy good past, but our future is threatened by our participation in demonic othering of young and welfare-dependent mothers, a threat that comes from outside the community.

In a moment when welfare mothers, young mothers, and single-parent families are under relentless attack, the presence of such a rap song is poignant. It serves as an antidote to widely available discursive poison about black female and black family pathology and unites the comfort of that antidote with a desire for a future better than the present.

Why subject such a song to criticism? Because this kind of positive rap, which comes out of conventional madonna-whore narratives, beautifully plays out the black equivalent of family-values discourse and is therefore more disturbing than gangsta rap. It is more disturbing precisely because it is so easily accommodated, so easily routinized in ways that reproduce the problematic status quo. It does this in large part because it is beautiful. It is because it is not transgressive, not dramatic and sensational, that it doesn't draw our attention to its ideological content. Its contrast to the rhetoric of gangsta rap—a form explicitly and deliberately situated outside civil mores—lulls our critical faculties as it helps contribute aesthetically to the pleasure of consuming family values, differently styled.

Not least, the song betrays black women and the possibility of center-ing their own sexual desire, insofar as it reiterates the confined space in which they must exist in order to be venerated, to be respected. It re-asserts the primacy of motherhood in our imagining of female importance.

Imagine a coalition of antichoice factions: Ralph Reed's (and Pat Robertson's) Christian Coalition, Newt Gingrich, and the reigning gov-ernment elite managing to acquire some degree of cool. Together they produce a few sixty- and ninety-second TV spots supporting more restric-tions on reproductive rights and intensifying the coercive rhetoric of nominal respect for women by insisting that every reproducing woman have a husband and be barred from contraceptive devices and abortion. The spots are beautifully produced and photographed with absolutely gor-geous black people dressed either in 'hoodwear or kentewear. Tupac Shakur's "Keep Ya Head Up" provides the sound track.

To draw attention to the ways in which the state or any other coercive power, or elite group, or the routine operation of capitalism, can make use of the cultural production of a marginalized group in order to aid in re-pressing that group is to draw attention to dynamics that have been in use for a very long time. Still, it is important to understand how such deploy-ments take new form and acquire added resonance given particular cir-cumstances.

■

I want to close with another brief example of black nationalism's dangers with a reminder that black nationalism and black popular culture—like all of our formations—are products of history. A man's voice is saying,

> We've got to start policing and patrolling our own neighbor-hoods. There's got to be a day when we go into the drug house and kick down the door. Snatch the drug dealer, take his drugs. De-stroy his drugs. Take the money and put it into the movement. That's what we gotta do. We can't dial 911, call Sheriff Bill or Deputy Tom who don't care about the community or drugs.[17]

This is the rapper Ice Cube being interviewed by Angela Davis. Through-out the interview, Ice Cube deifies the Nation of Islam and Louis Farrakhan. The Nation and Farrakhan become the light that will lead black people into the nationalist promised land—history reclaimed, the present controlled, and the future ensured. The Nation, with its entrepreneurial and security operations, functions as the role model for black community action and for imagining the roles of black men.

Ice Cube is intensely contradictory throughout the interview, but this quote is especially chilling, and not because it expresses rage toward drug dealers. It calls on the history of black interaction with the police and it depends on our remembering that we are often not among those protected by the judicial system. But at the same time that Ice Cube is reminding us of this history, he is also suggesting that we imitate those police functions, that we replicate disregard of civil liberties, that we participate in the demonization of the drug dealer—the rationale for larger and more vicious intrusions by the state into black American life. Inexplicably, we are supposed to understand that if we are called to do these things, we do them in the name of history, in the name of the "movement"—the civil rights movement, the black power movement.

Of course, there is a difference between Ice Cube talking in an interview to Angela Davis, and the LAPD using tanks to break down doors. These are the words of a black rapper trying to express outrage about the depredations a hypercapitalist drug trade is wreaking on ordinary black people who are trying to live their lives. But the current climate and its hysteria about the drug war not only produces disinformation in the larger public imaginary, it feeds fantasies of desire for repressive freedom from fear. Something dangerous is happening in the interstices between Ice Cube's language—with its evocation of what has become black common sense—and the larger U.S. narrative of underclass pathology, of the drug culture, of inner-city chaos, of the need for black Americans to "police themselves." Ice Cube, and by extension black Americans who want an end to the drug war at any price (as if drugs and the black underground economy of which they are a part are what is determining the contours of our lives and not the operation of an unfettered and capitalist political economy that has declared war on jobs, poor people, and black people) are being persuaded to consent to dangerous excesses of external and internal policing, of community marginalization, in the name of helping "the community," the black family.

The demonic "other"—the drug dealer—is an entity generated by the judicial system in its choice to treat certain drugs (crack, cocaine, marijuana, heroin) differently from other drugs (alcohol, tobacco), despite the higher social and human costs of the legal drugs. It is generated by the banking systems that launder the money, by the scarcity of legal employment possibilities, and by the conservative opinion-making that is determined to keep our attention away from a powerful elite's control of the economy. That drug dealer is eerily and easily available as a "symbol" of what's "wrong" with the black community. The visibility of that symbol is intensified by the absence of other demons: with very rare exceptions within the mainstream press there is no presentation of demonic figures who stand in for what is wrong with the white upper class, or no demonic corporate figures that stand in for what is wrong with the corporate elite running this country and responsible for the human immiseration of millions.

Here, within the terms of Ice Cube's analysis, the drug dealer falls outside of the black family—the bedrock of black American common sense. The drug dealer has no connection to the community, no connection to larger economic or political forces. And in the black nationalist/commonsensical vigilante-wannabe embrace of this pathology narrative, black common sense cozies up to the state and its imperatives of political dominance and assaults on civil rights and liberties.

From the middle of this century, beginning with Moynihan's call for black males to learn manhood in the army, through the current love affair between politicians and the judicial system, to the rapidly spreading use of prison labor to undercut wages and employment in the private sphere, there has been an intensification of the state's policing of certain segments of the country. If we consider also the thoroughly ingrained disciplining of women within the larger polity and its aestheticized disciplining within the black nationalist family narrative, then we can watch the evolving control over black Americans that rivals slavery and segregation for its efficacy. It will remain successful so long as it continues to acquire the consent of the group at which it is aimed.

If the Nation of Islam—with its call for "policing" the black community, its instantiation of black male leadership and responsibility, its marginalization of black women, its aesthetics of precision group control, rituals of self-effacement in the presence of strong, charismatic leadership, and moral asceticism, its centering of black male bonding at the expense of gender and sexual orientation inclusiveness, is the answer—what on earth is the question?

What represents the aesthetics of state repression dressed up in black-face, in slogans of black responsibility, in increased attention to black self-help, in black military or militarylike trappings, in the valorization of black male self-reassertion predicated on the silencing of women, of black gay males, of anyone who falls outside of the parameters of the black nationalist "family"? Here are two more answers:

The Million Man March
Colin Powell

NOTES

1. James Kavanagh, "Ideology," in *Critical Terms for Literary Study*, ed. Frank Lentricchia and Thomas McLaughlin (Chicago: University of Chicago Press, 1990), 310.
2. Laurie Langbauer, "The City, the Everyday, and Boredom: The Case of Sherlock Holmes," *differences* 5, no. 5 (Fall 1993): 86.
3. "Being-as-a-group" is taken from Stuart Hall et al., "Subcultures, Cultures, and Class: A Theoretical Overview," in *Resistance Through Ritual: Youth Subculture in Postwar Britain*, ed. Stuart Hall et al. (London: Hutchinson, 1976).
4. This definition draws on the work of several theorists of nationalism, among them Max Weber, Ernest Renan, Elie Kedourie, Bernice Reagon, and Benedict Anderson.
5. Max Weber, *Economy and Society*, ed. Guenther Roth and Claus Wittich (Berkeley: University of California Press, 1978).
6. Bernice Reagon, "Coalition Politics: Turning the Century," in *Home Girls*, ed. Barbara Smith (New York: Kitchen Table—Women of Color Press, 1983), 359. Reagon's language implicitly draws attention to the ways in which a group storytells itself against a larger, pervasive, context. If we consider that understandings about the world are forged in the midst of and with the language of larger discourses, then it follows that the means by which one makes an impact might be the means of one's moment. In other

words, I don't know what black American cultural logic would be called if it hadn't forged itself over the past couple of hundred years in the fire of both worldwide nationalism and white American nationalism.

7. Wilson Moses, *The Golden Age of Black Nationalism 1850–1925* (New York: Oxford University Press, 1978).

8. Timothy Mitchell, "The Limits of the State: Beyond Statist Approaches and Their Critics," *American Political Science Review* 85, no. 1 (March 1991): 81. My understanding of the state also draws on Nico Poulantzas, *State, Power, Socialism*, trans. Patrick Camiller (London: New Left Books, 1978).

9. Oliver Cox, *Caste, Class, and Race* (New York: *Monthly Review Press*, 1970 [1948]), 319.

10. Here I'm borrowing from Fredric Jameson's formulation that postmodernism is the cultural logic of late capitalism. Fredric Jameson, "Postmodernism: Or, the Cultural Logic of Late Capitalism," *New Left Review* 146, no. 1 (July–August 1984).

11. Manning Marable, *Blackwater: Historical Studies in Race, Class Consciousness, and Revolution* (Niwot, Col.: University Press of Colorado, 1993), 93–128.

12. Gina Dent, ed., *Black Popular Culture* (Seattle: Bay Press, 1992).

13. Tupac Shakur died September 13, 1996, of injuries he sustained from a drive-by shooting. His death occurred after this essay was written.

14. Avery Gordon, "The Work of Corporate Culture: Diversity Management," *Social Text* 44 (Fall 1995): 3.

15. "Political imaginary" comes from Raymond Williams, *Marxism and Language* (New York: Oxford University Press, 1977), 99.

16. Cora Kaplan, *Sea Changes: Essays on Culture and Feminism* (London: Verso, 1986).

17. Angela Davis and Ice Cube, "Nappy Happy" (an interview), in *Transition* 58 (n.s. 2, no. 4) (1992): 174–92.

THE ETHNIC SCARRING
OF AMERICAN WHITENESS

Patricia J. Williams

■

REPRESENTATIONS OF RACE and gender inequality in the United States are endlessly complicated. While I have spent most of my career thinking and writing about the social history packed into being "black" and "female," I am increasingly absorbed by the extent to which Europeans and European-Americans consider and battle among themselves as "minorities." It has been too easy, perhaps, to allow the relative freedoms found by some European immigrants in the "New World" of the United States to obscure the experiences of terrible discrimination in the "Old World," against women, Jews, gays, and certain ethnic groups. And in a time of reawakened national and ethnic warring abroad, it is easy to overgeneralize from the privileges of the United States's great wealth, by making money or its lack, the explanation for all divisions here. In doing so, however, one underestimates the extent to which markets themselves may be deeply distorted by racial and gender prejudice; one loses sight of the fact that some "successfully assimilated" ethnics in the United States have become so only by paying the high cost of burying forever languages, customs, and cultures.

Sometimes I wonder how many of our present American cultural clashes are the leftover traces of the immigrant wars of the last century and the beginning of the twentieth, how much of our reemerging jingoism is the scar that marks the place where Italian kids were mocked for being too dark-skinned, where Jewish kids were taunted for being Jewish, where poor Irish rushed to place lace curtains at the window as the first act of climbing the ladder up from social scorn, where Chinese kids were tortured for not speaking good English.

I think of some Russian neighbors of ours when I was growing up (most of the whites in that section of Boston at that time were first-generation immigrant working-class). There were two girls in the family, the older of whom was an excellent student and who went on to attend college. Her accomplishment, however, was met with great ambivalence within her family—much of which was no doubt provoked by the elder sister's affecting a bourgeois snobbishness that cast continual aspersion upon the traditions and education of her family for what she perceived as their provincialism. She found embarrassing their conformity to old ways (cast paradoxically as nonconformity to "the mainstream"—her term for a naturalized, universalized, upwardly mobile middle class). While this young woman's accomplishments were indeed the source of much pride in her family, they were also the source of at least as much anxiety. As her younger sister once expressed it to me, she became a kind of "chafing agent" in the family's already insecure and somewhat self-effacing sense of how it fit into the social order of the United States. The elder sister, who lost her rich Russian-inflected Boston Irish accent for a tersely monitored version of Boston Brahmin the first semester of college, was pretty hard to take, I do remember. She was endlessly promoting herself as a citizen of the world, able to wade in all waters, tasting widely, knowing all, possessing everything. She became suffused in a passion for openness, a compulsion for boundlessness that is all to the good, but compulsive because so tied to fear of being bounded, so linked to fear of being made fun of for being "too ethnic," too closed, too ignorant of "the larger society." While this should in no way be taken as a necessarily bad thing, it can also signal a lost balance, a sacrifice of appreciation for the bonds, the links, the ties that bind, that make family, connection, identity.

I wonder, in these times of heated put-down, about the genealogy of so much of what sometimes leaps out as quite irrational fears of what has been dismissively labeled "identity politics." Some identity politics are genuinely fearsome, genuinely rooted in neofascist tendencies—but the larger measure of concern strikes me as a not-yet-resolved peculiarly American anxiety about our immigrant, peasant, sharecropper roots. Some of it strikes me as being a demand for conformity to what keeps being called the "larger" American way, a tyrannical rather than a willing assimilation in which there is little room for accounts of the Ellis Island variety of the past as contiguous with the present. Rather all such accounts are thought to be in tension with some static image of a monolithic, pre-existing rather than vividly evolving, American culture.

This genealogy of status regard might be suggested more easily by the following example: I was purchasing rugs in a store in New York City. The rug salesman was an amiable young man, whose ethnicity I couldn't begin to guess, but who in the assimilative order of most parts of the United States generally would be identified as "white." The rugs I was considering were in a huge heavy heap in the middle of the floor, and the store had positioned two men on either side of the pile to peel the layers of rugs back for customer viewing. The two rug turners were handsome brown men, perhaps East Indian, but, again, I'm a bad guesser. They spoke very halting English, although with a very distinct British rather than American inflection. At one point they apparently misunderstood which rug I had wanted to see; the salesman curtly corrected them, and then turned to me, rolled his eyes, and sighed in all apparent seriousness: "It's so hard to find good help these days."

Now I am definitely the wrong person with whom to lodge such a complaint, but before I could start in with what he would have undoubtedly found to be a very annoying little disquisition, the salesman reached over and carelessly, messily, flipped back the edge of the top rug. One of the rug turners, who was clearly seething, snapped at him to "take his hands off" that rug, that that was their job; and then said, very carefully, but with great passion: "What's the matter, don't you understand English?!"

I was struck by how quickly and completely, in the context of this apparent employment hierarchy, the lower-status person had learned the lesson of stealing the power and thunder of the high-status person's insult by turning it back on itself. There was something about this exchange that marked a ritual of assimilative initiation: Did someone hurl those words to the salesman's great grandmother as she scrubbed floors, or did he just see it in a movie? Will the high sarcasm of the rug turner's remark lose its irony and retain only its demand as the rug turners or their children lose their accents but keep the gesture of power?

The ability to see the commonalities of a hand-me-down heritage of devalued humanity, even as our specific experiences with that devaluation may differ widely with time and place, is in need of serious cultivation. The ability to fully understand the desperate socioeconomic circumstances of blacks in the United States is, I think, intricately linked with the tangled and evolving histories of oppression throughout the world, and the analytical conundrums that they present for us all.

Against this backdrop, and in view of the relatively advantaged situation of whites and particularly white men in the United States, the constantly bunkered sense of transgressed rights that appears to be the chief theme of much of today's right-leaning radio and television probably needs more excavation to be understood as the powerfully appealing narrative of "white" (versus ethnic) neonationalism that it appears to have become. I think that the appeal is attributable to at least two factors: (1) the persuasive form of the narrative itself, and (2) the ennobling romantic vision of its content in which tropes of local inclusion or representation are played out against the backdrop of intense global debates about democracy, citizenship, and community.

There are any number of junctures in history where a shift in the boundaries of law or some political movement has been signaled by very particular uses of rhetoric, peculiar twists of the popular imagination. American presidents, for example, routinely attempt to harness the irresistible rhetorical movement of the Puritan jeremiad as a persuasive form by intertwining the language of divine proclamation and political mission. At the same time, the appeal for equality, of African Americans and many others, has always been boosted by the power of great rhetorical moments. During the entire civil rights movement social activists were at their most effective when they were able to capture certain material events within the metaphoric unfolding of destiny, or of apocalypse, or of nature and "the natural." Martin Luther King's heart-wrenching vision of the mountaintop owes many a tip of the hat, of course, to the oral traditions of Africa, but also to the forms of political discourse that influenced the Boston missionaries and New England abolitionists whose words have so necessarily infiltrated the expression of black aspiration.

But it is also true that the deepest of our social divisions have been powerfully perpetuated by precisely such devices. From the earliest Supreme Court cases, the authority of the law was hitched to a myth of compelling mission and sacred vision, an endowment emanating from God but ultimately speaking through the naturalized logic of positivism. The dispossession of aboriginal people from their land was accomplished by legal opinions that figured the land in question as "virgin," a holy female, a queen whose honor is upheld in the very fact of conquest. The legal awards of "charter" "title," "fee" and "possession" wrested land not from Native American people but from "idleness," "wilderness" and "emptiness."[1]

This particular way of imagining is not just "how the west was won," but has characterized much of the "impersonal" discourse of conquest and exclusion throughout our jurisprudence. If "the wilderness" was a term whose use effectively obliterated the existence of the humans who lived there, "the underclass" is a contemporary device to achieve very much the same end. This issue of class is underscored by the vocabulary of the so-called taxpayer revolt, which, while rooted in the sober reality of a stunning national deficit, has found unfortunate expression in a bitter discourse of deservedness in which the deserving are those whose material accumulation identifies them as those who "can't" "keep on" paying taxes, while the undeserving are figured as those who supposedly "don't" pay taxes. Making the streets "safe for taxpaying citizens," for example, has become a rallying point for the criminalization or institutionalization of the homeless in cities as supposedly "liberal" as San Francisco and New York. Author Mike Davis observes that "restaurants and markets have responded to the homeless by building ornate enclosures to protect their refuse. Although no one in Los Angeles has yet proposed adding cyanide to the garbage, as happened in Phoenix a few years back, one popular seafood restaurant has spent $12,000 to build the ultimate bag-lady-proof trash cage: made of three-quarter-inch steel rods with alloy locks and vicious out-turned spikes to safeguard priceless moldering fishheads and stale french fries."[2]

A friend tells the story of her young niece, who is growing up in New York City. The little girl and a friend were walking into their apartment building when they saw an old man who lived on the street. "Hi, Sam," said my friend's niece, for she and her parents saw him every day and had grown to know him. The other little girl ran at once to her parents and said, very distressed, "You can't call a homeless a name! Mommy, she called a homeless a name!"[3] It is telling, this story, the blanket anonym of "a homeless" revealing the extent to which a whole generation of children are being cultured not to see those who live all around us. The very simplest of social exchanges struck this little girl as something like a blasphemous epithet against the safe borders of what exists, of what *can* be known and named.

Similarly, if the "underclass" is a way of unnaming the poor, "whiteness" is a way of not naming ethnicity. And "blackness," of course, has been used as a most effective way of marking the African-American quest for either citizenship or market participation as the very antithesis: blacks are defined as those whose expressed humanity is too often perceived as "taking" liberties, whose submission is seen as a generous and proper "gift" to others rather than as involving personal cost.

The fraternal bliss of romanticized racism, in which professions of liberty and inseparable union could simultaneously signify and even reinforce an "American" national identity premised on deep social division is, again, the central paradox of our times. D. W. Griffith's filmic paean to the founding of the Ku Klux Klan, *The Birth of a Nation*, ends with all the features of a classic jeremiad, imploring the Invisible Empire of decent white people who care about their daughters to dare to "dream of a Golden Day when the Bestial War shall rule no more. But instead the gentle Prince in the Hall of Brotherly Love in the City of Peace." The last scene of that movie shows a hall full of industrious white citizens attired in togas, in an apparent state of fraternal bliss, a giant, ghostly figure of Jesus Christ hovering above them all. "Liberty and Union, One and Inseparable, Now and Forever!" reads the very last subtitle.

I would like to explore simultaneously the suggestion that at least part of the sense of victimization coalescing a class of "oppressed" or "trumped" white men is primed by a certain class coding in the appeals of many right-wing political and media commentators. I began to take this possibility seriously during the media blare about the attack on figure skater Nancy Kerrigan, allegedly engineered by the shady retinue of her rival,

Tonya Harding. I was startled by mainstream "respectable" print and television media's repeated characterization of Harding and company as "poor white" or even "white trash." Then, weeks into the debacle, I heard an interview with residents of East Portland, the Oregon neighborhood in which Harding grew up. In the eyes of these people, Tonya Harding was a heroine—and for precisely all the reasons the dominant media opinion attacked her. She was tough, she was crafty, she had muscles, she could throw back a few beers with the boys, wasn't too fanatic to have a cigarette every once and again; she was *not* America's sweetheart, *not* Cinderella, *not* Pollyanna, this little girl who knew trucks and could handle a chain saw. What could be better than that?

Indeed, I thought. Might really be handy to be able to overhaul an engine.

And with that interview I began to listen much more closely for the ways in which poor whites are depicted in insulting and dehumanized ways by mainstream media, even when it's too "respectable" to use overt markers like "white trash." The *New Yorker* magazine, for example, ran a piece about the community of Clackamas County, where Harding lives, where her fan club is based, where the rink at which she learned to skate is located. Even as the piece purports to air the felt sense of class division ("'Trailer trash is what they call people out here,' [said a member of Harding's fan club]"), it exudes a profoundly insulting barrier of voyeuristic condescension. The author lingers on the physical attributes of everyone she meets: the bodies of the natives range from "meaty" to "fleshy." "Ruddy faces" are set with "pinkish eyelids" that are, in the case of the girls, "rimmed in black liner." Their dispositions run from "weary" to "jittery." Their children are "restless," "shrill-voiced," and "strange." Their hair is "greased-back" or "frosted" or "fading" or "stringy blond." They wear "inexpensive-looking clothing" like "worn-out chambray work shirt[s]" and "plastic windbreaker[s]." Even as the natives insist that Clackamas is a "good neighborhood" and "a very warmy place," the author warns the gentle reader that while such words may "make it sound soothing and regular," it's really "more haphazard and disjointed." In fact, every evidence of habitation and community is read right out of existence in this piece: the author finds only a wilderness of "drab rooms," floors that "felt hollow," houses that "look as though they had been built for dolls or chickens," "tumbledown farmhouses," "idle pastures" and "weedy tracts waiting to be seized and subdivided." "There really isn't a town of Clackamas . . . ," opines the New Yorker–on–safari; ". . . there are pockets of businesses having to do with toys and mufflers and furniture, but there really isn't any town to speak of, or even a village to drive through."⁴

Once I developed an eye and an ear for it, I began to see the vast body of sitcoms, talk shows, editorials, and magazines as not just "mainstream," but class-biased and deeply hypocritical. The most interesting aspect of this hypocrisy rests, I think, in the wholesale depiction of "poor whites" as bigoted, versus the enlightened, ever-so-*liberal* middle and upper classes who enjoy the privilege of thinking of themselves as "classless." I can well imagine that this might encourage residents of white poor and working-class communities from East Portland, Oregon, to Charlestown, Massachusetts, to hear the word "liberal" as just another synonym for hypocrite.

If I hold in my mind this particular construction of a "powerful liberal media," then I begin to understand how poor whites could feel victimized in very much the same way—if to varying degree—that blacks do by their image in the media. But blacks, by and large, tend to call the identical phenomenon the product of "conservative" or "right-wing" rather than liberal media, perhaps because no one has ever tried to market bigotry against blacks (as conceivably they have in the case of bigotry against poor whites) as "liberalism." It is instructive to see how the experience of race puts enough of a spin on just this much of the vocabulary that without any other experience than an arguably shared one, blacks and poor whites end up on opposite sides of a right-left divide. And looking at it this way gives me some insight into the way in which those who are in one sense aligned with a powerful majority could feel so paradoxically threatened, *as* a "minority" in a world overrun *by* "minorities."

If this much has any validity, then the complex ideological overlays of everyday racial dramas can only confound the picture more. In one direction it might be argued that many African Americans identify with and understand the ways in which aspects of white blue-collar life are shared lifestyles. As media expert John Fiske observes, the cartoon character Bart Simpson's "defiance, his street smarts, his oral skills, together with his rejection, appeared to resonate closely with many African Americans. The Simpsons are a blue-collar family whose class difference from mainstream America is frequently emphasized, and as race is often encoded into class, so class difference can be decoded as racial. Bart's double disempowerment, by class and age, made him readily decodable as socially 'black.' "[5]

But from the other direction I think it is very hard for lower-class whites to decode *themselves* as socially black—there is simply too much representational force militating against it. I keep thinking back to the paradigm of *The Birth of a Nation*, in which upper-class whites were depicted not merely as suffering at the hands of out of control blacks, but also as suffering lowered status at the hands of northern "radicals" —a misfortune that eventually brought ladies to the point of having to trim their frocks with unprocessed cotton, or "poor man's lace." By the same token, in Margaret Mitchell's *Gone with the Wind*, Scarlett O'Hara is a woman of great "breeding" unjustly reduced by crazed Yankee social engineering, a point made most memorable by her having to tear down the velvet curtains in order to clothe herself according to her lost station. These images tap into powerful myths that invite the average American working-class dreamer—who is, after all, the intended consumer of such romantic pulp—to imagine a great and primeval fall from Edenic upper-class status, *and to do so in racial terms*.

The rhetoric of such southern Gothic dramas bears the earmarks of a poor man's jeremiad—the mythic sense of banishment from the classier classes, the pathetic grace of struggle against the odds, the conjunction of just deserts and a clever needle (or a shiny pair of ice skates) saving the day for a brighter tomorrow when North and South, rich and poor shall sit down at the same table and be properly waited on by you-know-who. But it is also a jeremiad in which the borders of the lower-class wilderness are guarded by federally funded "outsiders" who "don't understand" and who block exodus to the promised land by unleashing upon them running-dog hordes of black heathens and criminal "elements" who *belong* in a wilderness.

It is not surprising that empirical information has such a hard time standing up to the passionate desire to don crinoline; and it is not surprising, I suppose, that if a badly written rip-off sequel to the badly written original of *Gone with the Wind* can just about outstrip the Bible in worldwide sales, then some savvy disc jockeys spinning the same yarn could capture quite a lot of market share.

Let me end with a story about how I think the imaginary line drawing of national identity operates on the very local level, indeed, at home.

Some months ago I was riding on a train. In between napping and reading the newspaper, I languidly fell into overhearing the conversation of a very well-dressed, well-educated family seated across the aisle from me. Here was a family with traditional values *and* Ralph Lauren looks— mother, father, bright little girl, and a big, bearded friend of the family who looked like that seafaring guy on the clam chowder label. It was a fascinatingly upper-class conversation, about investments, photography, and Japanese wood-joinery. It was also a soothingly pleasant conversation, full of affection, humor, and great politeness. I enjoyed listening to them, and allowed myself the pleasure of my secret participation in their companionability. They they started telling redneck jokes.

There was no shift in their voices to warn me of it; they spoke in the same soft, smiling voices as before, with those deliciously crisp *t*'s and delicately rounded *r*'s.

The little girl, who was probably around seven or eight years old, asked, "What's a redneck?" (No longer napping, I leaned closer, titillated and intrigued by what this moment of sharp but innocent intervention promised in terms of drawing these otherwise thoughtful adults up short in a lifeboat of glorious contrition and renewed sense of social awareness.)

"Drinks beer, drives a pickup, low-class, talks bad," came the unselfconscious reply. Then the three adults told more jokes to illustrate. Being very bright, the little girl dumped innocence by the wayside, and responded promptly by telling a bunch of blond jokes and then one involving "black"—but I couldn't hear if she were talking about hair or skin.

The father told another joke—what's got ten teeth and something I couldn't hear. The answer was the front row of a Willie Nelson concert.

They were so pleasant and happy. Their conversation was random, wandering. They showed pictures of each other's kids, they played word games, they shared hot dogs. And yet they were transporting a virus.

This process of marking. No wonder it is so hard to get out of our race and class binds. It occurred to me, as I watched this family in all its remarkable typicality, that that little girl will have to leave the warmth of the embracing, completely relaxed circle of those happy people before she can ever appreciate the humanity of someone who drives a pickup, who can't afford a dentist. "Rednecks" were lovingly situated, by that long afternoon of gentle joking, in the terrible vise of the comic, defined by the butt of a joke.

The prevalence of how *givingly* social divisions are transmitted was brought home to me in an essay written by one of my former students: She described her father as a loving family man, who worked six and a half days a week to provide for his wife and children. He always took Sunday afternoons off; that was sacred time, reserved for a "family drive." Yet the family's favorite pastime, as they meandered in Norman Rockwell contentment, was, according to this student, "trying to pick the homosexuals out of the crowd." ("Bill Clinton would have *homosexuals* in his administration!" railed Pat Robertson in his speech to the 1992 Republican National Convention, during which convention homophobic violence reportedly rose 8 percent in the city of Houston.)

Hate learned in a context of love is a complicated phenomenon. And love learned in a context of hate endangers all our family.

NOTES

1. *Johnson and Graham's Lessee v. William M'Intosh*, 21 U.S. 543 (1823).
2. Mike Davis, *City of Quartz* (New York: Vintage Books, 1992), 233.
3. Ariella Gross, letter of March 14, 1994, on file with author.
4. Susan Orlean, "Figures in a Mall," *New Yorker*, February 21, 1994, 48ff.
5. John Fiske, *Media Matters: Everyday Culture and Political Change* (Minneapolis: University of Minnesota Press, 1994), 123.

RACE AND CRIMINALIZATION

Black Americans and the Punishment Industry

■

Angela Y. Davis

I N THIS POST–CIVIL RIGHTS ERA, as racial barriers in high economic and political realms are apparently shattered with predictable regularity, race itself becomes an increasingly proscribed subject. In the dominant political discourse it is no longer acknowledged as a pervasive structural phenomenon, requiring the continuation of such strategies as affirmative action, but rather is represented primarily as a complex of prejudicial attitudes, which carry equal weight across all racial boundaries. Black leadership is thus often discredited and the identification of race as a public, political issue itself called into question through the invocation of, and application of the epithet "black racist" to, such figures as Louis Farrakhan and Khalid Abdul Muhammad. Public debates about the role of the state that once focused very sharply and openly on issues of "race" and racism are now expected to unfold in the absence of any direct acknowledgment of the persistence—and indeed further entrenchment—of racially structured power relationships. Because race is ostracized from some of the most impassioned political debates of this period, their racialized character becomes increasingly difficult to identify, especially by those who are unable—or do not want—to decipher the encoded language. This means that hidden racist arguments can be mobilized readily across racial boundaries and political alignments. Political positions once easily defined as conservative, liberal, and sometimes even radical therefore have a tendency to lose their distinctiveness in the face of the seductions of this camouflaged racism.

President Clinton chose the date of the Million Man March, convened by Minister Louis Farrakhan of the Nation of Islam, to issue a call for a "national conversation on race," borrowing ironically the exact words of Lani Guinier (whose nomination for assistant attorney general in charge of civil rights he had previously withdrawn because her writings focused too sharply on issues of race).[1] Guinier's ideas had been so easily dismissed because of the prevailing ideological equation of the "end of racism" with the removal of all allusions to race. If conservative positions argue that race consciousness itself impedes the process of solving the problem of race—i.e., achieving race blindness—then Clinton's speech indicated an attempt to reconcile the two, positing race consciousness as a means of moving toward race blindness. "There are too many today, white and black, on the left and the right, on the street corners and radio waves, who seek to sow division for their own purposes. To them I say: 'No more. We must be one.'"

While Clinton did acknowledge "the awful history and stubborn persistence of racism," his remarks foregrounded those reasons for the "racial divide" that "are rooted in the fact that we still haven't learned to talk frankly, to listen carefully and to work together across racial lines." Race, he insisted, is not about government, but about the hearts of people. Of course, it would be absurd to deny the degree to which racism infects in deep and multiple ways the national psyche. However, the relegation of race to matters of the heart tends to render it increasingly difficult to identify the deep structural entrenchment of contemporary racism.

When the structural character of racism is ignored in discussions about crime and the rising population of incarcerated people, the racial imbalance in jails and prisons is treated as a contingency, at best as a product of the "culture of poverty," and at worst as proof of an assumed black monopoly on criminality. The high proportion of black people in the criminal justice system is thus normalized and neither the state nor the general public is required to talk about and act on the meaning of that racial imbalance. Thus Republican and Democratic elected officials alike have successfully called for laws mandating life sentences for three-time "criminals," without having to answer for the racial implications of these laws. By relying on the alleged "race-blindness" of such laws, black people are surreptitiously constructed as racial subjects, thus manipulated, exploited, and abused, while the structural persistence of racism—albeit in changed forms—in social and economic institutions, and in the national culture as a whole, is adamantly denied.

Crime is thus one of the masquerades behind which "race," with all its menacing ideological complexity, mobilizes old public fears *and* creates new ones. The current anticrime debate takes place within a reified mathematical realm—a strategy reminiscent of Malthus's notion of the geometrical increase in population and the arithmetical increase in food sources, thus the inevitability of poverty and the means of suppressing it: war, disease, famine, and natural disasters. As a matter of fact, the persisting neo-Malthusian approach to population control, which, instead of seeking to solve those pressing social problems that result in real pain and suffering in people's lives, calls for the elimination of those suffering lives—finds strong resonances in the public discussion about expurgating the "nation" of crime. These discussions include arguments deployed by those who are leading the call for more prisons and employ statistics in the same fetishistic and misleading way as Malthus did more than two centuries ago. Take for example James Wooten's comments in the *Heritage Foundation State Backgrounder*:

> If the 55% of the estimated 800,000 current state and federal prisoners who are violent offenders were subject to serving 85% of their sentence, and assuming that those violent offenders would have committed 10 violent crimes a year while on the street, then the number of crimes prevented each year by truth in sentencing would be 4,000,000. That would be over 2/3 of the 6,000,000 violent crimes reported.[2]

In *Reader's Digest*, Senior Editor Eugene H. Methvin writes:

> If we again double the present federal and state prison population—to somewhere between 1 million and 1.5 million and leave our city and county jail population at the present 400,000, we will break the back of America's 30 year crime wave.[3]

The real human beings—a vastly disproportionate number of whom are black and Latino/a men and women—designated by these numbers in a seemingly race-neutral way are deemed fetishistically exchangeable with the crimes they have or will allegedly commit. The real impact of imprisonment on their lives never need be examined. The inevitable part played by the punishment industry in the reproduction of crime never need be discussed. The dangerous and indeed fascistic trend toward progressively greater numbers of hidden, incarcerated human populations is itself rendered invisible. All that matters is the elimination of crime—and you get rid of crime by getting rid of people who, according to the prevailing racial common sense, are the most likely people to whom criminal acts will be attributed. Never mind that if this strategy is seriously and consistently pursued, the majority of young black men and a fast growing proportion of young black women will spend a good portion of their lives behind walls and bars in order to serve as a reminder that the state is aggressively confronting its enemy.[4]

While I do not want to locate a response to these arguments on the same level of mathematical abstraction and fetishism I have been problematizing, it is helpful, I think, to consider how many people are presently incarcerated or whose lives are subject to the direct surveillance of the criminal justice system. There are already approximately 1 million people in state and federal prisons in the United States, not counting the 500,000 in city and county jails or the 600,000 on parole or the 3 million people on probation or the 60,000 young people in juvenile facilities. Which is to say that there are presently over 5.1 million people either incarcerated, on parole, or on probation. Many of those presently on probation or parole would be behind bars under the conditions of the recently passed crime bill. According to the Sentencing Project, even before the passage of the crime bill, black people were 7.8 times more likely to be imprisoned than whites.[5] The Sentencing Project's most recent report[6] indicates that 32.2 percent of young black men and 12.3 percent of young Latino men between the ages of twenty and twenty-nine are either in prison, in jail, or on probation or parole. This is in comparison with 6.7 percent of young white men. A total of 827,440 young African-American males are under the supervision of the criminal justice system, at a cost of $6 billion per year. A major strength of the 1995 report, as compared to its predecessor, is its acknowledgment that the racialized impact of the criminal justice system is also gendered and that the relatively smaller number of African-American women drawn into the system should not relieve us of the responsibility of understanding the encounter of gender and race in arrest and incarceration practices. Moreover, the increases in women's contact with the criminal justice system have been even more dramatic that those of men.

> The 78% increase in criminal justice control rates for black women was more than double the increase for black men and for white women, and more than nine times the increase for white men. . . . Although research on women of color in the criminal justice system is limited, existing data and research suggest that it is the combination of race and sex effects that is at the root of the trends which appear in our data. For example, while the number of blacks and Hispanics in prison is growing at an alarming rate, the rate of increase for women is even greater. Between 1980 and 1992 the female prison population increased 276%, compared to 163% for men. Unlike men of color, women of color thus belong to two groups that are experiencing particular dramatic growth in their contact with the criminal justice system.[7]

It has been estimated that by the year 2000 the number of people imprisoned will surpass 4 million, a grossly disproportionate number of whom will be black people, and that the cost will be over $40 billion a year,[8] a figure that is reminiscent of the way the military budget devoured—and continues to devour—the country's resources. This out-of-control punishment industry is an extremely effective criminalization industry, for the racial imbalance in incarcerated populations is not recognized as evidence of structural racism, but rather is invoked as a consequence of the assumed criminality of black people. In other words, the criminalization process works so well precisely because of the hidden logic of racism. Racist logic is deeply entrenched in the nation's material and psychic structures. It is something with which we all are very familiar. The logic, in fact, can persist, even when direct allusions to "race" are removed.

Even those communities that are most deeply injured by this racist logic have learned how to rely upon it, particularly when open allusions to race are not necessary. Thus, in the absence of broad, radical grassroots movements in poor black communities so devastated by new forms of youth-perpetrated violence, the ideological options are extremely sparse. Often there are no other ways to express collective rage and despair but to demand that police sweep the community clean of crack and Uzis, and of the people who use and sell drugs and wield weapons. Ironically, Carol Moseley-Braun, the first black woman senator in our nation's history, was an enthusiastic sponsor of the Senate Anticrime Bill, whose passage in November 1993 paved the way for the August 25, 1994, passage of the bill by the House. Or perhaps there is little irony here. It may be precisely because there is a Carol Moseley-Braun in the Senate and a Clarence Thomas in the Supreme Court—and concomitant class differentiations and other factors responsible for far more heterogeneity in black communities than at any other time in this country's history—that implicit consent to antiblack racist logic (not to speak of racism toward other groups) becomes far more widespread among black people. Wahneema Lubiano's explorations of the complexities of state domination as it operates within and through the subjectivities of those who are the targets of this domination facilitates an understanding of this dilemma.[9]

Borrowing the title of Cornel West's recent work, race *matters*. Moreover, it matters in ways that are far more threatening and simultaneously less discernible than those to which we have grown accustomed. Race matters inform, more than ever, the ideological and material structures of U.S. society. And, as the current discourses on crime, welfare, and immigration reveal, race, gender, and class matter enormously in the continuing elaboration of public policy and its impact on the real lives of human beings.

And how does race matter? Fear has always been an integral component of racism. The ideological reproduction of a fear of black people, whether economically or sexually grounded, is rapidly gravitating toward and being grounded in a fear of crime. A question to be raised in this context is whether and how the increasing fear of crime—this ideologically produced fear of crime—serves to render racism simultaneously more invisible and more virulent. Perhaps one way to approach an answer to this question is to consider how this fear of crime effectively summons black people to imagine black people as the enemy. How many black people present at this conference have successfully extricated ourselves from the ideological power of the figure of the young black male as criminal—or at least seriously confronted it? The lack of a significant black presence in the rather feeble opposition to the "three strikes, you're out" bills, which have been proposed and/or passed in forty states already, evidences the disarming effect of this ideology.

California is one of the states that has passed the "three strikes, you're out" bill. Immediately after the passage of that bill, Governor Pete Wilson began to argue for a "two strikes, you're out" bill. Three, he said, is too many. Soon we will hear calls for "one strike, you're out." Following this mathematical regression, we can imagine that at some point the hard-core anticrime advocates will be arguing that to stop the crime wave, we can't wait until even one crime is committed. Their slogan will be: "Get them before the first strike!" And because certain populations have already been criminalized, there will be those who say, "We know who the real criminals are—let's get them before they have a chance to act out their criminality."

The fear of crime has attained a status that bears a sinister similarity to the fear of communism as it came to restructure social perceptions during the fifties and sixties. The figure of the "criminal"—the racialized figure of the criminal—has come to represent the most menacing enemy of "American society." Virtually anything is acceptable—torture, brutality, vast expenditures of public funds—as long as it is done in the name of public safety. Racism has always found an easy route from its embeddedness in social structures to the psyches of collectives and individuals precisely because it mobilizes deep fears. While explicit, old-style racism may be increasingly socially unacceptable—precisely as a result of antiracist movements over the last forty years—this does not mean that U.S. society has been purged of racism. In fact, racism is more deeply embedded in socioeconomic structures, and the vast populations of incarcerated people of color is dramatic evidence of the way racism systematically structures economic relations. At the same time, this structural racism is rarely recognized as "racism." What we have come to recognize as open, explicit racism has in many ways begun to be replaced by a secluded, camouflaged kind of racism, whose influence on people's daily lives is as pervasive and systematic as the explicit forms of racism associated with the era of the struggle for civil rights.

The ideological space for the proliferations of this racialized fear of crime has been opened by the transformations in international politics created by the fall of the European socialist countries. Communism is no longer the quintessential enemy against which the nation imagines its identity. This space is now inhabited by ideological constructions of crime, drugs, immigration, and welfare. Of course, the enemy within is far more dangerous than the enemy without, and a black enemy within is the most dangerous of all.

Because of the tendency to view it as an abstract site into which all manner of undesirables are deposited, the prison is the perfect site for the simultaneous production and concealment of racism. The abstract character of the public perception of prisons militates against an engagement with the real issues afflicting the communities from which prisoners are drawn in such disproportionate numbers. This is the ideological work that the prison performs—it relieves us of the responsibility of seriously engaging with the problems of late capitalism, of transnational capitalism. The naturalization of black people as criminals thus also erects ideological barriers to an understanding of the connections between late-twentieth-century structural racism and the globalization of capital.

The vast expansion of the power of capitalist corporations over the lives of people of color and poor people in general has been accompanied by a waning anticapitalist consciousness. As capital moves with ease across national borders, legitimized by recent trade agreements such as NAFTA and GATT, corporations are allowed to close shop in the United States and transfer manufacturing operations to nations providing cheap labor pools. In fleeing organized labor in the U.S. to avoid paying higher wages and benefits, they leave entire communities in shambles, consigning huge numbers of people to joblessness, leaving them prey to the drug trade, destroying the economic base of these communities, thus affecting the education system, social welfare—and turning the people who live in those communities into perfect candidates for prison. At the same time, they create an economic demand for prisons, which stimulates the economy, providing jobs in the correctional industry for people who often come from the very populations that are criminalized by this process. It is a horrifying and self-reproducing cycle.

Ironically, prisons themselves are becoming a source of cheap labor that attracts corporate capitalism—as yet on a relatively small scale—in a way that parallels the attraction unorganized labor in Third World countries exerts. A statement by Michael Lamar Powell, a prisoner in Capshaw, Alabama, dramatically reveals this new development:

> I cannot go on strike, nor can I unionize. I am not covered by workers' compensation of the Fair Labor Standards Act. I agree to work late-night and weekend shifts. I do just what I am told, no matter what it is. I am hired and fired at will, and I am not even paid minimum wage: I earn one dollar a month. I cannot even voice grievances or complaints, except at the risk of incurring arbitrary discipline or some covert retaliation.
>
> You need not worry about NAFTA and your jobs going to Mexico and other Third World countries. I will have at least five percent of your jobs by the end of this decade.
>
> I am called prison labor. I am The New American Worker.[10]

This "new American worker" will be drawn from the ranks of a racialized population whose historical superexploitation—from the era of slavery to the present—has been legitimized by racism. At the same time, the expansion of convict labor is accompanied in some states by the old paraphernalia of ankle chains that symbolically links convict labor with slave labor. At least three states—Alabama, Florida, and Arizona—have reinstituted the chain gang. Moreover, as Michael Powell so incisively reveals, there is a new dimension to the racism inherent in this process, which structurally links the superexploitation of prison labor to the globalization of capital.

In California, whose prison system is the largest in the country and one of the largest in the world, the passage of an inmate labor initiative in 1990 has presented businesses seeking cheap labor with opportunities uncannily similar to those in Third World countries. As of June 1994, a range of companies were employing prison labor in nine California prisons. Under the auspices of the Joint Venture Program, work now being performed on prison grounds includes computerized telephone messaging, dental apparatus assembly, computer data entry, plastic parts fabrication, electronic component manufacturing at the Central California Women's facility at Chowchilla, security glass manufacturing, swine production, oak furniture manufacturing, and the production of stainless steel tanks and equipment. In a California Corrections Department brochure designed to promote the program, it is described as "an innovative public-private partnership that makes good business sense."[11] According to the owner of Tower Communications, whom the brochure quotes,

> The operation is cost effective, dependable and trouble free. . . . Tower Communications has successfully operated a message center utilizing inmates on the grounds of a California state prison. If you're a business leader planning expansion, considering relocation because of a deficient labor pool, starting a new enterprise, look into the benefits of using inmate labor.

The employer benefits listed by the brochure include

> federal and state tax incentives; no benefit package (retirement pay, vacation pay, sick leave, medical benefits); long term lease agreements at far below market value costs; discount rates on Workers Compensation; build a consistent, qualified work force; on call labor pool (no car breakdowns, no babysitting problems); option of hiring job-ready ex-offenders and minimizing costs; becoming a partner in public safety.

There is a major, yet invisible, racial supposition in such claims about the profitability of a convict labor force. The acceptability of the superexploitation of convict labor is largely based on the historical conjuncture of racism and incarceration practices. The already disproportionately black convict labor force will become increasingly black if the racially imbalanced incarceration practices continue.

The complicated yet unacknowledged structural presence of racism in the U.S. punishment industry also includes the fact that the punishment industry which sequesters ever-larger sectors of the black population attracts vast amounts of capital. Ideologically, as I have argued, the racialized fear of crime has begun to succeed the fear of communism. This corresponds to a structural tendency for capital that previously flowed toward the military industry to now move toward the punishment industry. The ease with which suggestions are made for prison construction costing in the multibillions of dollars is reminiscent of the military buildup: economic mobilization to defeat communism has turned into economic mobilization to defeat crime. The ideological construction of crime is thus complemented and bolstered by the material construction of jails and prisons. The more jails and prisons are constructed, the greater the fear of crime, and the greater the fear of crime, the stronger the cry for more jails and prisons, ad infinitum.

The law enforcement industry bears remarkable parallels to the military industry (just as there are anti-Communist resonances in the anti-crime campaign). This connection between the military industry and the punishment industry is revealed in a *Wall Street Journal* article entitled "Making Crime Pay: The Cold War of the '90s":

> Parts of the defense establishment are cashing in, too, scenting a logical new line of business to help them offset military cutbacks. Westinghouse Electric Corp., Minnesota Mining and Manufacturing Co., GDE Systems (a division of the old General Dynamics) and Alliant Techsystems Inc., for instance, are pushing crime-fighting equipment and have created special divisions to retool their defense technology for America's streets.

According to the article, a conference sponsored by the National Institute of Justice, the research arm of the Justice Department, was organized around the theme "Law Enforcement Technology in the 21st Century." The secretary of defense was a major presenter at this conference, which explored topics like "the role of the defense industry, particularly for dual use and conversion":

Hot topics: defense-industry technology that could lower the level of violence involved in crime fighting. Sandia National Laboratories, for instance, is experimenting with a dense foam that can be sprayed at suspects, temporarily blinding and deafening them under breathable bubbles. Stinger Corporation is working on "smart guns," which will fire only for the owner, and retractable spiked barrier strips to unfurl in front of fleeing vehicles. Westinghouse is promoting the "smart car," in which mini-computers could be linked up with big mainframes at the police department, allowing for speedy booking of prisoners, as well as quick exchanges of information.[12]

Again, race provides a silent justification for the technological expansion of law enforcement, which, in turn, intensifies racist arrest and incarceration practices. This skyrocketing punishment industry, whose growth is silently but powerfully sustained by the persistence of racism, creates an economic demand for more jails and prisons and thus for similarly spiraling criminalization practices, which, in turn fuels the fear of crime.

Most debates addressing the crisis resulting from overcrowding in prisons and jails focus on male institutions. Meanwhile, women's institutions and jail space for women are proportionately proliferating at an even more astounding rate than men's. If race is largely an absent factor in the discussions about crime and punishment, gender seems not even to merit a place carved out by its absence. Historically, the imprisonment of women has served to criminalize women in a way that is more complicated than is the case with men. This female criminalization process has had more to do with the marking of certain groups of women as undomesticated and hypersexual, as women who refuse to embrace the nuclear family as paradigm. The current liberal-conservative discourse around welfare criminalizes black single mothers, who are represented as deficient, manless, drug-using breeders of children, and as reproducers of an attendant culture of poverty. The woman who does drugs is criminalized both because she is a drug user and because, as a consequence, she cannot be a good mother. In some states, pregnant women are being imprisoned for using crack because of possible damage to the fetus.

According to the U.S. Department of Justice, women are far more likely than men to be imprisoned for a drug conviction.[13] However, if women wish to receive treatment for their drug problems, often their only option, if they cannot pay for a drug program, is to be arrested and sentenced to a drug program via the criminal justice system. Yet when U.S. Surgeon General Joycelyn Elders alluded to the importance of opening discussion on the decriminalization of drugs, the Clinton administration immediately disassociated itself from her remarks. Decriminalization of drugs would greatly reduce the numbers of incarcerated women, for the 278 percent increase in the numbers of black women in state and federal prisons (as compared to the 186 percent increase in the numbers of black men) can be largely attributed to the phenomenal rise in drug-related and specifically crack-related imprisonment. According to the Sentencing Project's 1995 report, the increase amounted to 828 percent.[14]

Official refusals to even consider decriminalization of drugs as a possible strategy that might begin to reverse present incarceration practices further bolsters the ideological staying power of the prison. In his well-known study of the history of the prison and its related technologies of discipline, Michel Foucault pointed out that an evolving contradiction is at the very heart of the historical project of imprisonment.

> For a century and a half, the prison has always been offered as its own remedy: . . . the realization of the corrective project as the only method of overcoming the impossibility of implementing it.[15]

As I have attempted to argue, within the U.S. historical context, racism plays a pivotal role in sustaining this contradiction. In fact, Foucault's theory regarding the prison's tendency to serve as its own enduring justification becomes even more compelling if the role of race is also acknowledged. Moreover, moving beyond the parameters of what I consider the double impasse implied by his theory—the discursive impasse his theory discovers and that of the theory itself—I want to conclude by suggesting the possibility of radical race-conscious strategies designed to disrupt the stranglehold of criminalization and incarceration practices.

In the course of a recent collaborative research project with U.C. Santa Barbara sociologist Kum-Kum Bhavnani, in which we interviewed thirty-five women at the San Francisco County Jail, the complex ways in which race and gender help to produce a punishment industry that reproduces the very problems it purports to solve became dramatically apparent. Our interviews focused on the women's ideas about imprisonment and how they themselves imagine alternatives to incarceration. Their various critiques of the prison system and of the existing "alternatives," all of which are tied to reimprisonment as a last resort, led us to reflect more deeply about the importance of retrieving, retheorizing, and reactivating the radical abolitionist strategy first proposed in connection with the prison-reform movements of the sixties and seventies.

We are presently attempting to theorize women's imprisonment in ways that allow us to formulate a radical abolitionist strategy departing from, but not restricted in its conclusions to, women's jails and prisons. Our goal is to formulate alternatives to incarceration that substantively reflect the voices and agency of a variety of imprisoned women. We wish to open up channels for their involvement in the current debates around alternatives to incarceration, while not denying our own role as mediators and interpreters and our own political positioning in these debates. We also want to distinguish our explorations of alternatives from the spate of "alternative punishments" or what are now called "intermediate sanctions" presently being proposed and/or implemented by and through state and local correctional systems.

This is a long-range project that has three dimensions: academic research, public policy, and community organizing. In other words, for this project to be successful, it must build bridges between academic work, legislative and other policy interventions, and grassroots campaigns calling, for example, for the decriminalization of drugs and prostitution—and for the reversal of the present proliferation of jails and prisons.

Raising the possibility of abolishing jails and prisons as the institutionalized and normalized means of addressing social problems in an era of migrating corporations, unemployment and homelessness, and collapsing public services, from health care to education, can hopefully help to interrupt the current law-and-order discourse that has such a grip on the collective imagination, facilitated as it is by deep and hidden influences of racism. This late-twentieth-century "abolitionism," with its nineteenth-century resonances, may also lead to a historical recontextualization of the practice of imprisonment. With the passage of the Thirteenth Amendment, slavery was abolished for all except convicts—and in a sense the exclusion from citizenship accomplished by the slave system has persisted within the U.S. prison system. Only three states allow prisoners to vote, and approximately 4 million people are denied the right to vote because of their present or past incarceration. A radical strategy to abolish jails and prisons as the normal way of dealing with the social problems of late capitalism is not a strategy for abstract abolition. It is designed to force a rethinking of the increasingly repressive role of the state during this era of late capitalism and to carve out a space for resistance.

NOTES

1. See, for instance, the *Austin-American Statesman*, October 17, 1995.
2. Charles S. Clark, "Prison Overcrowding," *Congressional Quarterly Researcher* 4, no. 5 (Feb. 4, 1994): 97–119.
3. Ibid.
4. Marc Mauer, "Young Black Men and the Criminal Justice System: A Growing National Problem," Washington, D.C.: The Sentencing Project, February 1990.
5. Alexander Cockburn, *Philadelphia Inquirer,* August 29, 1994.
6. Marc Mauer and Tracy Huling, "Young Black Americans and the Criminal Justice System: Five Years Later," Washington, D.C.: The Sentencing Project, October 1995.
7. Ibid., 18.
8. *See* Cockburn.
9. *See* Lubiano's essay in this volume, as well as "Black Ladies, Welfare Queens, and State Minstrels: Ideological War by Narrative Means," in *Race-ing Justice, En-gendering Power: Essays on Anita Hill, Clarence Thomas, and the Construction of Social Reality,* ed. Toni Morrison (New York: Pantheon, 1992), 323–63.
10. Unpublished essay, "Modern Slavery American Style," 1995.
11. I wish to acknowledge Julie Brown, who acquired this brochure from the California Department of Correction in the course of researching the role of convict labor.

12. *Wall Street Journal*, May 12, 1994.
13. Lawrence Rence, A. Greenfield, Stephanie Minor-Harper, *Women in Prison* (Washington, D.C.: U.S. Dept. of Justice, Office of Justice Programs, Bureau of Statistics, 1991).
14. Mauer and Huling, "Young Black Americans," 19.
15. Michel Foucault, *Discipline and Punish: The Birth of the Prison*, trans. Alan Sheridan (New York: Vintage, 1979), 395.

COLOR BLINDNESS, HISTORY,
AND THE LAW

Kimberlé Williams Crenshaw

■

ANTHROPOLOGIST BRACKETTE WILLIAMS has said "only a fool stands in the middle of an intersection."[1] Well, having been that foolish for some time now in my own work, today I entertain yet another folly in order to share with you some loosely formed or, as my colleague Kendall Thomas might say, "mushy thoughts" about the relationship between law and the contemporary bid to consolidate and render unremarkable racial hierarchy. I say folly, of course, because my fantasy when I began this project was to present to you a tightly drawn, illuminating, and provocative analysis that pulls together themes of critical race theory and which is theoretical yet practical, sophisticated but accessible, collective yet original, antiessentialist yet grounded, with refrains from intersectionality and interesting interventions on structure and agency; and all in a nice, original, and neat package.

My starting point is actually two somewhat disparate social texts: the popular political discourse on race and particularly the developing discourse on victimology, and 1994's celebration of the fortieth anniversary of *Brown v. Board of Education*.[2] In 1994 we had reproduced for us again and again by the media a particular celebratory narrative about how that case marks the historical moment when African Americans were finally granted full citizenship status within the American political community. According to that narrative, it will no longer be possible to say that the national subject can only be described in white terms. *Brown* completed a narrative about the ultimate inclusion of African Americans facilitated importantly by law. I suspect that along with the celebratory rhetoric there also will be attempts to address what will be called "contemporary racial anomalies"—like the continuing material and political disparities between African Americans and the white community.

My particular interest here is to examine how this apparent contradiction is rationalized by neoliberal and conservative forces, and indeed how *Brown* itself has been deployed to do the ideological work of legitimating racial hierarchy. The project of legitimation has created a growth industry for a few ambitious African Americans who can provide the salve to soothe lingering doubts about whether the promise of *Brown* has really been fulfilled. Enterprising individuals such as Clarence Thomas, Thomas Sowell, and others fill that demand, providing a racially correct voice-over to narrate the story of black pathology and dependence that is produced by predictable social consequences.

Key exhortations to eschew victim-based demands are behind the appropriation of *Brown* as constituting a fundamental break with white supremacy. Through the force of this ahistoricism, this willful inattention to the historical operations of white supremacy, contemporary race hierarchy is assured of its historical grounding and represented as a natural outgrowth of cultural disability and economic dependence. My specific concern here is how law has come to endorse this narrative and how in doing so, it, too, presumes a discontinuity between the past and the present that its own analytics simultaneously deny.

Part of my goal, then, is to challenge the use to which *Brown* has been put, to reveal the continuity in law between the former period of explicitly endorsed, state-sponsored white supremacy, and today's more benign version of formal equality. Key to this project is uncovering the continuing viability and vitality of *Plessy v. Ferguson*, the case that enshrined the doctrine of separate but equal, rendering segregation consistent with the commands of the Fourteenth Amendment.[3] I seek to trace *Plessy*'s continuing presence in terms of its formalistic analytics, which illustrate the manipulability of concepts such as equality, and perhaps more important, I seek to name the social vision it endorses: the notion of a pre-private sphere in which some version of the market works to produce fair outcomes.

My point, however, is not simply to show that *Plessy* lives, but to suggest how law in its almost infinite flexibility can assist in legitimating hierarchy simply by labeling the realm of the social equal, declaring victory, and moving on. To state it more simply, the same interpretive strategy deployed to legitimize segregation is now being deployed to immunize the racial status quo against any substantive redistribution.

I'd like to demonstrate this argument by returning to *Plessy* and by connecting its analytics and social visions to perhaps the definitive case in the postreform contemporary era, specifically *Richmond v. Croson*.[4] I want to suggest as well that *Plessy* shares the same ideological plane as another case, *Lochner v. New York,* that embodied the doctrine of freedom of contract that functions quite similarly to contemporary color-blind jurisprudence.[5] While *Lochner* has fallen into disrepute, color blindness and its social vision is resurrected in contemporary race jurisprudence. I conclude by suggesting the relevance of law in shaping discourse about race, and by placing critical race theory in opposition to this race jurisprudence.

Homer Plessy was the plaintiff in *Plessy v. Ferguson,* an 1896 case that challenged the constitutionality of a segregation statute in Louisiana. Homer Plessy was defined by the state of Louisiana as an octoroon. He challenged the segregation statute under the Fourteenth Amendment and actually made two separate arguments: first, that the race classification system that classified him as black basically deprived him of equal protection of the law due to the irrationality of the classification system, and second, that the statute was unconstitutional in that it segregated those defined as black from those who were defined as white.

Despite the rather clear design of these statutes to relegate blacks to a status of second-class citizenship, the Supreme Court upheld the constitutionality of the statute requiring segregation on trains. In order to do this, the court had to decide how to rationalize forcing African Americans into hot, noisy, engine cars as consistent with equality. The strategy they chose was to formalize equality basically to constitute only symmetrical treatment and then to render the social, material context of segregation as well as its effects—in this case, discomfort in unpleasant cars—private or unknowable. This strategy would be achieved through distinguishing between the civil, which was protected, and the social, which was not.

Civil equality, then, required formal equality—satisfied here by the symmetrical treatment of blacks and whites under the statute. Whites were not permitted to go to black cars and blacks were not permitted to go to white cars. No inequality there. But of course, the cars were not equal, nor was the meaning of segregation for blacks and whites. The inequality of material dimensions did not figure in the analysis, apparently having been relegated to the private sphere to be worked out between blacks and the railroad (without noting that African Americans had little if any means of persuading the railroads to work out these problems). As far as the *meaning* of the statute was concerned, there was nothing in the statute that warranted the interpretation of its intent to imply inferiority. As the Court saw it, if blacks chose to interpret segregation in that way, then that was their choice. Whites would certainly not view the statute that way, had it been adopted by Reconstruction-era legislators.

Yet the heart of *Plessy*, in my view, was its admonition that law could not be looked to in order to bring about social equality. In the nature of things, the Fourteenth Amendment could not have been intended to ensure actual social equality. If social equality were to be achieved, blacks would essentially have to earn the respect of whites within the private social sphere. I call this racial marketplace ideology. In this market the state cannot interfere to redistribute racial value. Such redistribution is an illegitimate end that would upset the natural outcomes of the market. If blacks wanted social equality, they would have to get in there (in the market) and work for it. What interests me about this analysis is the ability to sustain a belief, in the face of massive racial subordination, that such a market was somehow free and that the social subordination of blacks was a neutral evaluation of their group work within that market. With all avenues for achieving a producing, competitive racial power foreclosed, this conceptualization was simply fantastical, yet it worked, at an interpretive level, to consolidate white racial power and to insulate that power for more than five decades.

The legal strategy of the pre-*Brown* civil rights cases was essentially to overturn the logic of *Plessy v. Ferguson*. In contemporary periods we tend to characterize *Brown* as having successfully interred *Plessy*. Quite clearly, separate but equal is no longer the law of the land. But I think it would be a mistake to focus solely on the rejection of the formal doctrine while failing to uncover the continuity of *Plessy*'s social vision and its analytic. By interrogating its contemporary race jurisprudence, it becomes clear that the social vision and the analytics that constitutionalized the massive inequality of separate-but-equal is reincarnated in color-blind jurisprudence.

I can illustrate this claim by using one of the more controversial post-reform cases, that of *Richmond v. Croson*. Some of you may know that *Richmond v. Croson* was a case in which the Supreme Court struck down an affirmative action program that was adopted by the Richmond city council. The program was adopted in light of gross disparities between Richmond's black population, which was 50 percent of the total population, and the percentage of city contracts awarded to minority-owned businesses, which was less than 1 percent.

Richmond's majority black city council, based on their belief that this was not a natural consequence of some market but the reflection of substantial discrimination, adopted an affirmative action program that required 30 percent of state contracts and city contracts to be set aside for minority firms. The Supreme Court's first move in reviewing the constitutionality of this affirmative action program was to determine whether race classifications that burden whites would be subject to the same level of review as traditional classifications that burden people of color. The Court essentiality decided that race would be narrowly construed to basically represent simply skin color—devoid of any historical, political, or economic value, or determination, or history.

Having determined, then, that everyone was equal in the sense that everyone had a skin color, symmetrical treatment was satisfied by a general rule that nobody's skin color should be taken into account in governmental decision-making. Justice Sandra Day O'Connor, who wrote the opinion, then considered whether there was a compelling state interest to justify these classifications. She indicated that the city might have a compelling state interest if it could prove that the disparities were in fact the result of some kind of discrimination. Therefore, the question was whether or not those disparate numbers were simply the natural result of some undetermined market force, or whether they were actually the result of some past discrimination.

Richmond was no stranger to the Supreme Court. It had long been one of the most racially entrenched southern cities in the country and often came before the Supreme Court in regard to race doctrine. It had been in front of the Court on any number of occasions on questions of discrimination in voting, discrimination in housing, and discrimination in schools—Virginia actually closed its schools rather than integrate them. Yet, in the Court's view, none of these examples of de jure discrimination had any bearing on the disparities that the programs sought to address. According to the Court's view, affirmative action, absent any factual base, was designed merely to correct for social discrimination and to privilege a few minorities at the expense of more deserving whites.

O'Connor's final pronouncement on the dearth of minority contractors was to feign ignorance and postulate that perhaps minorities simply didn't choose to become contractors in lockstep proportions to their percentage in the population (recall here *Plessy*'s discussion about choice). Thus, affirmative action was struck down, and if the logic stands, few other programs will stand constitutional muster.

When one examines *Croson* and *Plessy* together, their analytical similarities are striking. Both reduced the question of racial equality to mere formalism, completely abstracted from history or contract. The different meanings and experiences of whiteness and blackness are completely erased, with the categories formally construed to represent an ahistorical essential view of skin color. Both *Plessy* and *Croson*, then, required that the two categories be treated the same. That sameness in *Plessy* was to guarantee that blacks and whites were sent to separate cars; that sameness in *Croson* was to guarantee that the state must treat blacks and whites the same by not considering their race.

It is fairly obvious that treating different things the same can generate as much an inequality as treating the same things differently. Anatole France captured that inequality when he noted that the law in its majestic equality prevents the rich and the poor from sleeping under bridges.[6] Clearly, the law works in inequality when the rich will never seek that worldly pleasure, and the poor have no other choice. A similar denial of social power differentials between racial groups reproduces and insulates that very power disparity. Formal equality in conditions of social inequality becomes a tool of domination, reinforcing that system and insulating it from attack.

As troubling as Justice O'Connor's formalism was, what is more troubling is her distinction between public and private realms. Racial disparities in employment and housing and in other spheres absent some direct exclusive causal link are simply the consequences of a private market. Describing this as at best amorphous notions of societal discrimination, she determined that law cannot be deployed to alter those conditions unless there was a justification for assuming that those conditions were the result of some kind of defect in the market.

In this sense, this particular understanding of the market and the limitations of what state powers can do constitutes a key analytical move that also informs other Supreme Court doctrines—the particular image of the social spheres as free and open for individuals struggling to compete, unfettered by the state. This image of a private sphere was dominant in the pre–New Deal era in which the Court struck down, for example, labor legislation that sought to protect workers, by requiring wage and hour limitations, against exploitation at the hands of their employers. Freedom of contract is based similarly on a laissez-faire philosophy imagining a free market undisturbed by state power in which the individuals basically compete. In the Court's early view this free market necessitated that the state had to stay out of the competition. It could not adopt legislation that attempted to deal with some of the problems of exploitation. Thus, in a famous case, *Lochner v. New York*, the Supreme Court struck down as unconstitutional a health regulation limiting bakers' hours on the argument that the bakers freely chose to enter the contractual relations that resulted in their long hours. Such regulations violated their freedom of contract and constituted an impermissible attempt to redistribute bargaining power to employees from employers.

Legal realists showed that the competitive advantage the bakery owners had was neither natural nor prepolitical, but was a function of a preexisting set of rules of contract and property, rules that were the product of state power and just as easily could have gone the other way. It was, thus, no argument to say that the state could not get involved in the market because, in fact, the state was already there.

Laissez faire was to labor what color blindness is to African Americans. Justice O'Connor's statement in *Croson* that blacks simply choose not to engage in lucrative employment is essentially the same as the assumption in *Lochner* that bakers simply chose to engage in oppressive contracts. In both instances real material constraints are erased or ignored in the analysis in order to conclude that employees were free and that blacks and whites were treated equally.

Just as the realists showed that there was in fact no free market, much of critical race theory is attempting to show that there is no free market of race that determines relationships between blacks and whites. There is no free competition between blacks and whites in part because the law actually structures those relationships across a wide range of societal competitions over certain social resources.

To conclude, the doctrine of color blindness, along with the nineteenth-century market vision it endorses, uses and redeploys in the context of equal opportunity very narrow visions of equality and a specific contested vision of the notion of the private sphere. It not only works to legitimize material deprivations, but it also produces a particular ideological regime. That regime forces African Americans into articulating legitimate demands within the discourse of victimhood. Doing so is the only way that blacks can achieve political power: to show that there is a defect in the market and that the defect is constituted by an intentional, particular, state actor articulating its decision to discriminate solely on the basis of skin color—that is, essentially forcing black people to articulate themselves as perfect victims as against a perfect discriminator. Consequentially, when blacks are told that they should not be deploying the use of victimology as a way of articulating demands, they are essentially being forced into a catch-22. The only way one can achieve political power through this structure is to articulate ourselves as victims, yet the very articulation of ourselves as victims is a justification for rejecting our claim. In the law, it is clear that the end of interpretation is usually the exercise of state power. Such interpretation is produced by the ways state power, in fact, will be deployed in a particular context.

I think we need to be prepared to understand the distributive consequences of legal ideology, particularly legal ideology that produces social discourses of victimhood, and to reject the invisibility of law in structuring those discourses. In race matters, I think we need to be prepared relentlessly to show how, in fact, law matters.

NOTES

1. Opening remarks to her paper presented at the Race Matters Conference, Princeton, NJ, April 28–30, 1994. Intersection refers to Williams's conference panel's subject matter—the coming together of race, gender, and/or sexuality. It is also a word and a concept that I have used frequently in my own work to describe its focus on race, class, and gender.
2. *Brown v. Board of Education*, 347 U.S. 483 (1954).
3. *Plessy v. Ferguson*, 163 U.S. 537 (1896) (Harlan, J., dissenting).
4. *City of Richmond v. J. A. Croson Co.*, 488 U.S. 469 (1989) (Scalia, J., concurring).
5. *Lochner v. New York*, 198 U.S. 45 (1905) (overruled by *Ferguson v. Skrupa*, 372 U.S. 726 [1963]).
6. Anatole France, *Le Lys Rouge* (1894), in *Oeuvres* v. 2 (Paris: Editions Gallimard, 1987).

SUBJECTS IN HISTORY

Making Diasporic Identities

∎

Stuart Hall

I AM THE ONLY participant from another part of the "black diaspora," and, as a consequence, what we in England know as the "burden of representation" lies particularly heavy on my shoulders. As a consequence of that burden, it seems to me incumbent in some ways to try to add to an ongoing discussion; my function, it seems to me, is partly to bring to bear on the discussion a perspective that adds a transnational, global, "diasporic dimension," to what is inevitably U.S. terrain. I'm going to do so, in part, by referring to a number of points that have already arisen in the debate simply to bring to bear on them some experiences, some similar and parallel lines of approach and political work elsewhere in the "black Atlantic."

I don't want to get into details, into particular aspects of ideological analysis, or cultural production, although I'm going to draw some examples from cultural production. Instead, I want to outline something more general; I want to express some views about the place of cultural politics in the present racial conjuncture, about how it is shifting and changing, and about the problems thrown up in our attempts to theorize and define adequate strategies for dealing with the place of cultural politics. That is what is required by the moment the conference itself addressed, and to do so I want to return to that conference's "electric opening," which I'll never forget, not to rerun the West-Steinberg conversation,[1] but partly to explain the reason for my own brief intervention in that debate in order to spell out the grounds on which I made it. To those of you who weren't there, I simply said, "Please remember that questions of culture are not superstructural to the problems of economic and political change; they are constitutive of them!"

What does it mean to take seriously, in our present conjuncture, the thought that cultural politics and questions of culture, of discourse, and of metaphor are absolutely deadly political questions? That is my purpose. I want to persuade you that that is so. And that we ought to sort of preach on this occasion, no, not only to give up the bad habits of smoking and drinking and whoring and gambling, but to give up certain forms of political essentialism and the way in which it makes you sleep well at night.

There are two basic reasons at this point why I wanted to suggest to you why questions of culture and of representation, of cultural productions, and of aesthetics, politics, and power are of absolute centrality. There are many other reasons, but I can't deal with them now. I want to deal with two particular reasons because they are central to how we need to conceptualize the question of race itself. You see, if indeed, as we mouth the mantra, race is indeed a sociohistorical concept, not a transhistorical discourse grounded in biology, then it must function not through the truth of the "biological referent" but as a discursive logic. That is to say, as a logic in which, of course, the biological trace still functions even when it's silent, but now, not as the truth, but as the guarantor of the truth. That is a question of discursive power. Not a question of what is true, but what is *made* to be true. Such is the way in which racial discourses operate. To use a familiar Foucault phrase, it is a "regime of truth." I want to insist that its logic is discursive in this sense, that racial discourses produce, mark, and fix the infinite differences and diversities of human beings through a rigid binary coding. That logic establishes a chain of correspondences both between the physical and the cultural, between intellectual and cognitive characteristics; it gives legibility to a social system in which it operates; it allows us to decipher different signifiers from the racial fixing of the signifier "race"; and through that reading it organizes, regulates, and gives meaning to social practices through the distribution of symbolic and material resources between different groups and the establishment of racial hierarchy.

To say that is to say that race is a discourse, that it operates through the movement of the signifiers, and yet, at the same time, to say that the whole historical organization of human social practices through the binary coding of race is dependent on the meanings that it is able to give to the relationships of power and representation between human societies.

The second reason culture is absolutely central to our concerns, in my view, is that it constitutes the terrain for producing identity, for producing the constitution of social subjects. It is one of the social conditions of existence for setting subjects in place in historical relations, setting them in place, in position. They are unable to speak, or to act in one way or another, until they have been positioned by the work that culture does, and in that way, as subjects they function by taking up the discourses of the present and the past.

It is that taking up of positions that I call "identities." You see the consequence of turning the paradigm around that way, the political question (for there is always a political question, at any rate, in the way I pose the issue) is not "How do we effectively mobilize those identities which are already formed?" so that we could put them on the train and get them onto the stage at the right moment, in the right spot—an act the left has historically been trying to do for about four hundred years—but something really quite different and much deeper.

How can we organize these huge, randomly varied, and diverse things we call human subjects into positions where they can recognize one another for long enough to act together, and thus to take up a position that one of these days they might live out and act through as an identity. Identity is at the end, not the beginning, of the paradigm. Identity is what is at stake in political organization. It isn't that the subjects are there and we just can't get to them. It is that they don't know yet that they are subjects of a possible discourse. And that always in every political struggle, since every political struggle is always open, it is possible either to win their identification or to lose it.

Indeed, for those of you who have been in politics for as long as I have, usually it is possible both to win and to lose it, and then to win it again and to lose it again, in an infinitely recurring struggle. That is the open-ended, contingent nature of political struggle, and just as a warning to intellectuals, there isn't any final theoretical solution, any grand deconstructive scheme which we can pull out of the air, which we can ensure will tell us that the subjects are going to stay like that, that the subjects are in place and the moment is going to come. And then the intellectuals can go home and get on with their business. It isn't like that.

Remember: identifications, not identities. Once you've got identification, you can decide which identities are working *this* week.

I speak of the process of identification, of feeling yourself through the contingent, antagonistic, and conflicting sentiments of which human beings are made up. Identification means that you are called in a certain way, interpolated in a certain way: "you, this time, in this space, for this purpose, by this barricade with these folks." That's what is at stake in political struggle. And you can't ahead of time either know that or know how to recognize that, or know how to imagine the collectivity that all those folks together might make. For how else would you know them? They weren't there before, or they weren't gathered together in the proper place. You can only come as you were, come together because somehow you can represent yourself and begin to share an imagined community of some kind with others which without representation and culture you could not express to anybody else.

The idea that somehow, out of some space, a politics of antiracism will arise without our giving thought as to how the subjects of it are to be formed is, to my mind, unintelligible. So then the questions that arise are how and what kind? What are the natures of the cultural, social, and political identities that can and cannot be formed in these processes so as to conduct a political struggle, a cultural and social struggle that has the possibility of affecting something in the world? I want to insist that that is an open question, because I think at some level it remains more difficult than we think to take on the implications of what I've just been trying to say. Because when that rigid binary, racial logic is being used against us, we certainly know what's wrong with it. But when it seems to be working for us, we find that it's extremely difficult to give it up. We just can't let go of it in good moments, it makes us feel together; we can't imagine what a politics would be like if it wasn't there. How would you mobilize, what would you say to people, on what basis would you appeal to them, under what banner would you get them together? The whole thing begins to disintegrate, polarize, pluralize, get away from us, and we find ourselves confused by it. So, unfortunately, I think, people who know in their hearts that if you say race is not biological, that it is historical, cultural, and political, know you must follow the logic of that provision in terms of the alternative strategies you try to develop. Then, just at one minute to midnight, you're not beyond reaching for the final guarantee, and the whole biological fix actually slips back into place. Therefore, I want to explore what I think are the difficulties of what I'm going to call the end of the essentialized black subject, the end of an essentialist conception of the black experience.

One of the problems that confront a politics of this kind is that it effects some of our most central cultural and political concepts and images. Take the notion of tradition, for example. It is almost impossible to think of a cultural community as shared cultural meanings which exist over any period of time, which persist and have persisted over any period of time, which has managed to survive against all the odds, without thinking of the element of tradition that has enabled that community to hold together. Nevertheless, I think one of the implications of what I've just been saying is, indeed, that the question of tradition itself has to be conceptually rephrased.

Let me (walking dangerous waters, I know) talk about civil rights. Could one imagine the civil rights struggle of the sixties without the long traditions of black struggle that historically go back at least as far as the beginning of slavery? And yet, is there anybody here who wouldn't want to describe the civil rights movement as a movement that produced new black subjects? But new black subjects—now, what is that "new" then in the light of the tradition? Would it have happened without that tradition? Absolutely not. Where would traditions of struggle, where would the accumulated knowledge, where would the expectivity of human values that kept people going in dark days, where would that have come from if there hadn't been languages and historical traditions of one kind or another that sustained them across times? That sustained human beings in their lives of struggle across time—and yet the particular way that black people occupied that identity, lived that identity, and struggled around it, produced something which had never been seen before.

This is not the game you know, of trading "your victimage is bigger than mine," "my heroism is bigger than yours"—you don't have to say it's greater than what has happened before. That's not my argument; but my argument is that it was, and is, significantly different. And what was different about it was a particular reworking of that tradition under the force of the present conjuncture, not of a tradition which is simply a transmission belt that takes you from the past teleologically marching through to the future. A reworking that precisely delivers the much more complex idea that is a phrase you know well, "the changing same." That reworking transmits the capacity to be both the same and different, both located in a tradition and yet not constrained by it. Able to think freely on the basis of the particular ground. That reworking is almost musical and it has to be. What else is any successful blues, any successful jazz standard, or any gospel song but the given ground and the performance that translates it? But you couldn't listen to it if all there was was just the same damn thing once over again. It has to be that process of reworking the elements of a tradition, of taking forward what has been left, or engaging what is new, and of trying to put together a new kind of configuration. If you don't believe me because you think civil rights belongs to you, let me tell you that it didn't simply belong to you and it didn't simply produce some new black subjects here, it produced a lot of new black subjects elsewhere.

In the place where I came from in Jamaica, the conjuncture of the civil rights movement and the black consciousness movement of decolonization, the naming—the possibility at last to name the unspeakable fact of slavery and the imaginative, metaphorical connection with Africa—made Jamaica, where I was born, a black country for the first time in the 1960s. I don't mean it was the first time any black people were there. I mean black as a political category. I mean black as a culture. I mean black as a sociohistorical fact. It was the first time that I ever called myself that. I had called myself thousands of things before, but until that historical moment, it had been a word that I would never have applied to my own identity. So, if your own identities don't change, believe me, mine certainly have. They keep going on and on, and not only that, I most recognize them when other people say something different. In the sixties, after having been in England for ten years over that period when Afro-Caribbeans came to Britain for the first time, I went home and my mother said to me, "I hope they don't think you're one of those immigrants over there." I had never called myself an immigrant in all my life, and suddenly I said, "That's what I am." After all, I've gone to the people's place, I'm going to stay whether they like it or not, I intend to get a job if they're going to give me one. What am I but an immigrant? My life, far from the unfolding of this great identity I always knew about, this fabric endlessly unfolding but not changing toward some particular end, changes drastically, and when I get to the end, I can't say "There you are, you've always been like that, God help me, always been like that." No, the transformations have made me something different. Because historically, to say suddenly that you know we are black people, and to name the names, meant that the cultural terrain on which those names worked and struggled was thereby transformed. Cultural change is constitutive of political change and moral awareness of human consciousness.

And I want to say a word about political history as a way of passing on to another element and its complexity. In the 1970s, the signifier "black" was adopted as a political category of struggle, both by Afro-Caribbean migrants and by migrants from the Asian continent. People who manifestly were not, in any of the significant ways in which the term "race" had ever been used, the same race, called themselves by the racial signifier. They said, "Since the British can't tell the difference between us, we must be the same." We might as well call one another by the same name. That's what identity is; it always has a constitutive outside. Those people didn't know about a "constitutive outside," but they knew one when they got it. Since they were manifestly not white, they were black. They called themselves black. They organized under that *political* roof.

It was a very important moment politically in Britain. It isn't the moment that we're in now. That significance has gone. It is partly dissolved into a variety of new, more ethnically specific signifers. People now call themselves not only Asians, but Indians, Bangladeshis, Pakistanis, and indeed, South Indians. Things have moved into a new kind of ethnicized politics of difference. And that has presented certain profound difficulties of political organization when the signifier "black" has disappeared.

Still, I want to speak about this moment that I've just mentioned. What is this moment of the pluralization of cultural difference? Sometimes it is a racialized kind, sometimes an ethnicized kind—which is in my view increasingly characteristic of social antagonisms on a world scale. These antagonisms are a product of huge, planned, and unplanned world migrations—the greatest and most constitutive cultural fact of the late modern world. The planned and unplanned, forced and unforced movements of peoples, taking up hundreds of years later after that first forced migration of slavery with which modernity began. Here we are in late modernity, and what is happening is exactly the same kind of proliferation of movement as peoples. They are torn apart by poverty, by drought, by civil war, by the international arms trade, and they are moving, moving, moving from their settled homes to somewhere else.

Let me put that in cultural terms. They're moving like we have done before into the narratives, through which they will have to tell their history of migration, loss, displacement, redefining themselves, of home, of another home, of the question of where is home, of all of the images and metaphors of a perpetually unsettled people. That is the modern fact that is transforming this society; it is transforming Europe, Western European society. It is a world-historical fact of astonishing proportions and partly because it goes by different names—now refugees, now economic migrants, etc. And partly because it happens in this completely unplanned late-modern way, where people just calculate for themselves that the only thing to do is to buy a one-way plane ticket and get on a plane for paradise or, you know, the South Bronx, or wherever paradise is these days. In that way trying to resolve what is the global maldistribution of material and symbolic goods.

One of the consequences of that fact, within different national societies, has been to pluralize and complicate the terrain of social struggle. For what you find in each society is the integration of different forms of racialized and ethnicized difference, marked in different ways with very different and discrete histories. Nevertheless, it is part of the long history of the dialectics of "othering": these are all others of one kind or another, those that weren't othered through slavery were othered through colonialism or othered through imperialism. And some were othered through all three. Each of these people cling to the particular homes and identities that were formed through those histories. But what is most dramatic about them is that they are now convened in the very center of modernity, in the very "hotbed" of the modern, and what we find then as a consequence is that what the modern itself now means is precisely this conflict, this struggle, this complicated and differentiated line of struggle, between those who have had to move, and go on moving to survive, who have constantly been "the racialized other" of some system of supremacy, and on the other hand, the cultural nationalist racism that is the backlash against this multicultural drift, which is evolving in every society of the advanced, modern, Western industrial world.

I won't at this stage try to tell you what it means to us to see active fascism in the streets of London, to see the fascist right in alliance with a respectable center, to hear what we've heard before said about blacks, now said about North Africans, now said between peoples who call themselves European, who are hastily cobbling together in these societies that are hybridized and mongrelized to their roots. I couldn't find a "pure folk" anywhere. One would have to go into the museum to dig up the pure Bosnian-Serbian folk. Haul him out, mount him, etc.

Nevertheless, cobbling is a kind of defense against the modern world, a defense against living with difference, this retreat into the bunker of cultural and racist nationalism. I call it by that name, because although in its many respectable forms it doesn't recognize itself as such, this racism exists as a defense of "Englishness," of "Britishness," and of "Americanness." How could anybody object to Americans, or some Americans, defending a certain kind of "Americanness"? Who could argue against the possible claim that American children might not speak the "American language" first in American schools, and what is racist about that, what could possibly be racist about that?

I told a story recently in the Du Bois Lectures at Harvard, of a very close friend of Mrs. Thatcher's, Lord Tebit, who has devised a simple kind of handy test for deciding who culturally belongs to whom and who does not (call it "the Tebit test"). It is a very simple one. It's a question of whether or not the migrant families cheer the Pakistanis and the West Indians when they come touring for cricket. You have only to go to the cricket match and pavilion, and look around when the West Indians get to six hundred or whatever it is, and the "black stands," the ones closest to the oval, start to jump and down, you know you can identify them. Because clearly their hearts cannot be in the right place. On the other hand, it is a very serious business indeed, this question of reconstructing a little

"Englandism," reconstructing a little Americanism, through the struggles that are sometimes called "the culture wars."

Don't fool yourself that this is some superstructural, marginal question. At the center of this is the question of who can belong, who has access to the transmission belt through which Britishness, Englishness, is carried and can be inculcated. And who doesn't belong. And whether or not they have yet arrived at the moment when the lines are going to be drawn in blood and fire. Symbolic lines are being drawn, and what we know about culture is that once the symbolic difference exists, that is the line around which power coheres. Power uses difference as a way of marking off who does and who does not belong.

That is the shape of a new kind of cultural difference that impacts and sits atop another older kind: the politics of cultural difference. Today people sometimes say, "Of course, politics is a very confusing game, because there aren't those old stabilized identities around which we used to mobilize, and there aren't exactly those old kinds of struggles that we used to know how to fight." It is not, I warn you, because things are going through a little postmodern shake, and then they're going to settle down; then we're going to go back to the stabilized, well-organized, clearly demarcated frontiers of the past. We are in a new political conjuncture not without racism, not a conjuncture without difference; it is not a conjuncture without poverty and deprivation and marginalization on a world scale. But it is one in which the marking of difference, the careful and overlatticed marking of finely drawn distinction, can't be easily convened under a single political roof and fought in a simple battle. It is a much more differentiated, sophisticated, positional kind of struggle that has to be developed, to be conducted, if we are serious about refusing its human cost.

Sometimes the term "diaspora" is used as a way of conjuring up a kind of imagined community that would cut across the configurations of cultural nationalism. And I'm not only very much in favor of that, having contributed in some way to giving the term "lift off." But let me warn you and warn myself that after all diaspora, too, has been the site of some of the most closed narratives of identity known to human beings. It is a word that has lodged there for a people who are not going to change, who sat on top of a sacred text and erected the barriers, and who then wanted to make the return exactly to the place where they came from. And who have gone back and sat on the head of all the other people who were there, too. If you open yourself to the politics of cultural difference, there is no safety in terminology. Words can always be transcoded against you, identity can turn against you, race can turn against you, difference can turn against you, diaspora can turn against you because that is the nature of the discursive.

I am trying to persuade you that the word is the medium in which power works. Don't clutch onto the word, but do clutch onto certain ideas about it. The diaspora is a place where traditions operate but are not closed, where the black experience is historically and culturally distinctive but is not the same as it was before. We are to move from one end of the diaspora to another and be ready to move from differently translated worlds, each with its own inflection, places where the law is almost certainly the law of syncretism, of taking in influences, of translating what has been given, of disarticulating and rearticulating, of creolization. And here I give my last injunction: to give up smoking and give up the idea, the commitment to the politically pure. The future belongs to the impure. The future belongs to those who are ready to take in a bit of the other, as well as being what they themselves are. After all, it is because their history and ours is so deeply and profoundly and inextricably intertwined that racism exists. For otherwise, how could they keep us apart?

NOTE

1. During the discussion following Stephen Steinberg's critique of Cornel West's ideas about the "underclass," and after a few additional criticisms leveled from the floor, I stood up to intervene in order to address what I saw as an unhelpful reduction of culture to the conditions of the economic.

AFTERWORD

Cornel West

∎

THIS VOLUME RESTS upon three fundamental claims. First, white supremacy is *constitutive*, not additive, to the makings of the modern world. Second, antiblack racism is *integral*, not marginal, to the existence and sustenance of American society. And third, race remains the most *explosive* issue in the country today. In this sense, race matters in regard to how we conceive what it means to be modern, American, and human in our contemporary world.

The very construction of "race" is a European creation rooted in attempts to rationalize European superiority in oceanic transportation, military technology, and capitalist expansion resulting in imperial conquests and colonial subordination of many non-European peoples. The distinctive feature of the precious experiment in democracy called the United States of America was its profound and pervasive investment in white supremacy—in the expropriation of indigenous peoples' land and African peoples' labor. And one glaring aspect of our present-day society is the depth and breadth of racial polarization, balkanization, and de facto segregation.

Yet, after two hundred years of refined discourses about "modernity," few philosophers, social scientists, or cultural critics give significant weight to the thoroughly modern construct of "race." So, we have sophisticated, yet truncated, interpretations of modern democracies, nationalisms, sciences, technologies, capitalist markets, bureaucracies, empires, colonies, and subjectivities. These *deracialized* discourses about modernity are disarming and deceptive in the face of the persistence of white supremacy here and abroad. The denial of race in these "color-blind" perspectives about the modern past or the postmodern present is the intellectual counterpart of the denial of the legacy of white supremacy in our society and world. As long as race is simply added to the *central* dynamics of modernity or glibly marginal to the emergence and sustenance of American society, this lethal denial persists. The powerful and provocative essays in this volume not only challenge these centuries-long frameworks of racial denial, they also reveal the frameworks themselves to be complicitous with and supportive of this denial. That is why these essays constitute an indictment of most contemporary intellectuals, who view race as a kind of peripheral phenomenon in modern times as manifest in their writings about modernity and America.

In returning to these essays again, after having heard them first as part of the Race Matters Conference at Princeton, I'm especially struck by the range of analysis here even as responding to this work allows me to consider again the trajectory of my own thinking.

My own work primarily has focused on the *existential* predicament of New World Africans in the United States—how they were made and remade themselves into colored, Negro, black, and African-American human beings in the face of their absurd circumstances. This focus puts a premium on black cultural agency as a precondition for black collective insurgency. Despite that element of my work, there are critics who equate a philosophic notion of "nihilism" with a sociological concept of "passivity" or an existential response with a pathological reaction. I believe this to be a category mistake that produces a misreading of my work and flies in the face of my two decades of writings that highlight structural and institutional analyses of white supremacy alongside my steadfast concern about the existential plight of black people.

Nonetheless, regardless of the disagreements productively aired at the conference, and the differences manifested in some of the work brought together herein, we came together to talk with each other, with the audience, and now, with the larger public. Whether our differences are explicitly stated or implied by the differing terms of our analyses, we agreed and agree that what is needed is all the talent and serious work available to understand and transform the ugly realities of white supremacy. The precious cause of racial justice requires this from each of us. Criticism and engagement are essential; hatred is crippling.

Nowhere is the difficulty of this work more elegantly articulated than in Toni Morrison's magnificent opening essay. And nowhere are the stakes for our being able to do this work more clearly set out. The crucial significance of this volume is that it marks the rise of a new generation of intellectuals who are willing to apply their formidable talent and courage to project visions, analyses, and strategies to grasp and undo the vicious legacies of white supremacy in our time.

We are the heirs of two hundred years and more of engaged antiracist intellectuals making moments to combat those legacies. I'm pleased to have been part of this moment's work.

ACKNOWLEDGMENTS

.

THIS BOOK COULD not have been conceived without the conference at Princeton University that preceded it; therefore, I thank Arnold Rampersad, past director of the Program in American Studies, and Cornel West, past director of the Program in African-American Studies, for making that conference possible. My work on the conference would have been impossible without the inspiration and camaraderie that Toni Morrison provided. And the contributors were splendid both in the moment of the conference and in providing the intellectual wherewithal for this project.

Finally, this book would not have come to fruition without Peter Dimock's vision, work, and belief in the project. In addition to his advice, his editing, and his prodding, his spirit animated this project from the beginning and kept it going when mine flagged. While I assume full responsibility for any errors or inadequacies herein, he is responsible for the collection's coming together. I dedicate it to him.

INDEX

■

Levine, Lawrence, 163–64
"Liberalism and the Negro" (discussion), 16–17
"Liberal Retreat from Race During the Post–Civil Rights Era" (Steinberg), 13–47
liberals, white:
  anti-poor-white biases of, 259–60
  capitulation of, 15, 19–20
  failure of, viii
  order vs. justice and, 14
  rift between blacks and, 18–19
  two schools of thought among, 17
  West's views on, 34–35
"liberal structuralism," 37
lining out, 161–62
Lipsitz, George, 53
literacy rates, 161
literary analysis, 5, 7, 178–79, 184–85
literature:
  combating racism through, 3–12
  as mode of knowledge, 191–93
  race, 162–63
"Living at the Crossroads" (R. Williams), 136–56
Lochner v. New York, 282, 286, 287
Lorde, Audre, 121
Los Angeles, Calif., 214
  crime in, 198–99
  racial divisions in, 76
  riots in, 34
Los Angeles Police Department, 199
Los Angeles Times, 73, 77, 78, 79
Lott, Eric, 58
Louisiana, 282
Lubiano, Wahneema, vii–ix, 143–44, 155, 231, 232–52, 269, 278
Lukács, George, 186–87

McGee, F. W., 166
"Making Crime Pay" (article), 274
Malcolm X, 117, 157
Malthus, Thomas, 266
Marable, Manning, 237
"Margo" (prostitute), 221–22
Marshall, Thurgood, 88

Martin, Sara, 167
Martin, Valerie, 142
Marx, Karl, Du Bois compared with, 93
Maryland, University of, 137, 152
masculinity:
  of aerosol artists, 212
  of color-blindness, 108
  in *Deep Cover*, 239–45
  gay male sexuality and, 119
  hegemony of, in production, performance and promotion, 218–19
  homophobia and, 123
  nationalist worship of, 144, 232, 239–46
  play and, 205
  privileges of, 152
Massey, R. M., 166
Meet the Press, 15–16
Messner, Michael, 204
Methvin, Eugene H., 266
middle class, black:
  black working-class vs., 157–59
  insecurities of, 177–78, 184–85, 186–87
middle class, gun-ownership by, 201
Midwestern Floods of 1993, 49
Million Man March, 129–30, 238, 251, 264
Miss Saigon (Schönberg, Maltby and Boublil), 77
Mitchell, Margaret, 261
Mitchell, Tim, 235
model-minority model, 71–72, 73–75, 76, 77–79
moderates, 13, 14
modernity:
  black religion's transition to, 169
  race and, 295–97, 301–2
Modern Prince, The (Gramsci), 182–83
Morris, Aldon, 41
Morrison, Toni, vii, 3–12, 302
  racism addressed in work of, 3–5
  revisions by, 5–8
  works of, 5–7, 9, 191–92
Moseley-Braun, Carol, 269

ABOUT THE CONTRIBUTORS

■

Kimberlé Williams Crenshaw is a professor of law at Columbia University School of Law, where she teaches constitutional law, civil rights, and race and gender in law. Crenshaw's recent publications include the co-editorship (with Kendall Thomas and Neil Gotanda) of *Critical Race Theory: A Reader*, "Mapping the Margins: Intersectionality, Identity Politics, and Violence Against Women of Color" (43 *Stanford Law Review*, 1241), and *Words That Wound*, co-authored with Mari Matsuda, Charles Lawrence, and Richard Delgado.

Angela Y. Davis is Professor of History of Consciousness at the University of California, Santa Cruz. Her published books include *If They Come in the Morning, Angela Davis: An Autobiography, Women, Race and Class*, and *Women, Culture and Politics*. She has published widely in a range of journals, scholarly as well as popular. Her most recent project is a forthcoming book entitled *Ma Rainey, Bessie Smith and Billie Holiday: Black Women's Music and Social Consciousness*.

Neil Gotanda teaches constitutional law at Western State University College of Law in Fullerton, California. Professor Gotanda has published in law journals such as the *Stanford Law Review* and the *Columbia Law Review*, and is co-editor (with Kimberlé Crenshaw and Kendall Thomas) of *Critical Race Theory: A Reader*.

Stuart Hall is a professor of sociology and head of sociology discipline at The Open University, London. His published works span three decades (1964 to the present) in the form of Centre for Contemporary Cultural Studies publications, numerous journals and general distribution magazines, and anthologies, and includes co-editorship of *Culture, Media, Language: Working Papers in Cultural Studies* (1980), *Resistance Through Ritual: Youth Subcultures in Post-War Britain* (with Tony Jefferson, 1976), and *New Times: The Changing Face of Politics in the 1990s* (with Martin Jacques, 1991), among many others. He has authored *The Hard Road to*

Renewal: Thatcherism and the Crisis of the Left (1988), and *Policing the Crisis: Mugging, the State, and Law and Order* (1978).

Evelyn Brooks Higginbotham is a member of both the Faculty of Arts and Sciences and the Divinity School at Harvard University. She is Professor of Afro-American Studies and African-American Religious History. She is currently writing a book of essays to be published by the University of North Carolina Press, and is the author of "African-American Women's History and the Metalanguage of Race," *Signs* (1992) and the award-winning book *Righteous Discontent: The Women's Movement in the Black Baptist Church* (1993).

Robin D. G. Kelley is a professor of history and Africana Studies at New York University. He is the author of the prize-winning volume *Hammer and Hoe: Alabama Communists During the Great Depression* (University of North Carolina Press, 1990), *Race Rebels: Culture, Politics, and the Black Working Class* (The Free Press, 1994), the editor (with Sidney J. Lemelle) of *Imagining Home: Class, Culture, and Nationalism in the African Diaspora* (Verso, 1994), and has been widely published in journals such as *The Journal of American History*, *The American Historical Review*, *The Nation*, *Monthly Review*, *Labor History*, and *Radical History Review*, among others.

Wahneema Lubiano teaches in the Program in Literature and the Program in African and African-American Studies at Duke University. Her work appears in such journals as *Cultural Critique*, *American Literary History*, *Social Text*, *Assemblage: A Critical Journal of Architecture and Design Culture*, and *Z Magazine Z Papers*. She has two books in progress: *Messing with the Machine: Modernism, Postmodernism, and Black American Fiction* (forthcoming from Verso) and *Like Being Mugged by a Metaphor: "Deep Cover" and Other Fictions of Black American Life* (forthcoming from Duke University Press).

Toni Morrison, Nobel Laureate (1993) and Pulitzer Prize-winning (1987) author of *The Bluest Eye, Sula, Song of Solomon, Tar Baby, Beloved*, and *Jazz*, is also the author of a collection of essays on American literature, *Playing in the Dark*, and the editor of a collection of essays on the Clarence Thomas-Anita Hill controversy, *Race-ing Justice, En-gendering Power*. She has also edited a forthcoming collection of essays on the O. J. Simpson trial.

David Roediger teaches in the history department at the University of Minnesota. His work includes the *Haymarket Scrapbook* (1986, with Franklin Rosemont) and *Our Own Time* (1989, with Philip Foner), the Merle Curti Prize-winning *The Wages of Whiteness* (1991), and *Towards the Abolition of Whiteness* (1994). He is currently at work on *Shades of Pale: Whiteness in the Last Century and the Next* for Free Press. His articles appear in *American Quarterly, International Review of Social History, New Left Review, American Literary History, Journal of Social History, Cultural Correspondence, Labor History, New Politics,* and elsewhere.

David Lionel Smith is dean of the faculty and a professor of English at Williams College. He is completing *Racial Writing, Black and White,* a study of how American texts have been shaped by racial notions and how their writers have deployed race for rhetorical purposes. His published essays on Mark Twain, Booker T. Washington, Amiri Baraka, and other writers have derived from this larger inquiry, and have been published in a wide variety of journals. His future projects include books on the Black Arts Movement and on theories of African-American culture. As the poet D. L. Crockett-Smith, he is author of *Cowboy Amok* (1987) and *Civil Rites* (1996), both published by *The Black Scholar* Press.

Stephen Steinberg teaches in the department of urban studies at Queens College and the Ph.D. Program in Sociology at the CUNY Graduate Center. In 1996 he published *Turning Back: The Retreat from Racial Justice in American Thought and Policy,* (Beacon Press), which was named co-recipient of the Oliver Cromwell Cox Award for Distinguished Anti-Racist Scholarship by the Race and Ethicity Section of the American Sociological Association. In the same year he published an expanded second edition of his book, *The Ethnic Myth: Race, Ethnicity, and Class in America* (originally published in 1989 by Beacon). He is also author of *The Tenacity of Prejudice* and *The Academic Melting Pot,* and co-author of *Writing and Thinking in the Social Sciences.* He has published articles in *The Nation, New Politics,* and *Reconstruction.*

Kendall Thomas is a professor of law at Columbia University School of Law, where he teaches courses in constitutional law, communications law, legal philosophy, Critical Race Theory, and law and sexuality. His writing has appeared in the Virginia, Columbia, and U.S.C. law reviews, as well as in *GLO: A Journal of Lesbian and Gay Studies* and *Assemblage: A Critical Journal of Architecture and Design Culture*. Thomas is a co-editor (with Kimberlé Crenshaw and Neil Gotanda) of *Critical Race Theory: A Reader*. He is currently working on *Corpus Juris (Homo)sexualis: Gay and Lesbian Sexualities in the Body of Law*, a book-length investigation of the strategies by which legal discourse produces and polices figures of "queer" sexuality.

Cornel West is a professor in the Harvard University School of Divinity and the department of African-American Studies. He has written on a variety of subjects drawing from a wide range of sources. He has authored *Prophesy Deliverance!* (1982), *Prophetic Fragments* (1988), *The American Evasion of Philosophy* (1989), *The Ethical Dimensions of Marxist Thought* (1991), *Race Matters in Postmodern Times*, and *Prophetic Reflections: Notes on Race and Power in America* (Common Courage Press, 1993), *Keeping Faith: Philosophy and Race in America* (1993), and *Race Matters* (1993). His recent work continues his effort to explore the intersection of philosophy, race, and culture. He is presently working on three books: *Being and Blackness: The Struggle Against Nobodiness* (the W.E.B. Du Bois lectures at Harvard, 1993), a critical (re)reading of the Scottish philosopher, David Hume, and a book on John Coltrane.

Patricia J. Williams, educated at Wellesley College (B.A.) and Harvard Law School, is a professor of law, Columbia University School of Law. Professor Williams has published widely in law journals, in academic journals, and in general distribution magazines and journals—such as *The Nation*, *The New York Times Book Review*, *Ms. Magazine*, and *The Village Voice*. She is the author of *The Alchemy of Race and Rights: Diary of a Law Professor* and *The Rooster's Egg*.

Rhonda M. Williams is a political economist and a professor of Afro-American Studies at the University of Maryland in College Park. Williams's work has appeared in the *Review of Black Political Economy*, the *Review of*

Radical Political Economics, and *Feminist Studies*. Her publications include "Accumulation as Evisceration: Urban Rebellion and the New Growth Dynamic" (a chapter in Robert Gooding-Williams's (ed.), *Reading Rodney King, Reading Urban Uprising*) and "Race, Deconstruction, and the Emergent Agenda of Feminist Economic Theory" (published in Marianne Ferber and Julie Nelson (eds.), *Beyond Economic Man: Feminist Theory and Economics*. Williams has co-authored a chapter on race, gender, and structural economic change with M. V. Lee Badgett that will appear in Adler and Bernstein (eds.), *Understanding American Economic Decline*.

Howard Winant teaches sociology and Latin American Studies at Temple University in Philadelphia. He is the co-author (with Michael Omi) of *Racial Formation in the United States: From the 1960s to the 1990s* (second edition, Routledge, 1994); he has also written *Racial Conditions: Politics, Theory, Comparison* (University of Minnesota Press, 1994), and *Stalemate: Political Economic Origins of Supply-Side Policy* (Praeger, 1988).

Grateful acknowledgement is made to the following for permission to reprint published material:

Beacon Press: Excerpts from *Turning Back: The Retreat from Racial Justice in American Thought and Policy* by Stephen Steinberg included in his new essay "The Liberal Retreat from Race During the Post-Civil Rights Era." Reprinted by permission of Beacon Press.

Harvard University Press: Excerpts from *The Rooster's Egg* by Patricia Williams. Copyright © 1995 by the President and Fellows of Harvard College. Reprinted by permission of Harvard University Press.

Quandra Prettyman: Excerpt from "When Mahalia Sings" by Quandra Prettyman. Reprinted by permission of Quandra Prettyman.

Songs of Polygram International, Inc.: Excerpt from "Paid in Full" by Eric Barrier and William Griffin. Copyright © 1987 Songs of Polygram International, Inc. All rights reserved. Reprinted by permission of Songs of Polygram International, Inc.

Excerpt from "Boom Bye Bye" reprinted by permission.